Jasper Ridley was edud
University.

After a successful car   n
writing historical biog   l
John Knox, Mary Tu
Palmerston (for which
Black Memorial Prize), Garibaldi and Napoleon III.

Jasper Ridley

The History of England

Futura
Macdonald & Co
London & Sydney

A Futura Book

First published in Great Britain in 1981
by Routledge & Kegan Paul Ltd

This edition published in 1983
by Futura Publications, a Division of
Macdonald & Co (Publishers) Ltd
London & Sydney

ISBN 0 7088 2369 6

Reproduced, printed and bound in Great Britain by
Hazell Watson & Viney Ltd, Aylesbury, Bucks

Futura Publications
A Division of
Macdonald & Co (Publishers) Ltd
Maxwell House
74 Worship Street
London EC2A 2EN

A BPCC plc Company

To My Son John

CONTENTS

BRITAIN
BEFORE THE
ENGLISH

In the five thousand years which have elapsed since some form of civilised life has existed in Britain, 175 generations of human beings have lived here. Most of them lived in a stable society, in which kings and noblemen often fought each other, but in which the ordinary men and women, from youth to old age, lived the same kind of life which their fathers and mothers had lived before them, and which their sons and daughters were to live after them. But 11 of these 175 generations have lived in a period of extraordinary change. Those members of these 11 generations – a small minority – who reached the age of eighty found themselves in their old age in a very different Britain from the Britain of their youth. They were the people who lived from AD 20 to 100; from 395 to 475; from 585 to 665; from 860 to 940; from 1030 to 1110; from 1310 to 1390; from 1460 to 1540; from 1540 to 1620; from 1630 to 1710; from 1780 to 1860; and from 1900 to 1980. They witnessed the most interesting periods of English history.

At the root of all history lie terrain and climate. In Britain, there is a considerable difference between the north and the south, and between the east and the west. In the south the average summer temperature is nearly ten degrees Fahrenheit warmer than the north. In the dry east, the average yearly rainfall is under 25 inches; in many places in the wet west, it exceeds 60, or even 80, inches. The south-east is relatively flat, the north-west is hilly. In the south, the harvest is usually reaped at the beginning of August, only a few weeks later than on the continent of Europe; in the north, it is sometimes not collected until October or even later. Throughout the whole of British history, the majority of the population has been concentrated in the south-east, which has always been in advance of the north in political and social, and usually in economic, development. Except for one strange interlude of 150 years between AD 450 and 600, the south has always been in close contact with Europe and has been politically and culturally a part of Europe. The north, for long periods, has been virtually isolated from all of Europe except Scandinavia.

As far as we can tell, the first immigrants came to Britain about five thousand years ago, having sailed here from Spain and Portugal and landed in Cornwall and Devon. Some of them went further north, but most settled on Salisbury Plain. Other immigrants came during the next three thousand years, until the population of Britain was about 400,000. The Iberians from Spain and Portugal were perhaps the ancestors of the small, dark-haired inhabitants of Cornwall and Wales today; the Celts from Brittany, Normandy, Flanders, the Netherlands and Denmark were tall, with red hair and blue eyes. Many of the immigrants went to Wiltshire, where they erected the great stone monuments of Stonehenge and Avebury. The inhabitants of the island were known as 'Pretani' to the foreign traders who bought their tin and sold them wine. The Romans later miswrote the name as 'Britanni' and called their country 'Britannia', which is why we call it 'Britain' now.

The Romans first came in 55 BC, when Julius Caesar, the Roman commander in Gaul, crossed the Straits of Dover with his army and landed near Deal; but though Caesar came again next year, and advanced as far as Hertfordshire, he made no attempt to conquer the island, and it was not until 97 years later that the Emperor Claudius invaded Britain, and the territory south of the Humber and east of the Severn was annexed to the Roman Empire.

The Romans were determined to conquer the whole island, and to invade the territory now known as Wales and Scotland.

Welsh resistance had collapsed by AD 77; but the Romans tried unsuccessfully for 130 years to conquer the Caledonians in Scotland. At the end of the thirteenth century, when the kings of England decided to conquer Wales and Scotland, they conquered Wales in three campaigns of a few months each, and tried for eighty years to conquer Scotland before giving up the attempt. Nineteen hundred years after Agricola and seven hundred years after Edward I, the movement for independence and devolution wins the support of large sections of the population of Scotland, but hardly any support in Wales.

Agricola marched as far north as Forfar, and after defeating the Caledonians, built a wall from the Forth to the Clyde to prevent them from raiding to the south of it; but after a hundred years of intermittent warfare, the Romans withdrew to the more formidable defensive barrier of Hadrian's Wall, which stretched from coast to coast just north of the Tyne, and became the northern frontier of the Roman Empire.

The result of the Roman occupation was to divide Britain into five separate regions – the south of England, Wales, the north of England, the Scottish Lowlands and the Scottish Highlands – which for the next eighteen hundred years were to have a different development and, to a considerable extent, a different history. The south of England, bounded by the Severn and the Humber, was incorporated into the Roman Empire, with the same Roman way of life as Gaul, Italy and North Africa. Wales, except for its eastern fringe along the present-day boundary with England, was outside the Roman Empire; its inhabitants, carefully watched by the Roman garrisons at Caerleon and Chester, left the Romans in peace and were left in peace by them, isolated from the life and history of the island. The north of England between the Humber and the Tyne was occupied by the Romans, who established their military high command in Britain at York; but though York was one of the great cities of the Empire, the Roman civilians who lived there hardly ever ventured beyond the walls of the city and the 10-mile strip of the Plain of York on both sides of it; and the Yorkshire moors and dales and the rest of the country north of the Humber were untouched by Roman civilisation. The area between the Tyne and the Forth and Clyde was a no-man's-land which was under Roman authority between 80 and 98 and between 142 and 184, but was then abandoned by the Romans to the ferocious Caledonians. The fifth region of Britain, the Highlands north of the Tay, was never conquered, though on two occasions Roman punitive expeditions penetrated into the territory, the Emperor Severus in 209 going at least as far north as Inverness, and possibly reaching John-o'-Groats.

In the south of England and the Plain of York, more than 100,000 Roman settlers – most of them soldiers or civil servants, but including some traders and other private individuals – fraternised and intermarried with the British aristocracy, many of whom were granted Roman citizenship and lived like wealthy Romans in villas. But most of the inhabitants of Britain worked on the land as serfs of their Roman or Romanised-British masters. The more oppressive labour in the nationalised iron, copper, tin, gold and coal mines, which the Romans developed much more systematically than the British of earlier times, was performed largely by convicted prisoners.

Great roads were built all across Britain; they were not as straight as they are traditionally supposed to have been. After being allowed to decay for 1200 years, they became the roads of modern England.

The Romans' greatest contribution to the development of Britain was the introduction of urban life and Christianity. Their towns were small compared with those of later centuries; the largest, London, covered 330 acres and probably had a population of about 15,000. None of the other towns had much more than 5,000 inhabitants; but unlike the villages and hilltop fortresses of pre-Roman Britain, they were towns with an urban life-style and culture like the other cities throughout the Roman Empire.

Jesus of Nazareth was crucified by Roman authority in Palestine about fourteen years before the conquest of Britain; but within a generation Christianity had spread throughout the Roman Empire, chiefly among the lower classes in the towns, although it was savagely persecuted by the Roman government. Many centuries later, the English Christians invented untrue stories about the early visits of Christ's followers to Britain; but there is no doubt that there were Christians in south-east England within a hundred years of Christ's death, and during the next two hundred years their faith spread. They had a few followers even beyond the bounds of Roman civilisation, in Wales, the North and Caledonia.

At the beginning of the fourth century, the Emperor Diocletian renewed the persecution of Christians throughout the Empire. According to later Christian writers a Roman soldier named Alban suffered martyrdom in Britain in 304. There is no contemporary record of his death, but the story was being told by British Christians 125 years later. Alban was stationed in the town of Verulamium, which is today called St Albans after him. He was not a Christian, but felt sympathy for a persecuted British Christian and hid him in his house. When he was arrested and charged with sheltering this fugitive from justice, he declared that he had decided to become a Christian himself, and was sentenced to death. He was taken to the place of execution, on a hill outside the town; but the soldier who was ordered to behead him refused to do so. The soldier and Alban were then both put to death by another soldier who was more amenable to military discipline.

Within ten years of Diocletian's persecution a remarkable change had taken place in the fortunes of the Christian Church. In 306 Diocletian's successor, the Emperor Constantius, died at York, after conducting a successful punitive expedition against the Caledonians. The army there chose his illegitimate son Constantine, who was with him at York, as the new emperor. Other claimants to the throne were supported by army units throughout the Empire, and Constantine had to fight them. His mother was a barmaid in Turkey, where Constantius had been stationed at the time; and it seems that, like so many other girls from the lower classes, she was a secret Christian. During his struggle for the imperial throne, Constantine decided to enlist the support of the Christians against his rivals; and after emerging as victor, he granted toleration to the Christians, and then established Christianity as virtually the official religion of the Empire, though he himself became a Christian only on his deathbed.

Under the Christian Empire the Church established a very efficient international administration, and the Christians in Britain were organised into dioceses under bishops who represented them at the international Councils of the Church at Arles and Rimini. It was a British theologian, Pelagius, who, early in the fifth century, put forward the doctrine of freewill which continued for over a thousand years to be denounced as the Pelagian heresy by the international Church. But the Roman Empire was decaying. By the beginning of the fifth century, barbarian tribes from Eastern Europe were overrunning the Empire and threatening Rome itself. The Roman government eventually withdrew all their armed forces from Britain, leaving their fellow-countrymen there, and the Britons, to their own devices.

Roman civilisation in Britain did not collapse overnight when the legions left; but almost immediately the Caledonians broke through Hadrian's Wall and ravaged the north of England, and they repeatedly ravaged south of the Wall during the next decades. The Romans and the Romanised natives in Britain lived on for another generation amid slow decay and growing fear of the future. When the Bishop of Auxerre, St Germanus, travelled from Gaul to Britain in 429, he reported that social and religious life was continuing in Britain; but he was worried about the demoralisation and the slow collapse. Things had become worse eighteen years later, when Germanus again visited Britain; and total disaster was at hand.

In 446 the government in Rome finally refused to send any military aid to protect Britain against the Caledonians. Meanwhile northern Gaul was overrun by barbarian tribes from Germany – by the Franks, who ultimately gave their name to the country which they conquered. These barbarians were not traders, and did not wish to have anything to do with the inhabitants of Britain, who were now cut off from Rome. For the first time for several centuries, Britain was totally isolated from Europe. After Germanus's second visit in 447, there is no record of any other traveller from Europe visiting Britain for 150 years.

CHAPTER 1

THE
ENGLISH
AND THE
CHRISTIANS
(446–686)

Students who study the history of events since 1500 can read, for every decade that they investigate, thousands of contemporary public records, private letters, diaries, books, pamphlets and newspapers; but we have only four sources of information about the history of Britain between 447 and 597. The earliest is a book written by a British monk, Gildas, in about 545; the second is the chronicle of an Anglo-Saxon monk, Baeda (the Venerable Bede), which he published in 731; the third is a book by a Welsh monk, Nennius, who wrote between 785 and 808; and the fourth is the *Anglo-Saxon Chronicle*, compiled under the direction of King Alfred in about 895. Gildas is the only one of these who is in any sense contemporary, and even in his case most of the incidents which he described took place before he was born; while Bede, Nennius and the authors of the *Anglo-Saxon Chronicle* were writing about events as far removed from them as the period stretching from the reign of Henry VIII to the Napoleonic Wars is from us. But both Bede and Nennius had read earlier written histories which have since been lost; and the four chronicles all agree on some basic matters, despite the fact that Gildas and

Nennius were Britons, and Bede and the authors of the *Anglo-Saxon Chronicle* were English.

These authors all state that after the Roman government in 446 refused the British request for military aid against the Caledonians, the Britons asked the Angles and Saxons in Germany and Denmark for help. Nennius provides more details. The British chieftain Vortigern, who in the vacuum which followed the departure of the Roman army had made himself king of south Britain, asked the Jutes of Jutland to send mercenaries to protect him against the Caledonians. The Jutes arrived under their leaders, the brothers Hengist and Horsa. They defeated the Caledonians, and as a reward were granted land in the Isle of Thanet. They proceeded to bring more Jutes and their families from Jutland, and expanded into other parts of Kent. The Britons then rallied under a general, Ambrosius Aurelianus, who was descended from an aristocratic Roman family. They defeated the Jutes in a battle near Aylesford in Kent, in which Horsa was killed; a great mound, which can still be seen today, is probably his tomb. Hengist and his defeated followers retreated to Jutland, but soon returned and reconquered Kent, where Hengist died at an advanced age, perhaps in 488.

The details of the conquest of Kent by the Jutes, supplied chiefly by Nennius, make a story as exciting as those of Homer, and show Hengist as a brave, cruel and cunning leader in the style of Odysseus. When he first persuades Vortigern to grant him territory in Thanet, he asks only for as much land as can be covered by a leather thong; but by cutting the hide of a bull into long thin strips, he makes a thong which is long enough to enclose a rocky hill on which he can build an impregnable castle. He contrives for Vortigern to fall passionately in love with his beautiful daughter Rowena, and consents to Rowena's marriage to Vortigern on condition that Vortigern grants him the whole of Kent. Realising that, despite the complaisance of the amorous Vortigern, resistance is to be expected from the British military leaders, he makes a show of friendship, invites them to come unarmed to peace negotiations, and arranges for every Jute to murder one of his British neighbours with hidden daggers. The chroniclers' stories, like Homer's, unwittingly show the puny power of their heroes and the small scale on which they operated. The final result of all Hengist's valour, cruelty and guile is to

2

acquire the Kingdom of Kent; yet the older inhabitants over whom he ruled there had in their childhood been subjects of an Emperor whose territories extended from the Tyne to North Africa.

Though we have very little reliable information about Hengist, we know even less about the other Anglo-Saxon invaders of Britain. Another band of Jutes, who had no connection with Hengist, sailed from Jutland and conquered the Îsle of Wight and Hampshire. Saxons from the district near Hamburg, under their leader Aella, landed on the Sussex coast, and in 491 captured the old Roman city of Anderida (now Pevensey) by storm, and massacred the inhabitants. Aella then proclaimed himself king of Sussex. We do not know even the names of the leaders of the Angles and Saxons who landed in Norfolk, Yorkshire and Northumberland, and between the Tweed and the Forth; but they established themselves along the whole eastern seaboard. The invaders of Norfolk were English, coming from the area of Schleswig-Holstein between the territories of the Jutes and the Saxons. Within two centuries of their arrival in Britain, these Jutes, Angles and Saxons, who were all members of the same race, were known as Anglo-Saxons, or English, and were indistinguishable from each other.

The English of the fifth century were the most destructive immigrants who have ever come to Britain. They were a nation of free peasants who were subject to no master or landlord, and cultivated farms which varied in size, in different parts of England, from 50 to 200 acres. They preserved their nation from anarchy and civil war by accepting the son of their leader as their hereditary king, and only departing from the hereditary principle in exceptional circumstances; but apart from the king and his family and relations, there was no aristocracy or class divisions. The free peasants all served in the army in wartime, paid contributions to the king for the maintenance of his court and retainers, and participated in the regular open-air meetings of the popular assemblies, where local problems were discussed. After winning a battle, they often killed their defeated enemies; but sometimes they spared their lives and took them as slaves.

The lawless instincts of the English were restrained by their respect for their customary laws. These were generally observed,

3

although there was no law-enforcement body, because the laws were simple, very few in number, and remained unchanged for generation after generation. One of the most important laws laid down that anyone who committed murder had to pay to the family, or master, of the murdered freeman or slave a fixed sum of money which varied according to the victim's age, sex and importance.

The English had no urban life, and had a special hatred for the decaying towns of Roman Britain. The people of some of them, like Anderida, were exterminated, and the towns disappeared. Later generations called the fifth and sixth centuries in Britain the 'Dark Ages'; and the barbaric condition of the island is especially remarkable when we remember that at the same time, during the sixth century, Theodoric in Ravenna and Justinian in Constantinople – cities which had recently been part of the same empire as Britain – were erecting splendid buildings and promulgating a great code of laws which have endured for centuries. Sometimes today we speak of another Dark Age being imminent, and use the term to refer to oppressive modern totalitarian regimes; but these have nothing in common with the Dark Ages of Anglo-Saxon England. Modern totalitarian society, with its technology, its cruelty and its forced labour camps, has much in common with the Roman Empire, but nothing with the English kingdoms of the Dark Ages, whose only modern parallel is Cambodia of the Khmer Rouge, where urban life and culture were similarly destroyed.

The surviving Romans and Britons in the island, as they fled to the west, naturally saw the coming of the English as an unqualified disaster. Gildas was probably a refugee in a monastery in Brittany when he wrote his *History of Britain*, which he described as an island 'situated on almost the utmost border of the earth, towards the south and west and poised in the Divine balance, as is said, which supports the whole world', and which 'stretches out from the south-west towards the North Pole'. Having a much better knowledge of the Bible than of geography, he compared the sufferings of the Britons with those of the Jews whose sins had brought on their own heads the disasters foretold by Isaiah and Jeremiah. He blames various kings of Britain, whose names are known to us only from his book, for having caused the disasters by their selfish internecine quarrels. His tone of despair shows the state of mind of the British refugees in the middle of the sixth century.

But the English invasion was a slow-creeping horror. The Romans, four centuries earlier, had taken seven years to conquer the area south of the Humber and east of the Severn; the English took a hundred and thirty years. Their advance across Britain was not a planned invasion launched by a strong centralised military command, but a slow encroachment on British territory by small English kingdoms or by less organised communities, advancing a few miles further west when the harvest failed or when pressure of population drove them to seek new soil. There must have been periods of peaceful coexistence with the Britons; and on at least two occasions the Britons defeated them and checked their advance by a successful counter-offensive. The first occasion was the British victory over Hengist under the leadership of Ambrosius Aurelianus; the second, a generation later, was at the Battle of Mount Badon. This great victory of the Britons over the English has been dated by historians, according to their different interpretations of an ambiguous sentence of Gildas's, and of other conflicting evidence, as either 493 or 516. The place is uncertain, but though sites in Scotland and in the north of England have been suggested, it was probably in Berkshire or Wiltshire.

The British commander at Mount Badon, according to Nennius, was King Arthur. Nennius in about 790 is the earliest known writer to mention Arthur; his stories were embroidered by Geoffrey of Monmouth, the future Bishop of St Asaph, in 1136 and by other twelfth-century writers, and changed almost beyond recognition by Sir Thomas Malory in 1469. There has been a great controversy among modern historians as to whether Arthur really existed; but though it has been suggested that there may have been a military commander with the Roman name of Arturius who led the Britons to victory over the English in about 500, the Arthur of Nennius and Geoffrey of Monmouth is a legendary figure. As for Malory's King Arthur, he was undoubtedly as much a medieval creation as was the Round Table, now at Winchester, around which Arthur and his knights are supposed to have sat at dinner, but which the experts have now shown, by their tests on the timber, was made in about 1335. If Arthur really existed, he had nothing in common with either the early Welsh, or the medieval, hero, except that he was a military leader and a Christian; and in view of this, it does not matter very much whether he is 100 per cent, or only 95 per cent, fictitious.

Eventually, in 577, the English reached the Bristol Channel and split the British territory into two separate parts. One section of the Britons retreated into Wales, and the other into Cornwall, where they maintained contact by sea with their kith and kin in Wales and preserved their independence for another 240 years. They continued to be Christians as they had been under the Roman Empire; but in their isolation from Rome and from Christian Europe, they developed a slightly different version of Christianity, with a different method of calculating the date of Easter, and their own original saints, whose names are preserved in many Cornish villages.

During the sixth century, Celtic Christianity also took root in Scotland, to which it came from Ireland. In the last years of the fourth century, a boy of fifteen named Patrick, living in Roman Britain in the neighbourhood of the Bristol Channel, was kidnapped by pirates and sold as a slave in Ireland. After some years he succeeded in escaping, and returned to his native land; but he had not forgotten the Irish, and was determined to convert them to Christianity. When St Patrick, after many years of missionary work in Ireland, died at an advanced age, probably in about 460, most of the Irish were Christians, including a tribe, the Scots, who inhabited the kingdom of Dalriada in Antrim. During the sixth century, the Scots invaded Caledonia, and seized the south-west of the country, driving the Caledonians, who were now usually known as the Picts, into the north and east, while the south-east of Caledonia was occupied by English invaders from Schleswig-Holstein. Christian missionaries from Ireland completed the conversion of the Scots in Caledonia, which soon became known as 'Scotland'. They established a monastery on the island of Iona off the south-west coast, and from there new missionaries went into Pictland and northern England, where they had considerable success in converting Picts and Englishmen.

By the end of the sixth century, Britain was divided into more than a dozen pagan English kingdoms: Kent, Sussex, Wessex (stretching from Hampshire to the Bristol Channel), the Isle of Wight, Essex, which included London, East Anglia (Suffolk and

Norfolk), a number of very small Middle Anglian kingdoms in the Midlands, Mercia, in the Trent Valley, Lindsey (north Lincolnshire), Deira (central and east Yorkshire), and Bernicia (Durham, Northumberland, and Lothian, from the Tees to the Forth). Three areas were still held by the Christian Romano-Britons: Devon and Cornwall, Wales, and a strip along the west coast in Lancashire and the Lake District. The Scots held south-west Scotland from Argyll to Cumberland, and the Picts the rest of Scotland north of the Forth.

The Christian Church in Rome had been the last group in Europe to remain in contact with Britain in the middle of the fifth century, and it was they who reopened the connection 150 years later. The Christians, having converted their persecutors, the Roman emperors, to Christianity in the fourth century, repeated the process in the sixth and seventh centuries with their heathen enemies, the Germanic kings. Their first success was in 496, when the heathen king of the Franks, Clovis, after defeating the Christian Romano-Gauls in the south of France, became a Christian at the instigation of his Christian queen. This was part of a policy by which Clovis replaced the simple egalitarian social system of the barbarian Franks by a more complex class structure with himself at the apex as an autocratic sovereign. During the sixth century the Germans were converted to Christianity by missionaries from both Rome and Scotland; and in 597 Pope Gregory I sent a group of Italian monks, under the leadership of Augustine, to convert the English in the kingdom of Kent.

Gregory, the witty, intellectual and compassionate son of a nobleman who owned large estates in Sicily, became a priest and an important official at the papal court in Rome. One day during the years when Benedict I was Pope (between 574 and 578), Gregory happened to see some English children being sold as slaves in the Forum in Rome; they had been captured in their homes on the Yorkshire coast by pirates, and had reached the slave-market in Rome. Gregory was moved by the plight and charm of the children. When he was told that they were English children from Deira, a kingdom ruled by a king named Aella, he said that they were more like *angeli* (angels) than *Anglii* (English), and promised that he would rescue their fellow-countrymen in Deira *'de ira'* (from the wrath of God), and that one day 'Allelujah' should be sung in Aella's land. This well-known story

7

is better substantiated than many of the famous historical fables, for Bede, who wrote it down a hundred and fifty years later, had almost certainly been told about it by a man who knew some of Gregory's friends; and it was recorded by another chronicler who wrote earlier than Bede.

It was a formidable task for the Christians to persuade barbarian heathen warriors, who had so recently conquered and massacred Christians, to abandon their faith in the gods of their fathers who had led them to victory and to embrace the religion of their defeated foes. It is not surprising that the Christians regarded their success as a miracle, and that it finally confirmed their confidence in their mission and their triumph. They had two factors working in their favour: feminine influence, and the desire of the barbarian chieftains to become respectable.

More than any of the other great religions of the world, Christianity has elevated the position of women. In the sixth century, Christendom had not yet developed the high regard for women which was shown in later centuries by the knights and troubadours of the Middle Ages and lords, gentlemen and poets of modern times; but the Christian emphasis on the merits of chastity and motherhood gave a minimum of protection to women in any society in which the dominating and lustful barbarian warriors could be persuaded at least to pay lip-service to Christian ideals. In France, in Britain, and in many parts of Germany, the Christians first converted the queen; then the queen persuaded the king to grant them toleration and protection; finally she converted the king by convincing him that it was thanks to the intervention of the God of the Christians that he had won a critical battle and that she had been safely delivered of a healthy male heir. The king then ordered his nobles to become Christians, and this was followed by mass conversions among the people.

The conversion of the Europe of the Dark Ages was the last and greatest of the benefits which the Church obtained from Constantine's decision to sponsor Christianity in 312. It gave to the Christian religion the aura of imperial splendour. The heathen kings knew that they could never achieve the status of the Caesars merely by conquering and exterminating their enemies; but by becoming Christians they could raise themselves above their fierce barbarian comrades-in-arms, both socially and

8

morally, by their piety, their culture, and by the respect which the churchmen were prepared to show to a Christian king who could bring about the victory of Christianity in his realm far more easily and quickly than could all the missionaries by decades of propaganda. So Christianity, which three centuries before had been a religion of oppressed slaves, played an important part in establishing and buttressing a new class system and the domination of royal autocracy.

For twenty years after he saw the slave-children from Deira in the Forum, Gregory was unable to undertake the conversion of their fellow-countrymen, for he was otherwise occupied, first on a mission to Constantinople, then with the government of his monastery in Rome, and finally with the work which followed from his elevation to the papacy; but eventually he sent missionaries, not to Deira but to Kent, where Augustine and a party of monks landed in 597. Kent was the most suitable kingdom to choose for the beginning of the mission to England, for not only was it closest to the Continent and to Rome, but the first vital step in the conversion process had already been achieved. The king of Kent had married the Christian daughter of the king of Paris. It did not take long to convert the king, and the Kentish chieftains and people soon followed his example.

Augustine does not seem to have been a very intelligent or enterprising man, but he carried out the instructions which he received from Gregory, who directed his every step in letters from Rome. One pressing problem, as Gregory knew, was the relationship to be established with the Celtic Christian Church of the Romano-Britons in the west. Soon after Augustine reached Kent, he and a few colleagues met representatives of the Celtic Church. We do not know where the meeting took place, except that it was under an oak tree; nor do we know how Augustine and his party, and the Britons, managed to travel to the meeting-place through hostile English heathen territory. The meeting was not a success. Bede, though he was a supporter of the Church of Rome against the Celtic Church, admits that Augustine's tactlessness was largely responsible for this, as Augustine annoyed the Britons by failing to rise from his seat when they first approached. The two sides did not resolve their differences, and no further meetings between their representatives took place.

Meanwhile, in the north, the kingdom of Deira had been

incorporated by marriage into Bernicia, and formed the kingdom of Northumbria, stretching from the Humber to the Forth; it was by far the largest English kingdom in the island. The king of Northumbria, Aethelfrith, was a pagan and a ferocious enemy of the Christian Britons. After winning a number of crushing victories over the Scots on his north-west frontier, he turned against the Christian Welsh to the south-west, and in 613 met them in battle at Chester. The Welsh sent two thousand monks from the great monastery at Bangor – by far the largest monastery in Europe – to walk at the head of their army; they advanced, unarmed, towards the heathen Northumbrians, singing psalms and praying to their Christian God for victory. Aethelfrith ordered his soldiers to massacre them; he said that if they were praying for his enemies' victory, they too were his enemies and deserved to be treated as such. The monks were killed, and the Welsh army was routed. The Christian historians would probably not have mentioned this disastrous failure of the efficacy of Christian prayer, had it not been for the fact that the praying monks were Celtic Christians, and the Roman Christians publicised the story to show that God had punished them for their failure to reach agreement with Augustine at the conference under the oak tree and for their defiance of the authority of Rome.

The Battle of Chester marks the end of an era which had lasted for 160 years since the arrival of Hengist and Horsa – the era of warfare between the heathen English and the Christian Britons. Within four years Aethelfrith had been killed fighting against English claimants to his throne, and Edwin, a descendant of the kings of Deira, was king of Northumbria, which he governed from the former Deiran capital, York. Edwin was the most powerful ruler in Britain, and his English neighbours in Mercia were as alarmed by his power as were the Welsh, the Scots and the Picts. He extended his kingdom to the south of the Humber by annexing Lindsey; and at the north-eastern limit of his realm he built a fortress on the Forth which soon developed into a town, and was named 'Edinburgh' after him.

In 625 he married Aethelburh, the Christian sister of the king of Kent. It was a condition of the marriage contract that toleration should be granted to the Christians in Northumbria, and Aethelburh arrived in York accompanied by an Italian monk,

Paulinus, who had been sent by the bishop of Canterbury from his monastery in the Kentish capital. Paulinus was as successful as Augustine had been in Kent. As Augustine had settled at Canterbury twenty-one years before Paulinus reached York, Augustine's see was superior by seniority, with the result that today the archbishop of Canterbury takes precedence in the Church of England over the archbishop of York; but Paulinus's success in the great kingdom of Northumbria was much more important than Augustine's in Kent.

Pope Boniface V assisted his efforts, and a letter that he wrote to Queen Aethelburh shows the method of approach, and the subtle mixture of flattery and sternness, adopted by the Roman Christian Church towards the heathen reigning houses. The pope wrote to the queen

> We have been informed that, with unimpaired devotion, you occupy yourself so much with the love of your Redeemer that you never cease from lending your aid in spreading the Christian faith. But when, in our fatherly love, we inquired earnestly about your illustrious husband, we learned that he was still serving abominable idols, and hesitated to hear and obey the words of the preachers. This caused us no small grief, that he who is one flesh with you should remain a stranger to the knowledge of the supreme and undivided Trinity. Therefore we do not hesitate, in accordance with our fatherly duty, to send a warning to Your Christian Highness: we urge you that, being imbued with the Holy Spirit, you should not hesitate, in season and out of season, to labour so that, through the power of our Lord and Saviour Jesus Christ, he may be added to the number of Christians, so that you may thereby enjoy the rights of marriage in undefiled union. For it is written: 'They twain shall be one flesh'; how then can it be said that there is unity between you if he continues a stranger to your shining faith, seeing that the darkness of detestable error remains between you? . . . We send you not only the blessing of St Peter, chief of the Apostles and your protector, but also a silver mirror and an ivory comb adorned with gold. We beseech Your Majesty to accept it in the same kindly spirit as that in which it is sent.

Queen Aethelburh set to work on Edwin, and the king became a Christian in 627. The nobility and the people followed suit, and there were mass conversions throughout Northumbria. Many years later, an old man told Bede that he remembered seeing Paulinus baptising hundreds of people beside a river in Lindsey; he remembered that Paulinus 'was tall, with a slight stoop, black hair, a thin face, and a slender aquiline nose'. In considering his extraordinary success, we must remember that we know about the conversion of Anglo-Saxon England only from Christian writers, who may have exaggerated the missionaries' achievements and failed to mention the degree of compulsion and pressure used by the kings; but there was obviously no serious resistance to the conversion, and no heathen backlash against the Christians. The pagan religion had largely lost its influence before Augustine and Paulinus arrived, and there seems no doubt that Christianity filled a void in the religious lives of the people of Kent and Northumbria.

The only pagan resistance which arose had nothing to do with popular feeling, but with power politics; for a new international alignment was about to be formed in England. The dread of Edwin's power created an alliance of English heathen Mercia and British Christian Wales against English Christian Northumbria. King Penda of Mercia refused to adopt the fashionable course of converting to Christianity, perhaps because he was already a middle-aged man of fifty when he became king and when the question of his conversion arose; but he worked closely with his Christian ally, King Cadwallon of Gwynedd in north Wales. In 632* Penda and Cadwallon defeated the Northumbrians at the Battle of Hatfield near Doncaster in which Edwin was killed and his army destroyed. Northumbria was then devastated by the victorious allies.

The Christian missionaries were saddened to see that, after Edwin's defeat and death and Penda's victory, many of the recent converts reverted to paganism. In later centuries, Christians shuddered at the name of Penda. In the nineteenth and early twentieth centuries, English children were given, as suitable bedside reading, little illustrated books which told the story of his cruel persecution; but the Christians of the seventh and eighth centuries were, not surprisingly, far more indignant at the conduct of the Celtic Christian King Cadwallon than at the

* The battle was fought on 12 October. Later historians gave the date as 633, overlooking the fact that the Anglo-Saxons dated the beginning of the year from 1 September.

activities of the heathen Penda. Racial hatreds proved stronger than religious hatreds or sympathies. A hundred years later Bede wrote:

> At this time there was a great slaughter both of the Church and of the people of Northumbria, one of the perpetrators being a heathen and the other a barbarian who was even more cruel than the heathen. Now Penda and the whole Mercian race were idolators, and ignorant of the name of Christ; but Caedwalla, although a Christian by name and profession, was nevertheless a barbarian in heart and disposition and spared neither women nor innocent children. With bestial cruelty he put all to death by torture, and for a long time raged through all their land, meaning to wipe out the whole English nation from the land of Britain. Nor did he pay any respect to the Christian religion which had sprung up amongst them. Indeed to this very day, it is the habit of the Britons to despise the faith and religion of the English and not to co-operate with them in anything any more than with the heathen.

A year after his victory over Edwin, Cadwallon was killed in a battle near Hexham by Oswald, who became king of Northumbria. Oswald was the son of the pagan King Aethelfrith, the merciless victor of the Battle of Chester; but when he escaped to Scottish territory after Edwin's seizure of the throne in Northumbria, he was converted to Christianity by the monks of Iona, and under his rule Northumbria again became a Christian country. In 641 Oswald was defeated and killed by Penda, who for the next thirteen years was the most powerful ruler in Britain; but he could not permanently hold up the triumphant advance of Christianity. He himself, in his last years, began to soften towards Christianity, and moved with the times so far as to allow his son Peada to take the fateful step of marrying the Christian daughter of Oswald's brother Oswiu, who had become king of Northumbria. Peada thereupon converted to Christianity; and Penda's daughter Cineburga, who married Oswiu's son, also became a Christian and founded a monastery near Peterborough.

In 654 a revolt against Mercian domination broke out in East Anglia, and all the other Anglo-Saxon kingdoms united against Penda. The energetic old warrior, who was aged about seventy-five, then invaded Northumbria. Oswiu sued for peace, and was prepared to accept the most humiliating terms; but Penda insisted on continuing the war, and was defeated and killed on the River Winwaed, which was probably near Leeds. Within a few years of his death, his children had made Mercia a Christian state, despite the fact that Peada had been murdered by his Christian wife.

The death of Penda caused the final victory of Christianity, and of Roman Christianity. In September 663 Oswiu summoned a synod near Whitby,* at which the representatives of the Roman and Celtic Churches argued the respective merits of their branches of the Christian religion. The Roman case was ably argued by Wilfrid, a local Northumbrian monk who had studied in Rome and Lyons; but Oswiu seems to have been influenced even more by other factors in giving his decision in favour of Rome. He himself had been brought up a Celtic Christian when he was a refugee at Iona; but his wife Eanflaed, the daughter of Edwin and Aethelburh, had escaped to Kent when Penda and Cadwallon overran Northumbria, and at Canterbury had continued to be taught the Roman Christianity which she had learned from her parents. Bishop Colman's arguments for Celtic Christianity stood no chance against the influence of his wife and the prestige of Rome; and Oswiu remarked, with a smile, that if he had to choose between St Peter and St Colomba, he would choose St Peter, as he held the keys to the Kingdom of Heaven. The Celtic cause cannot have been helped by the memories of Cadwallon's atrocities in Northumbria only thirty years before, and the fact that the Celtic Christians of Wales had been Penda's allies on the losing side in the recent wars.

After the Synod of Whitby, the Roman churchmen rapidly eradicated the influence of Celtic Christianity in Northumbria. In 668 the Pope appointed Theodore, an aged Greek theologian from Tarsus in Asia Minor, to be Archbishop of Canterbury, and sent him to England, together with Hadrian, a monk from North Africa, to organise the English Church. As a recent convert from Greek to Roman Christianity, Theodore was particularly zealous in eliminating Celtic deviations.

Sussex, cut off by the forests of the Weald from contact with neighbouring kingdoms, was the last bastion of paganism; but the king of Sussex became a Christian in 686. The whole island was now Christian, and under the authority of the Roman Church.

* The historians, again overlooking the fact that the Anglo-Saxons began the year on 1 September, give the date of the Synod of Whitby as 664.

CHAPTER 2

ALFRED, CANUTE
AND
WILLIAM THE
CONQUEROR
(686–1066)

The establishment of Christianity was only one of the symptoms of the changing nature of Anglo-Saxon society. Class divisions had reappeared in Britain. The kings surrounded themselves with a bodyguard, who formed a class of largely hereditary warriors, though outsiders who showed outstanding prowess were always able to enter it. They were the cavalry in the army. The free peasant proprietors were sometimes called up to serve as infantry in wartime; but the Anglo-Saxon ballads and legends told only of the heroic deeds of the cavalrymen of the king's bodyguard.

The influence of the Church increased. Theodore created new dioceses, and monasteries and nunneries were founded all over England. Many of the clergy, unlike all the rest of the population, could read and write, and they became the civil servants and secretaries of the kings, and governed their kingdoms for them. In return, they were granted protection and gifts of large tracts of land. They established a working compromise with the descendants of the barbarian English invaders. They exhorted the kings and warriors to lead godly lives, and reproved them if they failed to do so; but they were prepared to pardon, if not to overlook, the private sins and political crimes of Christian princes who advanced the cause of the Church.

The Christian kingdoms of Britain were usually at war with each other. These were not religious or racial wars, but were between national states, fought to acquire territory, power and prestige, and most of all, perhaps, in order to justify the existence of the ruling class, the warriors of the king's bodyguard. During the eighth century, King Offa of Mercia became the most powerful English ruler. He conquered Kent and most of south-east England, and built the bulwark known as Offa's Dike to contain the Welsh. He was the first English king to exert an influence in Europe, where his foreign policy was taken into account by the European rulers. He established very friendly relations with Charlemagne, but he refused to marry his daughter to Charlemagne's son unless Charlemagne agreed that his daughter should marry Offa's son. Charlemagne was annoyed that Offa should thus claim equality of status with him, and temporarily closed French ports to the Mercian ships. Offa thought that Mercia, like Kent and Northumbria, should have an archiepiscopal see, and persuaded the pope to elevate Lichfield into an archbishopric; but there was an archbishop of Lichfield for only fifteen years, for after Offa's death in 796 Lichfield relapsed into a bishopric in the province of Canterbury.

After Mercia, it was the turn of Wessex to become the dominant English power. King Egbert of Wessex conquered the Celtic regions of Cornwall and the English kingdoms of Kent, Sussex, Essex, East Anglia and Mercia. He also defeated Northumbria, and by 829 all the other kings in England had submitted to him as their overlord and supreme ruler. Egbert is therefore usually regarded as the first king of England; but this unity of the country under Wessex was only temporary. Mercia revolted against Egbert, and after his death England split up into four independent national states which incorporated the smaller kingdoms which he had conquered.

Wessex consisted of the whole of England south of the Thames from Dover to Land's End. Suffolk and Norfolk formed the kingdom of East Anglia. Mercia stretched from the Thames to the Humber, including London on its southern border, and Northumbria from the Humber to the Forth. Wales was divided into several small independent Celtic principalities. In Scotland, the king of Scots, Kenneth Macalpine, defeated and massacred the Picts in the middle of the ninth century; but the Picts were not totally exterminated, as the contemporary chroniclers made out, and many survived to intermarry with the Scots and become integrated into the kingdom of Scotland.

In the middle of the ninth century the Danes invaded England. The English in 870 viewed the Danish invasion with the same fear and horror that the Britons had felt when the heathen English came four hundred years before; but though the Danes were pagans, were cruel enemies, and had a simpler and more egalitarian social system than that which existed in the England which they invaded, they were on a higher level of civilisation than the bands of Hengist and of Aella of Sussex. They came in search of land and loot. In the countries where they settled, they became, like the English, a nation of free independent peasant smallholders, with a ruling class of professional fighting men.

After raiding England spasmodically for thirty years, the Danes launched a formidable invasion in 865, and during the next few years overran Northumbria, Mercia and East Anglia. In 869 they defeated and captured the young king of East Anglia, Edmund, who was afterwards known as St Edmund the Martyr. According to the story which is said to have been told to Dunstan, the archbishop and statesman, many years later by Edmund's standard-bearer, the Danes called on Edmund to repudiate Christianity and worship their pagan gods; when he refused, they tied him to a tree and shot him to death with arrows, prolonging his sufferings by shooting first at his arms and legs and postponing the death-shot for as long as possible. In later centuries, the King's shrine at Bury St Edmunds became a famous place of worship and pilgrimage. If the traditional story is true, it was an isolated instance of its kind. Ordinarily the Danes made no attempt to convert the Christians to paganism, though they could certainly sometimes treat their prisoners-of-war with great cruelty.

In the late autumn of 870 they penetrated into Wessex as far as Berkshire. Here they encountered a determined resistance from the men of Wessex under their King Ethelred and his brother Alfred. Alfred was born in 848, the fourth son of King Aethelwulf of Wessex. Having three elder brothers, his chances of succeeding to the throne were remote. This may have been the reason why he was educated to be a scholar and taught to read and write, and twice taken to Rome on a pilgrimage before he had reached the age of eight. But when he was twelve, his father died. His eldest brother, who succeeded as king, died two years later; and the second brother died after a reign of five years, leaving the third brother, Ethelred, as king. Alfred became Ethelred's second-in-command, and took part in his first campaign against the Danes when he and Ethelred led their army to the assistance of the men of Mercia who were defending Nottingham. He fought again under Ethelred in the desperate national resistance of the men of Wessex to the Danish invasion.

Between Christmas 870 and the following Easter, Ethelred and Alfred fought four battles against the Danes in Berkshire, winning two victories and suffering two defeats. Then Ethelred died, probably from a wound received in action, leaving a small son. The people of Wessex believed that at such a time they needed an adult warrior as their king, and set Ethelred's son aside and chose Alfred in his place. Alfred fought five more battles against the Danes in the summer of 871, but was glad to gain a breathing-space before the end of the year by agreeing to peace terms under which the Danes withdrew from Wessex on condition that Alfred paid them a large sum of money.

It was obvious that the peace would be no more than a truce, and in 875 the Danes again invaded Wessex. They outflanked Alfred and entered Devon, and for two years the armies fought each other between Gloucester and Exeter. But Alfred for once was caught napping during the Twelve Days of Christmas. In January 878 he was celebrating Twelfth Night at Chippenham when the Danes suddenly attacked the town and nearly captured him. He escaped, just in time, and took refuge with a small band of followers on the high ground to the south-west of Glastonbury in Somerset which at that time was cut off from the surrounding country by marshes and streams and was known as the Isle of Athelney. His secretary, Asser, who wrote his biography, tells us that he was able to obtain food and supplies for his men only by seizing them from the Danes and from those Englishmen who collaborated with the invader.

The famous story of his burning the cakes is said to have

18

occurred during his stay in Athelney. According to the story, Alfred took shelter in the house of one of his cowherds. The cowherd's wife, who had gone out, had left her cakes baking. When she returned she saw Alfred, whom she did not recognise, sitting by the hearth preparing his bow and arrows and other weapons and not noticing that her cakes were burned black. She scolded him, saying that he might have prevented the cakes from burning, as he would have been glad enough to have eaten them if they had been nicely cooked. The authenticity of the story is doubtful, as it is not referred to by Asser and was first written down by a chronicler about the year 1000, a hundred and twenty years later. There is nothing very improbable about it, but if it gives the impression that Alfred was a wandering fugitive in Athelney, it misrepresents his position, for he was always in command of a body of soldiers during the few weeks that he stayed there. It is more difficult to believe the other famous story, which was first recorded by William of Malmesbury in 1136. He described how Alfred went alone, disguised as a minstrel, into the Danish camp, where he stayed for several days and over-heard them discussing their military plans. It would have been most unwise for Alfred to have undertaken this spying mission in person, for there was no one else who could have succeeded him as king and general if he had been caught.

The tide of war soon turned, and in the summer of 878 Alfred won a great victory at Edington near Chippenham, and forced the Danes to agree to a peace under which the Danish king Guthrum and Alfred divided England between them. One of the terms of the peace treaty was that Guthrum should become a Christian, and Alfred acted as his godfather at the baptism ceremony. Although Alfred had clearly won the war, he was not in a strong enough position to dictate terms and impose a forcible conversion on Guthrum; so it is plain that Guthrum had no strong objection to becoming a Christian. He was doubtless eager, like the English kings two hundred years before, to achieve respectability by adopting Christianity as he transformed his nation of sea-raiders into members of a more settled community.

Six years later, the Danes renewed the war. By this time, Alfred had built a powerful navy which he could send into the North Sea to attack the Danes in their rear. During the course of the war Alfred captured London, and by the peace treaty of 886 the frontiers of 878 were altered in Alfred's favour. Alfred was to have all Wessex, and Mercia south-west of a line drawn from the mouth of the Thames to Chester, including London, while Guthrum retained Mercia to the north-east of the line, and all East Anglia and Northumbria, except for the area north of the Tees, which held out as an independent English kingdom.

It was primarily because of military exigencies that Alfred restored urban life to England after four hundred years. The Roman towns were almost completely destroyed by the English invaders in the fifth century. In the course of the years, foreign traders came to London, York, Southampton, Canterbury and Rochester, and made these places important urban centres; but there were no other towns. The kings had no fixed capitals, but constantly moved throughout their kingdoms with their courts and bodyguard. The Christian Church had established its bishops' seats in the old Roman towns which had often been the diocesan centres under the Christian Empire in the fourth century; but in most cases only the two simple wooden structures, the bishop's house and the cathedral, distinguished the place from any of the other agricultural villages.

As the Danish armies ravaged through the Wessex country-side, Alfred called on his subjects to leave their villages and settle together in strong places where they could build fortifications on natural defensive sites. These strong-points were called *burhs*, and were the origin of the walled towns, or boroughs, which survived for nine hundred years, and after losing their walls and gates during the urban expansion and industrialisation in the late eighteenth century, still remain as the towns of England. The men in these towns earned their livings not as agricultural workers, but as silversmiths and other craftsmen. Merchants also appeared in the towns, and carried on a growing trade with other towns and with France and Scandinavia.

Apart from his success in war, Alfred promulgated a code of laws and acted as a great patron of literature. Having learned to read and write Anglo-Saxon as a child, he now learned Latin, and translated a number of books from Latin into Anglo-Saxon, including treatises by Pope Gregory I and the sixth-century Roman philosopher, Boetius and Bede's *History*. He also super-vised the writing by various priests and scholars of the *Anglo-*

Saxon Chronicle. The *Chronicle*, following Bede's *History* and other works which are now lost, traced the history of the English in Britain from the date of the arrival of Hengist and Horsa right up to the days of Alfred himself. Like Offa, Alfred was eager to play a part in European affairs; and he even sent envoys to the Arab rulers of Jerusalem, and to India.

In 892 the Danes attacked Alfred and began the fourth war. They had brought reinforcements from Scandinavia, and Alfred found himself in the most serious situation which he had faced since his days in Athelney. A Danish army invaded Mercia and advanced as far as Welshpool and Chester before it was defeated and driven back by the English and the Britons of Wales, with whom Alfred had made an alliance. After four years of warfare, Alfred was everywhere victorious; but the Danes still retained all the territory which they had held at the start of the fourth war when Alfred died on 26 October 899 at the age of fifty-one. There has never been any doubt that he died on 26 October, but there has been a good deal of controversy about the year. Until the beginning of the twentieth century, it was believed that he died in 901; more recently, 900 has often been given as the date. There is, however, no doubt that he died in the year which he and his contemporaries called 900, owing to the Anglo-Saxon practice of starting the year on 1 September, but which, by our modern computation, was 899.

Alfred was succeeded by his son Edward the Elder, who conducted a series of very successful campaigns against the Danes, in which he made good use of the fleet which Alfred had left him. When he died in 924, the frontiers of Wessex were on the Humber, and the Danes held only the old kingdom of Deira, between the Humber and the Tees. Edward was succeeded by his son Athelstan, who extended still further the frontiers of Wessex. Athelstan was only four when his grandfather, King Alfred, died; but Alfred had loved the precocious child, and had foretold that he would accomplish great things when he grew up. Athelstan captured York, and became king of all England. In 937 he defeated an invasion by the Irish and the Danes from Ireland at the Battle of Brunanburh, the site of which has not been identified, but was probably in Lancashire. He played an important part in European diplomacy. His sister, Edith, married the son of the German King, Henry the Fowler; but she did not live to see her husband become the Holy Roman Emperor, Otto the Great.

Athelstan's successors, with the archbishop of Canterbury, Dunstan, acting as their counsellor, maintained the overlordship which Athelstan had won, and the four Anglo-Saxon kingdoms were never again to be separate states. The Danish kingdom in England was destroyed; but the Danish settlers in eastern Mercia were allowed to retain their own local customs and laws in the area known as the Danelaw, in the neighbourhood of the 'Five Boroughs' of Stamford, Leicester, Derby, Nottingham and Lincoln. The superiority of the kings of Wessex was formally recognised in 975 when all the kings in Britain, including the king of Scots, assembled at Chester and paid homage for their lands to King Edgar of Wessex. According to a chronicler of the next century, the other kings, during the meeting at Chester, rowed Edgar for a short way along the River Dee, with each king toiling at an oar while Edgar sat at the prow, in token of his overlordship. In return for the submission of the king of Scots, Edgar granted him the Northumbrian provinces of Lothian and Cumberland.

The tenth century was a period of important social change. The Danish wars of Alfred and Edward the Elder had caused social and economic disruption over a long period. In his campaigns against the Danes, Alfred had ordered the people to leave their farms and man the defences of the boroughs; and he had repeatedly called out the local peasants to assist the warriors of his bodyguard and serve for prolonged periods in the army. A large number of farms were devastated by the Danes; and during the last Danish war, Alfred had destroyed the crops in Mercia to deprive the invaders of supplies. As in most wars, a few people became richer and most people became poorer. Many peasants were therefore compelled to surrender their land to the large landowners, and to deliver themselves into personal slavery in return for a promise of protection from some powerful lord. Other peasants agreed to hold lands from a lord in return for working on his land for several days in the week or rendering other services to him. By the end of the tenth century, slavery had become established throughout England on a much larger scale than in earlier times; a form of serfdom and the manorial system had appeared; and the power of the leading noblemen had increased.

The popular local assemblies of the early Anglo-Saxons had developed into the 'communal courts', the Court of the Shire and the Court of the Hundred, the hundred being probably a collection of a hundred farms, and covering an area which included several ecclesiastical parishes. These courts were presided over by the king's sheriff, or a subordinate royal officer, who consulted the local inhabitants about the business of the district and the guilt or innocence of persons suspected of crimes. During the tenth century the great landowners increasingly took over the administration of justice in their districts. The king granted to more and more of them the right to establish their own courts in which they could try disputes between their tenants, serfs and slaves, and punish them for crimes that they had committed. The lords also tended to control the communal courts which continued to exist alongside their own courts.

By the end of the tenth century, the king's officers were selecting twelve men in each district to decide whether there was a *prima facie* case to justify the prosecution of a defendant before the communal courts or the courts of the local lord. This was the origin of the Grand Jury, which continued until 1933. If the jury decided that the defendant must face trial, his guilt or innocence was determined by either ordeal or compurgation. The ordeal referred the decision to God. In the ordeal by fire, the defendant's hand was burned with a hot iron, bandaged up, and examined three days later; if the burn had healed he was innocent; if not, he was guilty. In ordeal by water, the defendant was bound hand and foot and thrown into a pond. If he sank in the usual way, he was held to be innocent, and was rescued and set free; if he floated, it was a proof that he was sustained by the devil, and he was convicted.

The defendant could escape the ordeal if he could prove his innocence by compurgation. He was required to produce a certain number of compurgators – the number varied with the gravity of the crime with which he was charged – who would swear that they believed him to be innocent. If the necessary number of compurgators came forward, he was automatically acquitted. It was not an altogether ridiculous method of procedure in an age when people believed in the binding validity of an oath and dreaded the consequences which befell the immortal soul of a perjurer.

At the end of the century, the English faced a new threat from the Danes, who came in increased strength from Scandinavia. The king of England, Ethelred II, had come to the throne at the age of ten in unfortunate circumstances when his half-brother, King Edward, a boy of fifteen, was murdered by the servants of Ethelred's mother as he rode into the courtyard of Corfe Castle in Dorset on 18 March 978. The story told by the later chroniclers was that Edward's stepmother planned the murder in order to put her son Ethelred on the throne, and that she handed Edward a cup of wine on his arrival, while he sat on his horse in the courtyard of the castle, in order to distract his attention while her servants stabbed him in the back. This is probably untrue; but public opinion was horrified at the assassination of the young king, who was worshipped as Edward the Martyr; and the fact that Ethelred was the beneficiary of the crime was one of the reasons for his great unpopularity during his life and after his death, despite the fact that he was only a child when his half-brother was killed. He increased his unpopularity by his policy of paying money to the Danes on the condition that they left his realm in peace, and raising the money by a tax on his subjects which was known as the Danegeld; for the payment of this money seemed only to encourage the Danes to return and demand more. He has become known in history as Ethelred the Unready, though the word '*unraed*' in the Anglo-Saxon language referred not to his unpreparedness but to his failure to follow good advice.

The Danes had increased in power and civilisation during the previous century. King Sweyn had become a Christian, though a rather doubtful one, as he was greatly under the influence of a fanatically pagan wife. In 992 Sweyn invaded England. Ethelred made peace with Sweyn, but in 1002 treacherously murdered the Danes living in England. The victims included Sweyn's sister, the brave and beautiful Gunnhild, and her husband and son. Sweyn then invaded England again, and fought a savage war of revenge. When he died in 1014 he was succeeded as commander by his son Cnut (Canute), who was aged nineteen.

Ethelred died two years later. His son, Edmund Ironside, was a far more heroic figure than Ethelred, and at first he more than held his own against Cnut in the fighting in England in 1016. But after Cnut had won a decisive victory near Ashingdon in Essex,

24

the two young kings decided to make peace. Edmund was to have Wessex, and Cnut everything north of the Thames. A few months later, Edmund Ironside died suddenly, and Cnut became king of all England. Edmund's death was probably due to natural causes, but the chroniclers' story of his assassination might have become accepted in English legend had it not involved unpleasant lavatory details which made it unsuitable for retelling in modern times. He is said to have been stabbed as he sat on a privy by the murderer who was concealed in the pit below.

Cnut consolidated his position by assassinating several prominent English nobles – Edmund Ironside's sons succeeded in escaping to Hungary – and by marrying Ethelred the Unready's young widow, Emma. She was herself of Norse origin, being the daughter of the duke of Normandy. The Norsemen had settled there during the ninth century and had become assimilated into feudal Christendom. The dukes of Normandy were vassals, but very powerful vassals, of the kings of France.

For nineteen years, England was part of Cnut's Scandinavian empire, which included Denmark, Norway, and Northern Germany from the Elbe to the Polish frontier on the Oder, while Cnut exercised overlordship over the Danes who had conquered and settled in the Orkneys and Shetlands, the mainland in the extreme north of Scotland, the Isle of Man, and parts of Ireland. Macbeth, whose title was not thane of Glamis, as Shakespeare states, but mormaer of Moreb, did homage to Cnut, not to Duncan, King of Scots, for his lands in Moray and Ross-shire.

Cnut spent most of his reign fighting in Norway against a formidable rebellion; but he visited England from time to time, and travelled throughout his English kingdom. He governed England through regional governors, who taxed the people to pay for his Norwegian campaign, but otherwise interfered very little with the economic and social way of life of Anglo-Saxon England. Some of these governors were Danes; but the governors of Mercia and Wessex, and several of Cnut's other officials in England, were native-born Englishmen. The governor of Wessex was Earl Godwin. According to some of the later chroniclers, he was the son of a swineherd; as a little boy he had attracted the attention of a Danish officer who called at the swineherd's hovel to demand food and shelter, and the officer granted the boy's request to be allowed to serve in Cnut's army. Other writers say that Godwin was the son of a Sussex gentleman; but whoever his father may have been, it is certain that Godwin rose rapidly, through service in Cnut's bodyguard in the Norwegian campaigns and by his marriage to the sister of Cnut's brother-in-law, the regent of Denmark, to become the most powerful noble in England.

Cnut's extensive northern territories made him an influential power in European politics, and he established his international prestige by becoming a prominent benefactor of the Christian Church. He endowed many abbeys, and worshipped at the shrine in Bury St Edmunds of Edmund the Martyr, whom his Danish predecessors had tortured to death a hundred and fifty years earlier. He travelled in great state to Rome to attend the coronation of the Holy Roman Emperor, Conrad II, and married his daughter to Conrad's son, the future Emperor Henry III. Although he lived more or less openly with two wives, the Church extolled his virtues and could rely on his support.

The story of his encounter with the waves was not written down until more than a hundred years after his death; but the chronicler Henry of Huntingdon probably recorded a well-established tradition, for he obtained much of his information from old men who had been young children during Cnut's reign. The story was typical of the attempts by the chroniclers to praise his piety. According to the story, on one occasion when Cnut was in Hampshire, his courtiers, praising him as a powerful and invincible king, told him that if he were to order the sea to go in or out he would be able to control the flow of the tides, as even the waves would obey him. Cnut was shocked and disgusted by their flattery. In order to expose them, he ordered them to place a chair of state on the sands on Southampton Water, and, taking his seat there, surrounded by his courtiers, he ordered the tide not to come in and wet his feet. He remained seated on the chair until the waves lapped all over his feet, and then upbraided his courtiers, pointing out that the waves had not obeyed him because only God could control the waves. It is ironical that this famous story is often incorrectly remembered today, and that many people think of 'King Canute' as an old fool who was stupid enough to believe that he could control the waves. Evidently there is a limit to the efficacy of the Church's propaganda on Cnut's behalf.

In November 1035 Cnut was travelling through the south of England and stayed the night at Shaftesbury. Here he had a stroke while playing chess, and died at the age of forty. He had chosen his son by Queen Emma, Harthacnut, as his successor; but as Harthacnut was in Denmark preparing to meet a Norwegian invasion, his half-brother Harold, the son of Cnut's other wife, seized the throne of England. As possible successors to Cnut, apart from Harold and Harthacnut, there were Queen Emma's sons by her first marriage to King Ethelred the Unready. Godwin, as the ruler of Wessex, was the key figure in the situation. He placed Harold on the throne; and when Emma's English son, Alfred, who had been living in Normandy, returned to England to visit his mother, Godwin arrested him. While Alfred was in his custody, some of his officers put out his eyes, and soon after- wards he died of his sufferings. Godwin always swore that Alfred had been blinded without his authority or knowledge.

Harthacnut was on the point of invading England when Harold died in 1040. Harthacnut succeeded him, but fell dead while drinking at a wedding feast two years later. King Magnus of Norway then claimed the throne of England under the terms of a treaty which he had made with Harthacnut; but Godwin used his influence to obtain the crown for Alfred's brother Edward, the son of Ethelred the Unready and Emma, who was in exile in Normandy. Edward's religious enthusiasm earned him the title in history of Edward the Confessor, and during the first years of his reign he was completely under the influence of Godwin, who governed the country while the king concerned himself with his religious devotions and the building of Westminster Abbey.

Edward the Confessor was too devout and spiritual to be interested in worldly affairs, but he resented the domination of Godwin; and though he owed his throne to Godwin, and married Godwin's daughter Edith, he suspected him of having been responsible for the blinding and death of his brother Alfred. He turned for support to Queen Emma's great-nephew, Duke William of Normandy, at whose court he had lived as a refugee; and he invited Norman and other nobles from France to stay with him in London and Winchester. Godwin, who felt that his power was threatened by the French influence, became the leader of the English opposition to it.

In 1051, the count of Boulogne and his retinue were attacked by the people of Dover on their journey home, and several of them were killed. King Edward ordered Godwin, as earl of Wessex, to punish the citizens of Dover in the customary way by sacking the town; but Godwin refused to do so. Edward turned for support to other nobles who were jealous of Godwin's power, first and foremost to Siward, earl of Northumbria (the 'Old Siward' of Shakespeare's *Macbeth*) – a Danish warrior who had risen to prominence under Cnut, and whose heroic exploits, according to his admirers, included the slaying of a dragon in the Orkneys. Godwin was overthrown, and fled to Flanders. Edward now came completely under Norman influence. William of Normandy visited England, and Edward apparently promised him that he would appoint him as his heir to the crown of England.

But a few months later, Godwin returned from exile with a strong naval force, and re-established himself in power. Edward's Norman friends fled for their lives. Godwin was in complete control of England when he died in 1053 of an apoplectic stroke while drinking heavily at a banquet; and his son Harold succeeded him as earl of Wessex and as the unofficial ruler of the whole country.

One of the first acts of Harold's government was to go to war with the Scottish king, Macbeth. He had become king after killing the former king, Duncan – not, as Shakespeare made out, by murdering him in his sleep, but in battle. Macbeth claimed the throne of Scotland through his wife, Gruach (Shakespeare's Lady Macbeth), who was entitled to succeed under the very complicated provisions of the old Celtic law of succession, though under the Anglo-Saxon law, which was gradually replacing it, Duncan was the lawful king. After Duncan's death his son Malcolm Canmore (Big Head) fled to England and was given asylum by Edward the Confessor. Macbeth retaliated by granting asylum to the Norman refugees who escaped to Scotland when Godwin returned to power.

The tensions between England and Scotland led to war in 1054. Siward invaded Scotland in order to overthrow Macbeth and put Malcolm on the throne; but after Siward had won a victory, in which his son was killed, the matter was settled by a compromise which left Macbeth as king of Scotland but granted Cumbria to Malcolm as an independent kingdom. Three years later, Malcolm renewed the war against Macbeth, who was defeated and killed, and Malcolm became King of Scotland.

The death of young Siward in the war against Macbeth enabled Harold to extend his power; for when old Siward died in 1055, there was no heir to succeed him as earl of Northumbria. The earldom was given to Harold's brother, Tostig. Soon afterwards, another brother, Gyrth, was made earl of East Anglia. But Tostig's misgovernment provoked a serious revolt in Northumbria. Harold was compelled to sacrifice Tostig, and he fled to Norway, vowing revenge against Harold, whom he thought had betrayed him.

It was felt on all sides that the death of Edward the Confessor was likely to be the signal for a bitter struggle for the succession. Harold had no blood relationship with the king; but he was Edward's brother-in-law and the most powerful man in England, and there were rumours that he would persuade the Witan, the great council of the nobles, to choose him as king when Edward died. William of Normandy claimed the throne, by a rather far-fetched argument, through his great-aunt, Queen Emma; and Harald Haardraade, who had become king of Norway after an adventurous life as a mercenary in Russia and Constantinople, put forward an equally questionable claim under King Magnus's treaty with Harthacnut.

In 1064, Harold went on a journey to France, and was seized near Abbeville and imprisoned by the count of Ponthieu, who was a vassal of William of Normandy. William insisted that the count should set Harold free. He entertained Harold as his guest at his court in Normandy, and Harold served in his army against his rebellious vassals in Brittany. But Harold felt that he was being held as a virtual prisoner by William; and before he sailed for England he took an oath at Bayeux, promising that when Edward the Confessor died, he would uphold William's claim to the English throne. Harold afterwards protested that he had taken the oath under duress, and that William had tricked him by concealing the fact that the box upon which Harold held his hand as he took the oath contained the bones of some saints.

Edward the Confessor died on 5 January 1066. On his death-bed he apparently chose Harold as his successor, and this was confirmed by the Witan, who proclaimed Harold as king. William of Normandy denounced him as a violator of the oath which he had taken at Bayeux, and prepared to invade England and seize the crown as the lawful heir of Edward the Confessor. He raised an army composed of his own Norman knights and tenants, his vassals in Brittany, and mercenaries from Flanders, the South of France, and Norman Sicily. He won the goodwill of the two most powerful rulers of Western Europe, the Holy Roman Emperor and the pope. Relations between the pope and Harold were very bad, because, during Godwin's lifetime, the pro-Norman Archbishop of Canterbury had been expelled without the pope's consent and replaced by Godwin's nominee, Stigand, who had been excommunicated by the pope. At the papal court, the powerful dignitary Hildebrand, who later became Pope Gregory VII, was relying on the support of the Normans from Normandy to Sicily in his campaign to reform the abuses of the Church and to increase the power of the papacy, which ultimately led to his spectacular humiliation of the Emperor Henry IV at Canossa. Hildebrand was William's strongest supporter at the papal court, and he persuaded the pope to condemn Harold as an oathbreaker and to give his blessing to William's invasion of England.

Meanwhile Harold's brother Tostig had placed his services at the disposal of Harald Haardraade. During the summer of 1066 he ravaged the coast of England from the Isle of Wight to the Humber. Both William and Harald Haardraade were fitting out a fleet to invade England, while Harold mobilised an army, calling up the levies from the shires throughout England. He also maintained a fleet in the Channel to prevent William's invasion.

William and Harold showed their different characters in their generalship. William, having taken the very daring decision to invade England with a force far inferior in numbers to that which Harold could raise against him, proceeded slowly and cautiously, consolidating his position at every step. Harold showed courage, initiative and dash, but committed several blunders, and seems to have underestimated his enemy. Throughout most of the summer, William's fleet remained inactive in the Seine estuary; when at last he was ready to launch the invasion, northerly winds prevented him from sailing beyond the mouth of the Somme. Harold's seamen in the Channel became impatient and almost mutinous; so in the middle of September he disbanded them, believing that William could not invade that year. He was also taken by surprise when he was told at about the same time that Harald Haardraade had landed in Yorkshire, for he had thought that the only threat from Scandinavia was Tostig's raiding parties.

Harald Haardraade captured York, and encamped his army at Stamford Bridge while he planned his advance to the south. He had no idea that Harold was marching north with his bodyguard and the local levies whom he had picked up in the districts through which he marched on the road from London. The Norwegians were taken completely by surprise when Harold's troops suddenly attacked their encampment on 25 September. They were utterly defeated, and both Harald Haardraade and Tostig were killed.

Two days later, the wind having changed at last, William's invasion fleet sailed for England on the night of 27 September. He himself became separated from the fleet during the crossing, and he might easily have been killed or captured if Harold's navy had still been patrolling the Channel; but he and his 6000 soldiers landed safely near Pevensey on the morning of 28 September. He knew that Harald Haardraade had invaded Yorkshire, but had not heard the news of Stamford Bridge, and did not know whether he would have to fight Harold or Harald Haardraade for the crown of England. Meanwhile he consolidated his position on the Sussex coast, having decided not to advance inland until he knew what opposition he would have to face.

When the news of the landing reached Harold at York, he summoned the levies of all the shires of England to assemble to fight William, and marched south. He moved with great speed, covering the 190 miles from York to London in less than nine days. Instead of waiting in London until the levies from the shires arrived, he decided to attack William at once with his bodyguard and the levies that had joined him on the march from Yorkshire. This was taking an unnecessary risk, because, though the army at his disposal was slightly larger than William's, it was not so well equipped, and had no cavalry or archers to match the horsemen and bowmen whom William had brought from Normandy. But he was eager to get at William, and remembered the success of his rapid advance and surprise attack at Stamford Bridge. On 11 October he left London and marched into Sussex.

At the last moment it was William, not Harold, who had the advantage of surprise. Hearing that Harold was advancing against him, he marched north to meet him. When the armies

31

came into contact 'at the grey apple tree' some seven miles north of Hastings, just south of the place which afterwards became the village of Battle, on the morning of Saturday 14 October 1066, Harold was taken unawares, and forced to fight in a place where his army was in a rather cramped position and deprived of full freedom to manoeuvre. But William's first attack was beaten back, and the English had the best of the first hours' fighting. It was only William's courage and coolness which prevented his men's retreat from being turned into a rout.

The Norman commanders showed superior tactical skill on the battlefield. On several occasions, by pretending to retreat, they tricked the English into pursuing them too far, and then cut them off and destroyed them. Late in the afternoon Harold was killed, apparently by a chance shot from a bowman; and soon afterwards the English broke and fled. A small group of them put up a final desperate resistance in a hollow, but they were wiped out, though William himself was nearly killed in overcoming their last stand.

This battle, which was somewhat inaccurately named the Battle of Hastings, has been rightly remembered as one of the most decisive events in English history. Nine hundred years later, there is an accepted national myth that 1066 was the last occasion on which England was invaded. This is untrue, because England was successfully invaded by foreign armies from the Continent in 1101, in 1153, in 1216, in 1326, in 1470, in 1471, in 1485, and in 1688,* without counting the occasions when a Scottish army crossed the border. But none of these later invasions, except that of 1688, caused so fundamental a change in the way of life of the English people.

* Not in 1399, when Bolingbroke landed accompanied by only fifteen armed men.

32

CHAPTER 3

THE
NORMAN RULERS
AND
HENRY I
(1066–1135)

It took William five years of almost continual fighting to conquer England; for the English continued to resist, and chase Edgar Atheling, a grandson of Edmund Ironside, as their king. After his victory over Harold, William marched east along the coast, took Dover and Canterbury, and advanced on London; but after capturing Southwark, he hesitated to storm his way across London Bridge, which was stoutly defended by the citizens. Instead, he adopted the strategy to which he usually resorted when he wished to capture a well-defended town; he wasted the country all around in order to frighten and starve the townsmen into surrender. He burned Southwark, marched west, forded the Thames at Wallingford, and moved along the north bank of the river towards London, devastating the countryside. When he reached Berkhamstead he received the surrender of the Londoners and of many of the English nobility, and he was crowned king of England in the recently built Westminster Abbey on Christmas Day 1066.

He felt secure enough to pay a visit to Normandy in the new year, but during his absence rebellion broke out in England. The rebels included not only the English but also his dissatisfied Norman knights in Kent, who thought that they had been inadequately rewarded for their valour at the Battle of Hastings. He suppressed the revolt, and in 1068 subdued the English resistance in the west by a campaign which culminated in the capture of Exeter; and in the next two years he crushed resistance in the north. But the Danes then intervened; seizing the opportunity to acquire loot, and perhaps territory, in England, the king of Denmark invaded eastern England, and in alliance with the English captured Peterborough and York.

William out-manoeuvred and out-marched them, suppressed a rising of the English in Mercia, and devastated the north of England to deprive his enemies of supplies and to terrify the native population into submission. By these means he defeated them without fighting a major battle. In 1070 the Danes sailed for home with their booty, leaving the English to their fate; and in the following year the last English resistance was overcome when the leader of a popular movement in East Anglia, Hereward – known to later generations, but not to his contemporaries, as Hereward the Wake – was finally driven out of his encampment in the Isle of Ely, where he had defied William's forces for many months.

William still had a war with Scotland on his hands. Malcolm Canmore had married Margaret, the sister of Edgar Atheling, had given shelter to Edgar in Scotland, and had raided Northumbria. William therefore invaded Scotland in 1072 and reached the Tay, where Malcolm submitted. He agreed to expel Edgar and the English refugees from Scotland, and did homage to William, though an ambiguity – perhaps a deliberate ambiguity – in the wording of the oath made it uncertain whether he was doing homage for his realm of Scotland or only for Cumberland and his lands in England.

Compared with the previous conquerors of Britain – the Romans, the English and the Danes – William was not vindictive towards his defeated enemies. The lands of the English who fought at Hastings were in many cases confiscated; but the supporters of Harold who submitted to William as he marched on London were pardoned and well treated. William gave quarter to the defenders of Exeter; and as late as 1070, four years after his coronation in Westminster Abbey had given him a plausible pretext for treating his enemies as rebels, he was still granting them pardon after his victories. By 1071 he was mutilating the captured followers of Hereward who had held out in the Isle of Ely; but Hereward himself, who escaped when William finally captured his redoubt, was pardoned and treated with honour when he surrendered some years later.

William always claimed that he became king of England, not as a foreign invader and conqueror, but as the lawful heir of King Edward the Confessor; but his victory brought continental institutions into England and caused important changes in English social life. He and his court spoke French, and to some extent at least French replaced Anglo-Saxon as the official and legal language, though many legal and other public documents were issued in both French and Anglo-Saxon. The English council of the great nobles and churchmen, the Witan, continued in existence and developed into the Great Council of the tenants-in-chief, the *Magnum Concilium*, and in due course became the House of Lords.

The growth in the wealth and power of the aristocracy in the tenth century had led to the introduction into England of many of the institutions of continental feudalism; but this process was greatly accelerated by the Norman conquest. The Anglo-Saxon communal courts continued to function for several centuries after 1066, but became increasingly unimportant, while the jurisdiction of the courts of the landowners was extended. The English procedure of ordeal by fire and water, and compurgation, was retained; but the Normans allowed the defendant to choose the alternative ordeal by battle, in which he fought his accuser and relied on God to give victory to the just. If the defendant was killed or forced to surrender before the end of the day, he was guilty; if he won, or held out undefeated until nightfall, he was innocent.

Instead of the social system which had prevailed in the rural areas of Anglo-Saxon England, with the large landowners, the independent peasant smallholders, the serfs and the slaves, the Normans, during the century which followed the conquest, introduced the feudal system of Normandy and continental Europe. The king, who was considered to be the lord of all the soil in his kingdom, granted land to his freehold tenants, who in return paid homage to him for their land and performed services for it. The tenants-in-chief who held their lands directly from the king granted parts of it to their own tenants, who likewise granted it to tenants, so that there might be seven or eight intermediary tenants between the ultimate occupier and the king; but there tended to be fewer degrees of subinfeudation in England than on the Continent.

There were four kinds of freehold tenure – knight service, sergeanty, frankalmoign and socage. The tenant holding by knight service was bound to serve his lord in war with a specified number of soldiers for up to forty days a year. Tenants holding by sergeanty performed personal services for the lord, varying from the grand sergeanty of high officials at court who acted as the King's carver or cup-bearer to the petty sergeanty of the village blacksmith or cobbler. The bishops, priests and monasteries held their land by frankalmoign in return for their prayers for the welfare and the souls of their lord and his family. The majority of the freehold tenants held by socage, or labour service, working for a specified number of days in each week in their lord's fields.

Tenants who held by any of these freehold tenures were all freemen; but the majority of the population were villeins, or serfs, living on the manors which the Normans introduced. The lord of the manor granted land not only to freemen, but also to villeins who held by copyhold, not freehold, tenure. The copy-holders were normally required to work in the fields of the lord of the manor, or sometimes to perform other services for him, in the same way as freehold tenants; but unlike the freeholders, who were free to leave if they wished and to try to make a better bargain for other land with other lords, the villein copyholders were compelled by law to continue working on the same plot of land for the lord or for any of the lord's successors who acquired the land.

The feudal system never existed in practice in its perfect form throughout any community at any time, and least of all in England after the Norman conquest, where the remnants of a past, and the germs of a future, system existed side by side with feudalism. Although the Normans, with the support of the Church, abolished slavery and freed the English slaves, they did not hurry the process unduly, and slaves were still to be found in England for a generation after 1066; and the system of commuting feudal services by payment of money had begun before slavery finally disappeared. As early as the reign of Offa in the eighth century there were isolated cases of tenants paying an annual rent in money to their landlords. By the thirteenth century, a large number of freehold tenants holding by socage, and in some cases even the villeins, were paying money rents instead of performing labour services; but the distinction between free churls and unfree villeins continued until the beginning of the fifteenth century.

The terms of the tenure of the villeins in their copyhold tenures were fixed by the custom of the manor. When the villeins' labour services were commuted into rents, the rents were also fixed by the custom of the manor. Copyhold tenure, with its almost complete protection against eviction, continued after serfdom had disappeared, and inflation reduced the copyholders' money rents into purely nominal payments; but the copyholder's obligation to surrender his best beast, or pay its value in money, to the lord of the manor when he succeeded to the tenancy at his father's death continued in some cases to be a burden to the copyholder until copyhold tenure was finally abolished on 1 January 1926. By this time a new class of tenant had appeared – the 'statutory tenant' of the Rent Restriction Acts, who, like the copyholder, was protected by law against rent increases and eviction.

The towns were partly within, and partly outside, the feudal system. The borough corporation usually held their land from some local landowner, or often as tenants-in-chief from the king, by socage or knight service, which from the earliest times were almost always converted into money rent. Many lords of the manor held tenements within the local borough from the borough corporation by feudal tenure commuted into money rent, and placed a freeholder or a villein in the tenement to operate a butcher's yard, a tannery or a shop for the benefit of the manor. But by the beginning of the twelfth century the boroughs were being granted charters by the king or the local nobleman which abolished serfdom in the boroughs, relieved them from feudal obligations, and exempted them from the jurisdiction of their lord's feudal court. The charters allowed the boroughs to set up their own courts, the courts merchant, which corresponded to the courts maritime in the ports.

The greatest deviation from pure feudalism in Norman England was deliberately introduced as a precautionary act of policy by William the Conqueror. He knew, from his own experience, that great feudal tenants-in-chief could threaten the power of the king, for he himself, as duke of Normandy, had weakened the power of his overlord, King Philip of France. He therefore avoided, as far as possible, granting large tracts of unbroken land to powerful noblemen, and did so only in favour of great dignitaries like the Earls of Northumberland, Hugh the Wolf, Earl of Chester, and Roger de Montgomery, Earl of Shrewsbury, whose lands were situated on the borders of Scotland and Wales, where it was necessary for the security of William's realm that there should be a powerful tenant-in-chief, and where this over-powerful magnate would probably be too busy fighting the Scots and the Welsh to have any spare time in which to challenge the authority of his king.

William adopted an even more important and unusual expedient to protect himself against rebellious tenants-in-chief. The usual practice under feudalism was for every tenant to swear fealty and pay homage only to his own overlord, so that only the tenants-in-chief took the oath directly to the King. A tenant-in-chief who violated his oath of loyalty to the king might nevertheless try to exploit the oath of allegiance which his own tenants had taken to him, in order to compel them to serve him, as their overlord, in his rebellion against the king. At Christmas 1085 William, after nearly forty years of almost continuous struggle against his feudal barons in Normandy and England, including his own son, alarmed his subjects by ordering the compilation of the Domesday Book as a census of land holdings in England. Having thus obtained an almost complete record of his subjects for the purposes of taxation and military service, he summoned every lord and knight in England who held land by knight service to meet him at Salisbury in August 1086 and to take an oath of allegiance to him personally as king, which in case of conflict was to prevail over any oath that they had taken to their immediate feudal overlord.

It is impossible to know how far the Norman conquest of England affected the lives of the ordinary Englishman, and how far he resented the Normans as oppressors. The population of the towns probably noticed little change in their way of life, though there was resentment, in the early years, over the great castles of wood and stone which the Normans built in the more important towns as a fortress for their garrisons in the locality; for the castles were not only a demonstration of Norman power over the conquered nation, but many of the townsmen's houses had to be demolished to make room for the castles within the city walls. Otherwise the changes which took place in the towns were for the better. William the Conqueror, once he had established his authority in a district, provided that firm government and the enforcement of law and order which throughout the history of Britain has always been highly valued by the middle classes and by the majority of the common people, especially by the citizens of the towns; and the increased contacts with Continental Europe caused an expansion of trade in the towns and a growth in the luxuries available to the wealthier classes there.

There were greater changes in the countryside, and not all of these were to the advantage of the common people. The chief losers by the Norman conquest were the English aristocracy, whose lands were usually confiscated and granted to Normans. Their free tenants, the churls, became in most cases freehold tenants by socage of the Norman landowners, and their labour obligations were often increased under the new feudal system. If there were many cases of free English churls becoming villeins of the Norman lords of the manor, their lot certainly worsened; but many of the villeins had already been serfs under English rule, and many others had been slaves. For the slaves, there was probably at least a slight improvement in the change from slavery to villeinage, for the villeins had clearly demarcated rights, as well as duties, under the feudal system.

Serfdom, as a status, was nevertheless resented by the villeins, and increasingly so during the following three centuries. In many cases, their feudal lords went far beyond their legal rights, claimed privileges to which they were not entitled, and violated the rights of the villeins, especially in times of civil war and when weak kings failed to enforce law and order with severity. The notorious *Jus primae noctis*, or *droit de seigneur*, by which the overlord was entitled to require the bride of any of his tenants to spend the first night after her marriage in his bed, is a figment of the imagination of the Liberal propagandists of the eighteenth and nineteenth centuries. It was never a recognised feudal right of the lord at any period in any country of Christendom; but there can be no doubt that it was one of many unlawful privileges which were sometimes claimed in practice by unscrupulous lords.

Feudal law and custom provided various loopholes through which villeins could gain their freedom. In ordinary circumstances this could only be done if the lord freed his villeins by a charter of manumission or in some other manner established by local custom. It was not uncommon for lords on their deathbeds to free villeins who had rendered loyal service, thus rewarding the villeins while depriving their heirs, not themselves, of the villein's services. At an early period the Church established the principle that no priest in holy orders, and no monk, could be a villein, and that any villein who was ordained or took his vows as a monk thereby automatically became a freeman; but in 1164 it was enacted that no villein could take orders or vows without the consent of his feudal lord – a law to which the Church did not object, as it prevented an abuse whereby undesirable characters had entered the Church for unworthy motives.

The easiest way, in practice, for a villein to gain his freedom was by running away illegally and seeking refuge in a town, for the law laid down that if a villein who escaped was not recaptured within a year and a day he became legally a freeman. The lord was only entitled to seize an escaping villein and bring him back by force if he caught him within four days of his escape; after this, the lord must bring legal proceedings in the court of the feudal lord or of the borough where the villein was found. This could sometimes cause delays which meant that the year and a day had elapsed, and the villein had gained his freedom, before the legal proceedings to recapture him had been completed.

The power of the Church in England increased after the Norman conquest, though the pope was disappointed in the expectations which had led him to support William's expedition so enthusiastically in 1066, for William double-crossed Hildebrand. He agreed to send the annual payment of Peter's Pence to Rome, but refused to do homage to the pope for England, as Hildebrand demanded after he became Pope Gregory VII in 1075. William insisted on his right to veto the appointment of any bishop in England, and informed Gregory that he would not allow any papal bull to be promulgated in England without his permission. Gregory, who could impose his authority over the Holy Roman

Emperor at Canossa, was powerless against William the Conqueror.

Though William successfully resisted Gregory's attempts to extend papal power over England, he and his Normans were devout Christians and willingly accepted the spiritual, as opposed to the temporal, authority of the Church. They took the Church's teaching about the wickedness of shedding blood sufficiently seriously that William's half-brother Odo, the bishop of Bayeux, took part in the Battle of Hastings wielding, not a sword or lance, but a great club with which he could crush the enemy soldiers' skulls but not, as a churchman, shed their blood; and when the Church imposed a fine as penance on every Norman who had killed an enemy soldier in the battle, as a condition of granting him absolution for wilfully causing the death of another human being, all the warriors of the victorious army paid up.

It was because of the Church's disapproval of the taking of human life that the Normans virtually abolished capital punishment, which had been very commonly applied under English rule. Only one man, the prominent rebel Waltheof, was executed during William the Conqueror's reign. Instead, the Normans punished the worst criminals by blinding or castrating them, and cutting off their hands or feet. This punishment by mutilation shocked the historians of the early nineteenth century, who thought it right that capital punishment should be applied for stealing and for 223 different categories of crime; but the eleventh-century Normans believed that, as compared with the death penalty, mutilation and castration were more humane punishments which, however severe, at least left the offender with some kind of a life and with time in which to repent of his sins before it pleased God to end his days on earth.

The greatest hardships suffered by the inhabitants of England as a result of the Norman conquest were caused by William's ruthless, but effective, way of waging war by ravaging a tract of country, burning all the houses and crops, in order to prevent the enemy or any prospective enemy from obtaining shelter or provisions there. In the autumn of 1066 he ravaged the country on both banks of the Thames between London and Wallingford; in 1069–70 he ravaged nearly the whole of Yorkshire and many parts of Mercia; and in 1085, hearing that the king of Denmark was planning to invade England during his absence in Normandy, he sent orders to ravage the coastal districts of Essex and Kent. Hardship was also suffered by those unlucky enough to live in a royal forest, for William ravaged land not only to defeat his enemies in war but also to ensure his pleasures in time of peace. He created the New Forest by expelling the local inhabitants from the area and destroying the villages and farms in order to provide himself with a good hunting ground, and made laws to punish poachers by blinding and mutilation and to prevent any residents in the forest from keeping dogs or any other animals which might interfere with the hunting. His successors continued the forest laws, and complaints about them, about the harsh way in which they were enforced, and the innocent people who had been wrongly convicted under them, were common throughout the twelfth and thirteenth centuries.

William the Conqueror spent the last twenty-one years of his life after the Battle of Hastings in almost continual warfare. As soon as he had finally defeated the English, the Danes and the Scots, he returned to Normandy to wage war against his Norman vassals and his powerful neighbours whom King Philip of France was constantly inciting to attack him. The rebels even included his eldest son, Robert, who on one occasion wounded him in the hand in single combat; but his queen, Matilda, succeeded in reconciling them. William invaded Wales in 1081 and penetrated as far as St David's; but he spent most of the time fighting in France.

He died in 1087 from injuries received when, after he had taken Mantes by storm and set fire to the town, his horse trod on a burning ember as he rode through the streets, and threw him. He was carried to Rouen where he died after lingering for several weeks. He granted Normandy to his rebellious son Robert, but left his realm of England to his second son, William, who was his favourite child and had always been loyal to him. His third son, Henry, received no lands but £5000 pf silver. William may have realised that this very intelligent young man of nineteen was more likely than any of the other members of the family to appreciate the increasing importance of money as a factor in royal statecraft.

The new king of England, William II, was aged about thirty when his father died. He was a short, stout, bull-necked man, who stammered when he became excited, as he often did. His contemporaries called him Rufus because of his red-blonde hair and ruddy complexion. He had been the pupil of Lanfranc, the highly respected archbishop of Canterbury, and after William the Conqueror died, Lanfranc had no difficulty in persuading the English people to accept Rufus as their king and to support him against the rebellious Norman barons who rose in revolt in support of Robert of Normandy's claim to the crown. Rufus promised to relieve the English from oppression, and particularly to relax the severity of the forest laws; and with English help he suppressed the rebellion. He allowed his brother Robert to retain Normandy, and pardoned the other rebels; but he broke his promises to his English supporters, and instead of relaxing the forest laws he made them more severe.

The ecclesiastical chroniclers state that after Lanfranc's death in 1089, Rufus turned to evil; and though he repented during a dangerous illness four years later, and appointed the aged St Anselm as archbishop, he reverted to his wicked ways as soon as he had recovered his health. He has been considered for eight centuries to be one of the worst kings of England; but though we know the precise accusations which have been levelled at the other wicked Kings and Queens – at King John, Richard III, 'Bloody Mary' and James II – it is more difficult to discover why William II has been denounced in vague and general terms by twelfth-century chroniclers and Victorian historians for unspeakable wickedness and unmentionable crimes.

But the churchmen who wrote about him give us some indication of the causes of his unpopularity. He was rude, and shouted at people in a bullying manner. He invited King Malcolm Canmore of Scotland to meet him at Gloucester to discuss how to promote peaceful relations between their two countries, and then insulted him and told him to go back to Scotland, with the result that Malcolm went home and declared war. He had a raucous sense of humour which the churchmen did not appreciate: whenever he had done something wrong, he made a joke of it. He would resort to any means to obtain money. He permitted his chief minister, Ranulf Flambard, whom he appointed bishop of Durham, to impose heavy taxes on the people, both rich and poor; he kept bishoprics vacant for years in order to appropriate the revenues for himself; and he pardoned malefactors who paid him bribes.

He was too friendly with the Jews for the churchmen's liking. The Jews had come to England after the Norman conquest, and carried on business in most of the large cities as moneylenders, usually charging interest at 43 per cent per annum, but sometimes at over 80 per cent. The chroniclers complained that moneylending was the only thing that flourished during Rufus's reign, and also accused him of forcing some Jews in Rouen, who had become Christians, to revert to Judaism after the rabbis had bribed him with a gift of gold. On another occasion he double-crossed a Jew who objected because his son had converted to Christianity; Rufus took the Jew's money while allowing the son to remain a Christian.

There seems to be little doubt that Rufus was a homosexual, though we do not know the names of any of his homosexual favourites. He never married, and has never been accused of having had mistresses or bastards. We are told that he had effeminate and luxury-loving courtiers who introduced the fashion of wearing elaborate pointed shoes, grew their hair long, and often went around half-naked. Anselm refused to grant them absolution for their sins unless they cut their hair; but they refused, and said that they would dispense with his absolution. There was nothing effeminate about Rufus himself, who was a tough and vigorous soldier, and spent most of his time hunting when he was not waging war.

Two of the allegations against Rufus probably explain the special hatred with which he was regarded by his subjects and by the ecclesiastical chroniclers. Although he sometimes punished murderers and robbers and enforced law and order with the vigour which the people expected of their king, he allowed the soldiers of his own bodyguard and his courtiers to loot and rape and maltreat the people in the districts through which they passed. Even worse from the clergy's point of view was his habit of mocking at religion. They were not amused when he told some Christian and Jewish theologians that he would attend a disputation between them and either remain a Christian or become a Jew according to which of them would put forward the most persuasive arguments. When his bishops asked his permission for them to pray that he might mend his ways, he burst out laughing and said that they could pray as much as they liked, as that could do him no harm. He also laughed when he asked

Anselm what sin he would be dealing with in his next sermon, and the archbishop replied: 'The sin of Sodom'.

His attitude seriously threatened the position of the clergy. Five hundred years after the establishment of Christianity in England, they held great power in the realm and throughout Christendom merely because everyone believed that they held the keys to the Kingdom of Heaven. The Church had been granted, in return for its prayers, large areas of land for which all other tenants would have had to pay by supplying a considerable number of soldiers in wartime or by many hours of toil in the fields; it could, sometimes at least, force the most powerful and brutal warriors to adhere to its code of morals by threats of eternal damnation; its supreme pontiff had recently made an emperor stand for three days in the snow at Canossa imploring him for forgiveness; and it was about to persuade thousands of knights to spend their fortune and risk the security of their lands at home by sailing to Palestine on a crusade to liberate the Holy Land from the infidel Muslims. This power would be reduced to nothing if the population, or the influential classes, followed Rufus's example and laughed at Christian values and the efficacy of prayer.

In 1095 Rufus was confronted with a serious revolt. The most prominent leader of the rebels was Robert de Mowbray, earl of Northumberland. Rufus marched against Mowbray and took him prisoner. When Mowbray's wife held out in Bamburgh Castle and defied attempts to capture it, he forced her to surrender by threatening to put out her husband's eyes if she continued to resist. Mowbray escaped with a sentence of life imprisonment; but William of Eu, another nobleman who had supported the rebellion, was blinded and castrated, and his steward, William de Alderi, was flogged at every church door in Salisbury before being hanged.

Rufus was successful in his foreign wars. His invasion of the principality of Gwynedd in mid-winter was a failure, as he was forced to retreat after sharing the hardships of his men in the snows of Snowdonia; but he captured Carlisle by storm from the Scots, and forced them to cede the province of Cumberland to England.

The campaigns in France were on the whole indecisive, though Rufus conducted them with great energy. He was hunting in the

New Forest when he received news that his town of Le Mans had been captured by the Count of Maine. He immediately rode to Southampton and crossed the Channel in a gale, telling his frightened attendants that kings do not drown, and recaptured Le Mans. Abbot Suger, who was afterwards chief minister of King Louis VI of France, believed that Rufus was planning to make himself king of France.

Rufus spent Lammastide in 1100 at Winchester, and next day, 2 August, went hunting in the New Forest. During the hunt he was killed by an arrow at a spot which is traditionally supposed to be the place which is now marked by the Rufus Stone. A contemporary record states merely that 'on the day after Lammas' he was 'shot off with an arrow from one of his own men in hunting'. William of Malmesbury, writing about thirty years later, gives a detailed account of the exact manner in which he was killed by Sir Walter Tyrrel, a knight in his party, who shot an arrow at a stag which accidentally struck the king; Rufus fell, and in falling drove the arrow further into himself, and died. It seems unlikely that William of Malmesbury would have given such precise details if he had not heard them from someone who had either seen, or been told, exactly how it occurred. Tyrrel immediately fled to France; but he later stated on oath to Abbot Suger that he had not killed Rufus.

Rufus's brother Henry was a member of the hunting party that day, and was in another part of the forest when Rufus was killed. Some modern historians have suggested that he may have connived at the assassination of Rufus; but none of the contemporary chroniclers suggested it, and it is perhaps more likely, from what we know of his character, that he quickly and unscrupulously took advantage of a fortuitous situation which he had neither planned nor expected. On the day that Rufus died, Robert of Normandy was on his way home from Palestine, where he had distinguished himself in the First Crusade, in which neither Rufus nor Henry had shown any interest. While Rufus's corpse was unceremoniously taken to Winchester in a peasant's cart, dripping blood all along the road, Henry rode on ahead and seized the royal treasure chest. Then, after attending with due reverence Rufus's funeral at Winchester, he travelled to London and within four days of Rufus's death had been proclaimed king of England. He made no attempt to take possession of his brother's duchy of Normandy, for seizing the lands of an absent crusader was a heinous sin, and Henry was determined not to antagonise the Church, as Rufus had done.

Henry was nearly thirty-two when he came to the throne; he was a man of medium height, with black hair which was already receding from his forehead. He was born at Selby during his father's northern campaign in the autumn of 1068, being the only one of William's sons to be born after the conquest; and this enabled him to claim that he was a native Englishman. Unlike his father and brothers, he learned to read and write, and was therefore called 'Beauclerc' by the appreciative ecclesiastical chroniclers. Not surprisingly, he had the vices of the feudal nobility. As a young man, before he came to the throne, he had several mistresses and bastards, and he continued to pursue women well into middle age. He could treat his enemies with the direct and personal brutality of a typical Norman warrior. When he discovered, during a campaign in Normandy in 1095, that a knight had betrayed him by handing over one of his towns to the enemy, he took the traitor to the top of the tower of his castle at Rouen, and with the help of a few friends lifted him up and threw him down from the tower into the Seine.

After he became king, he sometimes led his army into battle, and on one occasion killed an enemy knight in hand-to-hand combat on the battlefield; but he limited such feats of arms to the minimum necessary to maintain his image of a proper twelfth-century king. William of Malmesbury wrote that, like Scipio Africanus, he believed that he had been born to command, not to fight; and he achieved more by diplomacy and political finesse than by war. Four hundred years before Machiavelli wrote *The Prince*, Henry I was applying his principles in the government of England.

He worked consistently to win the support of the Church and of the English people, and succeeded in both objectives. As soon as Anselm, in his refuge in France, heard of Rufus's death, he returned to England, and Henry immediately reinstated him as Archbishop. He then issued a proclamation to the people, promising to free them from the 'oppressions' under which they had suffered in recent years, and issued a charter, guaranteeing their rights, which was very closely followed a hundred years later when Magna Carta was drafted. But he was under the disadvantage that Rufus had made promises to the people when he became king, and had broken these promises; so Henry, to convince them that he was sincere, arrested Rufus's minister Ranulf Flambard and imprisoned him in the Tower of London. He also decided to marry Princess Matilda, the daughter of Malcolm Canmore and his English Queen, St Margaret. Matilda had been sent to England as a child to be educated in a convent at Wilton, and it was generally believed that she had become a nun; but a marriage with a half-English Princess would strengthen Henry's position with his English subjects.

Henry consulted Anselm, and told him that Matilda had not taken her vows of her own free will. The nuns at the convent had insisted that she should do so, because there was no other way of protecting her from importunate suitors and from the lusts of the local nobles and knights; but she had repeatedly protested, and had torn off the veil whenever they placed it on her head. Anselm said that if she had truly become the bride of Christ, he would never consent to her becoming the bride of the king. Instead of laughing, as Rufus would have done, Henry appointed Anselm to preside at an investigation into the circumstances in which she had taken the veil; and Anselm reported that she had indeed been forced to do this against her will, and was therefore free to marry Henry. The Church was conscious of the weakness, as well as of the strength, of its position, and did not wish to offend a king, who, unlike his brother Rufus, acknowledged the authority of the Church.

After six months' imprisonment, Flambard escaped from the Tower. He made his warders drunk, and then took a rope which had been sent to him concealed in a wine-barrel, and lowered himself into a boat that was waiting for him in the river below. He made his way to Normandy and joined Duke Robert, who had now returned in triumph from the Crusade. They gained the support of many of the Norman barons and knights. The principle of primogeniture, which was well-etablished in Norman law and custom, would have made Robert in the ordinary way the heir to his father's English territories; and Henry could not claim, as Rufus could, that William the Conqueror had left him England in his will. Nor were the Normans overjoyed at Henry's attempts to ingratiate himself with his English subjects. In the summer of 1101, the commanders of Henry's fleet in the Channel

48

deserted to Robert, who landed with an army at Portsmouth, while Henry and his forces were waiting for him at Pevensey.

Henry's position was precarious; but the support of the English people placed him in a good bargaining position when he met Robert at Alton in an attempt to negotiate a peaceful settlement. The brothers agreed that Henry should be king of England and would pay Robert an annuity of 3000 marks (£2000, a mark being worth 13 shillings and fourpence) while Robert would remain duke of Normandy.

Robert was a gallant soldier and a charming, easy-going man who allowed his Norman friends a free rein. He made no attempt to enforce law and order in Normandy, and news reached England of the sufferings of the people there under his rule. His most powerful ally was Robert of Bellême, earl of Shrewsbury, who, according to the chroniclers, was a sadistic monster. He is said to have refused to ransom his prisoners because he got more enjoyment from torturing them, and on one occasion to have torn out the eyes of a child hostage with his own finger nails because the child's father had risen against him. Even allowing for the bias of the ecclesiastical writers against any enemy of Henry I, there is little reason to doubt that Robert of Bellême was guilty of the worst excesses which a powerful feudal baron could commit.

Henry, on the other hand, won the affection and respect of the English people by enforcing law and order. At most times throughout English history, the desire for freedom has come from classes and groups who were powerful enough to make use of freedom for their own advantage; the common people have usually preferred to be ruled by a strong government that would protect them against lawless criminals by so punishing and terrifying evil-doers that, as Bede had written about the reign of King Edwin of Northumbria in the seventh century, 'a woman with a new-born child could walk throughout the island from sea to sea and take no harm'. A monk of Peterborough wrote with equal enthusiasm that in the time of Henry I a man could carry a burden of gold and silver anywhere without being molested. Henry anticipated Machiavelli's precept of beginning his rule with severity and afterwards relaxing it. In the earlier years of his reign he often blinded and castrated criminals, and, reintroducing the Anglo-Saxon capital punishment, hanged many of them; but in later times he usually punished them merely by fines. He particularly pleased the people by requiring his body-guard to formulate rules as to what commodities they were lawfully entitled to take without payment from the people, and to pay for everything else. This was a welcome change from the behaviour of Rufus's retinue.

For four years after the settlement at Alton, Henry maintained order in England while Robert misgoverned Normandy. When Robert of Bellême led a revolt in England in support of Robert, Henry defeated him, seized his estates in Shropshire, and drove him into Normandy, where he continued his oppression of his Norman tenants. In 1105 Henry began a campaign to conquer Normandy with an army composed partly of Flemish mercenaries, whom he could pay with the treasure which he had accumulated, and partly of his English subjects. He made several raids on Normandy, and followed them up with a large-scale invasion.

On 28 September 1106 he defeated his brother's army at Tinchebrai; Robert of Normandy was taken prisoner, and Robert of Bellême fled into the king of France's realm. It was the fortieth anniversary of the day when William the Conqueror had landed at Pevensey; and the older generation of Englishmen, who remembered 1066, saw with enthusiasm their sons and grandsons invade Normandy and avenge Hastings at Tinchebrai. At Hastings, Harold had been defeated by the Norman archers; at Tinchebrai, the English bowmen in Henry's army won the first of many victories which were to establish their reputation during the next four centuries.

Henry held Robert of Normandy in honourable captivity for the rest of his life; he died at the age of eighty after twenty-eight years' imprisonment. In 1112, Robert of Bellême was sent as an ambassador to Henry by King Louis VI of France. Henry immediately had him arrested as a traitor; he was imprisoned at Wareham, and was never heard of again. Henry could afford to lay himself open to the accusation of violating diplomatic immunity when it was a question of punishing so hated an oppressor as Robert of Bellême.

Henry had enemies, particularly among those Norman knights who did not approve of his pro-English policy. According to Suger, who, unlike the English churchmen, was Henry's enemy, he mistrusted his bodyguard, and always slept with a sword and shield at his bedside in case there was an attempt to assassinate him during the night. One unsuccessful attempt was made on his life by his Chamberlain, who was blinded and castrated; but Henry I remained popular with his people. Apart from winning the goodwill of the Church, and therefore of the ecclesiastical chroniclers, he has rightly been remembered in history as one of the founders of English law.

Since the conquest, the law had been administered by the Anglo-Saxon communal courts and the seigneurial courts in which the churchmen who acted as judges in the court of the feudal lord dealt with crimes committed by the lord's tenants and with civil disputes between them. But from the earliest times, the king had acted as a judge in especially important cases, because sitting in judgment on his subjects, like leading his men into battle, was one of the essential duties of kingship. The Norman kings administered justice as they moved around the country. Edward the Confessor had spent most of his time in London and Winchester. William the Conqueror, Rufus and Henry I, like Athelstan and Cnut, were almost continually on the move, and did not have a fixed seat of government. They travelled through their realms accompanied by their court, their bodyguard and their officials. The Norman kings established the normal practice, when they were in England and not in Normandy, of spending Christmas at Gloucester, Easter at Winchester, and Whitsun at Westminster, though they sometimes went further afield.

These three great feasts of the Church were known as the three occasions in the year when the king wore his crown. His tenants-in-chief were summoned to Gloucester, Winchester and Westminster to attend on him, and apart from the religious ceremonies, the tournaments and the banquets, the king sat amid his tenants-in-chief as a judge to deal with important cases and also to hear a few humbler petitioners who had succeeded in gaining access to him. Henry I greatly increased the scope of the king's court. He not only sat himself as a judge, but also appointed clerics to sit as judges in his royal court when he was not there. He created the Court of Exchequer, composed of clerics and laymen of humble birth, whose duties were financial, administrative and judicial; they raised taxes, and adjudicated in disputes involving debts due to the crown, and sometimes in other litigation. Henry sent the judges of his royal court, and the barons of his Court of Exchequer, into every part of England to supervise local government and to try judicial cases.

The king's judges adopted the procedure of ordeal, compurgation and battle of the communal and seigneurial courts; but, unlike the other courts, they sometimes used a new method of deciding cases, requiring witnesses to give evidence on oath about things that they had seen. Several centuries elapsed before evidence completely replaced ordeal, compurgation and battle as a means of deciding judicial prosecutions.

It was in the reign of Henry I that the courts maritime in the ports and the courts merchant in the inland towns developed their own system of law for the shipowners and merchants who appeared before them. The judges in the courts merchant understood the law merchant which was developing throughout Western Europe, and they could therefore adjudicate in disputes between local traders, and, in the case of certain towns like London and Cambridge, between merchants who came from France, Flanders, Scandinavia, Germany and Italy to the great international fairs. The law merchant was completely alien both to the Anglo-Saxon law of the communal courts and to the continental feudal law of the seigneurial courts. The most important innovation of the law merchant was the negotiable instrument – the promissory note and the bill of exchange, of which the most common form today is the cheque. A negotiable instrument, unlike most other legal rights, can be assigned by a payee to a third person, who can then enforce the rights attached to the document against the party who originally executed it, with whom he had had no business relations. Negotiable instruments were well established in Italy by the eleventh century and in England by the reign of Henry I.

Henry reigned for more than thirty-five years, longer than any king of England had ever reigned except for Ethelred the Unready. For the last twenty-nine of these years, after Tinchebrai, there was peace in his English kingdom; but he was often engaged in waging wars and suppressing revolts in Normandy. His great enemy was King Louis VI of France. Louis ruled directly over only the relatively small area around Paris known as the Île de France, and his overlordship of the powerful rulers of Brittany, Maine, Anjou, Aquitaine and Provence, like his overlordship of Normandy, was more nominal than real. He gave refuge to Robert of Normandy's son William, and sponsored his claim to be the lawful king of England; but in his wars with Henry I he was always beaten before the fighting began by Henry's diplomacy; for Henry not only had the support of the pope, but built up an anti-French alliance with the Holy Roman Emperor and the German princes. In 1114 Henry married his nine-year-old daughter, Matilda, to the Emperor Henry V.

It was after a successful campaign in France that Henry I and his court sailed from Barfleur to England at the end of November 1120. Among the ships of his fleet was the pride of his navy, the *White Ship*, which was regarded as a great achievement of up-to-date shipbuilding, and was capable of travelling faster than any other ship. The King himself did not sail in the *White Ship*, but left it to the younger generation: his son and heir, Prince William, and two of his illegitimate children were on board, along with the emperor's nephew and other young men and women of the nobility. Before they left port they had a great banquet on board, and when they sailed at midnight the young lords and ladies leaned over the side of the ship, calling on the crew to go faster and overtake the slower craft ahead of them. The *White Ship* sailed on to the rocks at the harbour entrance and sank with only one survivor, a butcher from Rome. Henry's courtiers dared not tell him the news, but sent a young page to do so; when the king heard his report, he fell unconscious to the ground.

If a disaster of comparable magnitude had occurred in Rufus's reign, the ecclesiastical chroniclers would have written at length about this divine punishment which had been inflicted on the King for his sins; but though they said nothing about God's displeasure with Henry, the story of the loss of the *White Ship* made a profound impression on their contemporaries, and has been remembered for over eight hundred years as the most famous event of Henry I's time. It left the King without an heir. As Queen Matilda had died two years before, Henry remarried, choosing as a bride Adeliza of Louvain, the daughter of the Duke of Lower Lorraine; but she bore him no children. He therefore chose as his successor his daughter Matilda, the widowed empress, who returned to his court after the emperor's death. She married as her second husband Geoffrey Plantagenet, count of Anjou, by whom she had several sons. The nobles swore to

Henry that they would accept Matilda as their queen after his death; but he must have had forebodings about the future, especially as many of his lords in Normandy were in revolt in the last years of his reign.

He left England for the last time in August 1133, and after dealing with a rebellion in Normandy he died on 1 December 1135 as a result of eating too many lampreys, a fish he liked very much, though his doctors had warned him that it was bad for his health. He was aged sixty-seven, and had lived to a greater age than any king in England since Penda. The contemporary chroniclers turned a blind eye to all his faults, and had nothing but praise for him. Modern historians have reacted against their obsequiousness by emphasising the selfishness of his policy and the moral defects in his character, particularly his many mistresses; but there can be no doubt that he excelled at the art of statecraft, was a very successful politician, and showed great courage and imagination in initiating the revolutionary policy of appealing to the people of England for support against his Norman nobles. The chaos which followed his death caused the people to look back on his reign as a golden past, the good old days, which they remembered with perhaps an exaggerated nostalgia.

CHAPTER 4

LAWLESSNESS
AND
ORDER:
MAGNA CARTA
(1135–1216)

At Henry I's death, the Empress Matilda's claim to the throne was immediately challenged by her cousin, Stephen, count of Blois, whose mother was William the Conqueror's daughter. He had been one of the nobles who had sworn the oath to Henry I to accept Matilda as queen. He was a man in his late thirties, a generous and gallant soldier but with no aptitude for leadership, politics or diplomacy. His contest with Matilda led to a civil war which reduced England to anarchy and was remembered with horror by their contemporaries and future generations.

The majority of the nobles were conscious of the disadvantages of having a woman as their sovereign; they supported Stephen, and he had no difficulty in gaining control in England. But Matilda succeeded in entrenching herself in Normandy, and this encouraged her supporters in England to rise in revolt. She landed in England, and though Stephen captured her, he generously and unwisely released her and allowed her to join her followers. Her uncle King David of Scotland, the youngest son of Malcolm Canmore, repeatedly raided the north of England, ostensibly in order to champion her cause, but also to recover

Cumberland, which Rufus had annexed, and to take Northumberland, which had never been part of Scotland.

In the summer of 1138 the Scottish army swept through Northumberland and Durham and entered the North Riding of Yorkshire. Some units of King David's forces were men from Galloway, an area which had not been affected by the measures taken by Malcolm Canmore to civilise Scotland along Anglo-Saxon lines. The Scots from Lothian, and even more the English, considered the men of Galloway to be barbarians; and they committed many atrocities in the north of England. The people rose to oppose them and to support Stephen's forces.

The armies met near Northallerton in the battle which became known as the Battle of the Standard, because the English, before the battle began, erected a ship's mast, bearing the banners of three saints, in the midst of their army. The Scots were defeated, thanks to the indiscipline of the men of Galloway; but they remained in the north of England, doing great damage. When they eventually returned to Scotland, they took with them many English prisoners as slaves, for the Anglo-Saxon system of slavery still existed in Scotland, though it was soon to disappear.

Soon other districts of England, as well as the north, were suffering from the effect of the war between Matilda and Stephen. After eight hundred years it is still remembered, more than any of the other civil wars in England, as one of the darkest periods in our history. Apart from the horrors of warfare, such as the sack of Worcester by the men of Gloucester on Matilda's behalf, local lords and knights took advantage of the anarchy and of Stephen's weakness and tolerance to oppress the inhabitants of their neighbourhoods. The monk who completed the *Anglo-Saxon Chronicle* in Stephen's reign, after describing how the lords kidnapped members of the civilian population at random, and held them prisoners in their castles, where they starved and tortured them, until their friends paid a ransom for their release, ended his account with the famous statement that 'men said openly that God and His saints slept'. But it has been suggested that this gives an exaggerated impression of the situation in England as a whole, and applied only to the unfortunate inhabitants of the Fens in Cambridgeshire who were at the mercy of the brutal local nobleman, Geoffrey de Mandeville, earl of Essex. His sadism seems to have equalled that of Robert of

Bêlleme a generation earlier. But William of Malmesbury and Henry of Huntingdon were able to live and write in peace in their monasteries, for William finished, and Henry began, work on their great historical chronicles during the fighting in Stephen's reign.

After the war had continued indecisively for three years, Stephen was defeated by Matilda's generals in a battle near Lincoln in February 1141, and, after desperately defending himself with his battle-axe against superior numbers, he was taken prisoner. London then surrendered to Matilda. But she angered the citizens by imposing heavy taxes; and when Stephen's wife, Matilda of Boulogne, raised an army and marched on London, the Londoners rose in her support and drove out the Empress Matilda's army. A few months later, Stephen was exchanged for three leading noblemen of the empress's faction who had been taken prisoner, and he soon took the offensive. In September 1142 he attacked Oxford and captured the town; but Matilda took refuge in the castle, and held out for several months. It seemed as if the empress would certainly be captured when the castle fell; but on a December night, she escaped. Escorted by three knights, she walked undetected in the darkness through Stephen's lines in a snowstorm, the four of them having wrapped themselves in white sheets as a camouflage against the snow-covered ground; and after crossing the frozen Thames she reached her supporters at Wallingford.

The war continued for another six years, with Stephen in nominal control of most of England but unable to dislodge Matilda from her strongholds in Gloucester and Bristol and the surrounding country. By 1148 Stephen had driven Matilda from England; but she held Normandy. After five years of peace, Matilda's son, Henry of Anjou, restarted the war and invaded England. He was having the best of the fighting in Wiltshire and the Midlands when the death of Stephen's eldest son opened the possibility of a compromise peace. A truce was followed by lengthy negotiations, and a treaty was sealed at Winchester in December 1153. It was agreed that Stephen should reign as king for the rest of his life and at his death would be succeeded by Henry of Anjou, while Stephen's younger son, who, unlike his elder brother, had never been ambitious, was satisfied with the grant of lands in Sussex and elsewhere. Stephen survived for less than a year, and in October 1154 Henry of Anjou, at the age of twenty-one, ascended the throne of England as King Henry II.

In addition to England, Normandy and Anjou, Henry had acquired Aquitaine by marrying Eleanor of Aquitaine, the divorced queen of France. Eleanor had inherited from her father the duchy of Aquitaine, which included Poitou, Guienne and Gascony from the Loire to the Pyrenees. At the age of fifteen she had married the young King Louis VII of France, bringing to her husband a province which was larger than his own territories in the Île de France. Louis was profoundly religious, and renowned for his gravity; Eleanor was beautiful and gay, and complained that she had married a monk, not a king.

The First Crusade, in which England under Rufus had played no part, had ended in the capture of Jerusalem in 1099 and the establishment of the Christian feudal kingdom of Jerusalem, with Godfrey de Bouillon as its king and overlord of the Christian principalities of Tripoli, Antioch and Edessa. In 1144 the Saracens captured Edessa (the modern Turkish town of Urfa); and St Bernard, the abbot of Clairvaux, issued the call in France for the Second Crusade. All over Western Europe lords and knights answered the call and took the cross. Many came from England, preferring to fight for Christianity in Palestine than for either Stephen or Matilda. Religious enthusiasm was not the only motive which sent knights on a crusade, for the prospect of acquiring lands in Palestine and Syria was an incentive to landless younger sons.

King Louis of France led the crusading army. His wife went with him, and caused a scandal at the crusaders' headquarters in Antioch by having at least a flirtation with her uncle Raimund, the prince of Antioch. Louis decided to divorce her. Suger, who had been his tutor and continued as chief minister in France when Louis succeeded his father, advised against a divorce which would not only publicise the scandal but would lose France the province of Aquitaine; but Louis insisted, and in 1152 the pope dissolved the marriage on the usual grounds that it had been void because of the relationship of the parties. Eleanor, at the age of thirty, was the most famous beauty, and one of the greatest heiresses, in Christendom; but within two months of her divorce she had married the nineteen-year-old Henry of Anjou. It was undoubtedly a marriage in which love played a bigger part than diplomacy, and for Henry, who did not foresee his future matrimonial difficulties, it was in every respect satisfactory. With Normandy, Anjou and Aquitaine, he was lord of about half modern France, and the whole of the western part of the country. When he became king of England two and a half years after the marriage, his territories extended for nearly a thousand miles from the Tweed to the Pyrenees.

Henry II was a determined and passionate man, with a restless energy. He could not sit still, and was always pacing up and down the room; and he had a fiery temper, which sometimes led him into difficulties. He is usually considered to be one of the great English kings and the founder of the English legal system and the common law; but he suffered a series of disasters in his reign, and, at least in the short run, was unsuccessful in most of his undertakings. This was largely due to his poor judgment of character and his lack of ability in handling men. His worst troubles came from his quarrels with his friend Thomas Becket and with his wife. His feud with Becket led him into a disastrous conflict with the Church, and his rift with Eleanor into a series of civil wars with his sons.

During the horrors of Stephen's reign, the English people had longed for the law and order that they had known under Henry I, and with the advent of Henry II the growth of the jurisdiction of the King's courts resumed where it had left off in 1135. Increasingly under Henry II the king's judges encroached on the jurisdiction of the seigneurial courts by agreeing to hear cases which would otherwise have been brought in the court of the local lord. They also laid down the doctrine of the writ of right, which still exists under another name today. This established a limited system of appeal from the seigneurial courts, and from every other court, to the king's court, whenever some substantial or technical defect was found in the record of the court which had first tried the case.

Henry II extended the practice, which his grandfather Henry I had begun, of sending 'itinerant justices' of his royal court into every county of England to hold assizes – a system which continued until 1971. This brought the king's justice, both criminal and civil, within reach of many more of his subjects than had been able to resort to it when petitioners and plaintiffs had to travel to Gloucester, Winchester or Westminster; for the king's judges, with their escorts of armed bodyguards, could encounter the dangers from robbers on the roads with far less risk than could the humble litigant.

The leading part in the development of the administration of justice under Henry II was played by his justiciar, Glanvil, who, alone of all the leading lawyers of the Middle Ages, was not a priest, but a soldier. He led Henry's armies into battle as well as presiding in his court of law, and wrote the first textbook on English law, unless, as many historians believe, the book was written in his name by Hubert Walter, the archbishop of Canterbury.

The law enforced in the Anglo-Saxon communal courts, and to a lesser extent in the Norman seigneurial courts, varied from one district to another, according to local customs and the 'custom of the manor'. The king's itinerant justices, as they travelled throughout England, applied the same law in all the counties; and as the law of the king's courts was common to all England, it was known as the 'common law'. English common law developed to such a degree in Henry II's reign that in later centuries the judges held – though this was only a fiction – that it had been finally established by the time of his death. This is the origin of the doctrine, which still applies today, that in order to prove that the general principles of the common law are modified in a district by a local custom, it must be shown that the custom already existed at the date of Henry II's death, and had therefore already been incorporated into the common law before the common law was finally settled. By an illogical anomaly, the date fixed for this purpose is not the day of Henry's death, 6 July 1189, but the date on which his successor, Richard I, was crowned, 3 September 1189; for in the Middle Ages kings always dated their reign as beginning, not at the date of their predecessor's death, but from their coronation.

Henry's attempts to extend the jurisdiction of his courts brought him into conflict with the Church. This is another example of the clash which has so often arisen in English history between a powerful group fighting for its freedom – or, as others would express it, for its privileges – against the central government seeking to enforce law and order to the delight of the law-abiding section of the common people. The Church had won for all priests, and for those in the lower ecclesiastical orders, exemption from the savage penalties of royal justice and the seigneurial courts. A villein or a freehold tenant might be blinded or castrated by order of the judge in the court of his feudal lord; but if he had become a priest, or even merely a deacon, he could not be punished in this way, but could be tried only in the ecclesiastical courts. If he were found guilty there, he was sentenced only to suffer penances, or at worst to be unfrocked. If he was sentenced to be unfrocked, and then committed further offences, he could be punished next time as a layman; but the system was seen by its critics as a disgraceful anomaly by which priests were given two chances and allowed to commit crimes once with impunity. This 'benefit of clergy' was extended until it applied, not only to *bona fide* priests and deacons, but to everyone who could read. The practice arose, except in cases of treason and some other crimes, of giving every condemned criminal the chance to read the first verse of the fifty-first psalm, which was therefore called the 'neck verse'; if he was able to read it, he saved his neck; if he could not do so, he was hanged. The 'neck verse' was not abolished until 1706.

Early in his reign, Henry II appointed Thomas Becket to be his chancellor. Becket was the son of a Norman landowner and his wife – the story that she was a Saracen girl is an invention of later writers – who had settled in London in Henry I's reign. Becket studied in London and Paris, took minor orders, and became secretary to the archbishop of Canterbury in Stephen's reign, though he did not become a priest. The Church was delighted when Becket, with his links with the archbishop, was appointed lord chancellor; but they found, to their dismay, that he became a zealous instrument of Henry's policy and vigorously enforced the laws imposing taxes on the Church.

When the see of Canterbury fell vacant in 1162, Henry appointed Becket archbishop. Becket was very reluctant to accept the appointment, realising, as he warned Henry, that if he became archbishop of Canterbury he would owe his first duty to the Church, not to the king, and that this would lead to a quarrel between them. Henry so far misunderstood Becket's character that he did not take the warning seriously, and insisted on appointing him archbishop.

The clash which Becket had foreseen duly occurred. Henry was determined to extend the jurisdiction of his courts, and to stamp out an abuse which encouraged lawlessness, by abolishing the benefit of clergy, and bringing priests within the jurisdiction of his courts. Becket considered this a serious infringement of the rights of the clergy and the Church, and strenuously opposed it; and he stood firm when Henry demanded that a priest who had raped a girl and murdered her father should be tried a second time in the King's courts after the Church courts had imposed a very mild penance. Henry tried to reach an agreement, but Becket refused to compromise. After a bitter contest, in which both the king and the archbishop behaved in a tactless and provocative manner, Becket fled abroad, and, from the abbey of Pontigny in France, denounced Henry and excommunicated his ministers.

It was a common practice in Europe at the time for the king's heir to be crowned during his father's lifetime in order to ensure that he would be accepted as king after his father's death. In 1170 Henry arranged for his son Henry to be crowned, in Becket's absence, by the archbishop of York. Becket persuaded the pope to threaten to place England under an interdict for this encroachment on the prerogatives of the see of Canterbury. Henry gave way in order to avoid the papal censures, and allowed Becket to return to England; but as soon as he reached Canterbury, Becket suspended the archbishop of York from exercising his functions, and excommunicated other bishops who had suported the king.

Henry, who was celebrating Christmas in Normandy, was furious when he heard the news, and cried out, in the presence of his courtiers, that he wished he had a loyal servant who would get rid of Becket. Four of his knights, hoping to earn his favour, set out at once for Canterbury. Becket was warned that they were coming to kill him, but waited for them in the cathedral, where they stabbed him to death on 29 December 1170.

The murder of an archbishop in his cathedral outraged all Christendom. Becket was worshipped as a martyr throughout Europe, not least in Spain and Provence, where the king of Castile and the duke of Provence had both married Henry's daughters and were eager to dissociate themselves from the wickedness of their father-in-law. Henry's nobles, including his sons, rose in revolt. The kings of France and Scotland made a military alliance against England which was repeatedly renewed during the next 387 years, and went to war with Henry. Yet,

62

strangely enough, Henry's fortunes prospered better during the four years which followed Becket's death than at any other period of his reign.

In the first months after the murder, he escaped from the international uproar by invading Ireland and annexing the southeast of the country, where he established a 'Pale' of English settlers; it was the first step in the English conquest of Ireland. When the revolt of the nobles began, he more than held his own in the fighting against his sons in France; and when the king of Scotland, William the Lion, invaded the north of England, William was defeated and taken prisoner by Glanvil. Henry compelled him, as a condition of his release, to do homage for Scotland in terms which removed the ambiguity in Malcolm Canmore's homage to William the Conqueror as to whether Scotland, or only Cumberland, was a fief of the English crown. It is a remarkable tribute to the personality of William the Lion that he is remembered in Scottish history as a national hero, although he lost nearly every war in which he was involved during his forty-nine years' reign and was repeatedly forced to accept the most humiliating peace terms.

Henry tried in vain to disclaim responsibility for Becket's murder. The pope eventually agreed to pardon him after Henry had given way on most of the points at issue between him and the Church; but the popular indignation against him continued unabated. In 1174, at the height of the revolt against him, he performed a public penance at Becket's tomb, kneeling while he was whipped by the monks of the Canterbury priory. This was regarded by medieval Christendom as an inspiring symbol of the power of the Church to compel the mighty to repent; to Protestant Englishmen of the Reformation and the nineteenth century, it was a national disgrace, a shameful humiliation of England's king before an overweening foreign pontiff.

Soon after Henry's penance, the revolt against him collapsed; but he did not enjoy peace for long after his success in 1174. His troubles were largely due to his bad relations with his wife. She bore him five sons and two daughters, having had two daughters by her marriage with King Louis; but not long after his marriage to her, Henry began a notorious love affair with Rosamond de Clifford, 'the fair Rosamond', whom he installed at his hunting lodge at Woodstock. Eleanor established her court at Poitiers, where she was surrounded by poets and troubadours who adopted the cult of romantic love which was spreading from Provence all over Christendom. They wrote and sang of their passion for the beautiful lady they loved, and of their devotion and subjection to her, and especially to Eleanor. She was worshipped by troubadours all over Europe; a German poet wrote that if he were lord of all the land between the ocean and the Rhine, he would willingly surrender it if he could sleep one night with the queen of England in his arms.

In 1173 Eleanor incited her sons to revolt against their father. She tried to join them, but was caught escaping in man's clothes, and Henry imprisoned her for the next twelve years. Their sons took their mother's side, and for the rest of Henry's reign were usually fighting against him as allies of the young king of France, Philip Augustus. Henry, with his usual failure to judge character correctly, was on very bad terms with his son Richard, but loved his youngest son, John, although everyone else saw the vices in John's character from an early age. The king's eldest son, Henry, had died some years after his coronation, and Richard was now the heir to the throne; but his father insisted that when Richard succeeded him as ruler of England and Normandy, John should have Aquitaine, which Richard had governed for the previous ten years. This led to a war in France in which Richard and Philip Augustus fought as allies against Henry.

At a critical moment in the struggle, Henry learned, to his great grief, that John, for whose sake he had gone to war with Richard, had betrayed him, and was in secret contact with Philip Augustus and Richard. In a desperate campaign in the summer of 1189, Henry was out-generalled and defeated, and he was already dying when he was forced to agree to humiliating peace terms, by which he submitted to the arbitration of Philip Augustus the claims of his sons to his territories in France, and undertook to pay a heavy war indemnity. Two days later he died in despair, with only one of his bastards to solace his last moments.

Richard I, Coeur de Lion, was in his time one of the best-loved kings who have reigned in England. The people's admiration for him lasted for many centuries, and it was not until the nineteenth century that historians with very different moral values from Richard's regarded him with disapproval. His popularity is remarkable, because he spent so little time in England and was hardly in any sense an Englishman. He was born at Oxford, but during his father's reign he was nearly always at his mother's court in Aquitaine when he was not fighting against his father in other parts of France; and after he became king, he spent only four months in England during his nine years and nine months' reign. He not only spoke French as his principal language, as all the kings of England had done since 1066, but was in spirit, temperament and culture a Frenchman from south-west France. It is fitting that he should be remembered in England by his French nickname. Even Shakespeare, who, like all his contemporaries, anglicised foreign names and wrote 'Pandulph' for Pandolfo and 'Lewis' for Louis, referred to Richard as 'Coeur de Lion'.

Richard represented the ideal of feudal kingship, which in his case actually materialised in real life, although most kings typified the more sordid side of feudalism. He could be brutal in warfare, but always within the rules laid down by feudal doctrine. He was generous; he treated worthy foes with respect; and he had a warm and impulsive, not a calculating, temperament. The people in his time, unlike the nineteenth-century historians, did not think that it was reprehensible for a king to leave his kingdom and spend all his time fighting for the Cross in Palestine and for his feudal rights in France. His action in waging war against his father on the side of the king of France would today be an act of high treason; but by feudal morality he was justified in defending his province of Aquitaine, which his mother had given him, against the attempts of his father to deprive him of it; and there was nothing wrong in enlisting the support of his feudal overlord in Aquitaine, the king of France, and in fighting in support of his overlord's right to adjudicate in the disputes between him and his father as tenants-in-chief of Aquitaine and Normandy.

In 1187 the Saracens under Saladin captured Jerusalem and conquered the Christian kingdom which had survived for eighty-eight years. The Church in the West called for the Third Crusade. As soon as Richard Coeur de Lion became king, he devoted himself whole-heartedly to the Crusade, and the Holy Roman Emperor, Frederick Barbarossa, and King Philip Augustus of France also took the cross. Richard collected money for the expedition by taxing the people and by selling royal property and rights. He released William the Lion from his homage for Scotland in return for a large contribution by William to the cost of the crusade.

Richard came to England for his coronation at Westminster in September 1189, which the people of London celebrated by an attack on the Jews. Crusades always stimulated anti-Jewish religious zeal. The First Crusade had led to massacres of Jews in the Rhineland by crusaders on their way to the Holy Land. In 1144, when St Bernard was preaching the Second Crusade, the story spread in Norwich that a little Christian boy named William had been tortured and crucified by the Jews in the city at Easter in mockery of the crucifixion of Christ. At the time of the Third Crusade, the anti-Jewish riot in London on the evening of Richard's coronation was followed by attacks on Jews in Norwich, Lincoln and other towns in East Anglia in the spring of 1190. The worst case was in York, where the Jews barricaded themselves in a tower on a hill in the city and killed themselves in a mass suicide as their only way of escaping from the murderous mob. Richard and his ministers punished the rioters. In the case of the York massacre, the lord chancellor, William de Longuesépée, made it an excuse to dismiss from office and confiscate the lands of the officials of his rival, the bishop of Durham, whom he accused of inciting the outbreak.

Richard left England in December 1189, and after spending some time in France, Sicily and Cyprus, reached Acre in the summer of 1191. Philip Augustus went with him; but Frederick Barbarossa, who led an army overland, was drowned in crossing a river in Asia Minor. A small army of crusaders had been besieging Acre for two years before the main force arrived; but after Richard took charge of operations, the town was captured within a month. Philip Augustus then went home to France on the plea of illness, hoping to take advantage of the situation to seize the land of absent crusaders; Richard stayed in Palestine and advanced on Jerusalem. He defeated Saladin's army at Arsuf and captured Jaffa; but he was unable to take Jerusalem, though he came within sight of the city. He entered into negotiations with Saladin, and was very favourably impressed by his courage, charm and gentlemanly behaviour; he knighted the son of Saladin's brother Safadin, and considered giving his sister in marriage to Safadin. He discussed with Saladin the possibility of a peaceful partition of Palestine between Christians and Muslims;

but no agreement could be reached on this point, and in October 1192 he sailed for home after making a three-year truce with Saladin under which a Christian kingdom was established in a coastal strip around Acre and Jaffa.

He was shipwrecked in the Adriatic and cast ashore on the coast of Italy. He decided to make his way overland through the territories of the duke of Austria, with whom he had quarrelled in Palestine, and set off with a few friends, in disguise. They reached Vienna, and stayed at an inn on the outskirts of the city, where they attracted attention by their manners, and were arrested and identified. The duke of Austria imprisoned Richard in his castle of Dürenstein on the Danube. The well-known story, which was first recorded seventy years later, tells of how his troubadour Blondel set out to find him, and wandered from one German castle to another, singing songs that Richard knew in front of each castle until at last an answering voice singing the same song from within the castle revealed to Blondel that Richard was imprisoned there; but the time factor seems to disprove the story, because within two months of Richard's capture in Vienna the duke of Austria had reluctantly surrendered him to the Emperor Henry VI, who, as the duke's overlord, insisted on having Richard, although Philip Augustus offered money to the duke to continue holding him as a prisoner.

Philip Augustus hoped to take advantage of Richard's absence to seize his territories in France. He made an alliance with Richard's brother, John, and planned an invasion of England; but the realm was hurriedly placed in a state of defence, thanks chiefly to the energy of Eleanor of Aquitaine, who at the age of seventy-one saved her son's kingdom from the French. The emperor treated Richard as an honoured guest at Worms, but, in accordance with the accepted practice, would not release him until he had paid a large ransom. The money was raised with some difficulty in England by taxes and voluntary subscriptions from the people, and a heavy contribution was levied on the Jews. Richard returned to England in March 1194 after making an alliance with the emperor against France.

When Philip Augustus heard that Richard had been released, he said to John: 'The devil is loose; look after yourself.' But Eleanor of Aquitaine worked for a rapprochement between her two sons, and Richard, with his usual generosity, pardoned

John. After staying only two months in England, he sailed for France, where he spent the next five years making war against Philip Augustus and his rebellious vassals whom Philip had stirred up against him. He was killed in April 1199 by an archer who shot him while he was directing operations at the siege of the castle of Chalus. Before he died, he gave orders that the archer who shot him should be allowed to go free and given a pot of gold; but the captain of his guard, after capturing the castle, had the archer flayed alive and hanged every soldier of the garrison.

By the law of primogeniture, Richard's heir was his nephew Arthur, Duke of Brittany, the thirteen-year-old son of Henry II's third son, Geoffrey; but John, the youngest of Henry's sons, seized power in England and was crowned king. Arthur assembled an army and besieged the castle in Aquitaine in which Eleanor of Aquitaine was staying; but John marched to the relief of his mother, and took Arthur prisoner. Arthur died mysteriously in the castle of Rouen; it was widely believed that John had murdered him by stabbing him with his own hand.

John had always been disliked by the nobility, by the churchmen, and by most of the people who came into contact with him, though he could be charming. Although he was only five foot high, he was handsome and attractive to women, whom he pursued as tirelessly as his great-grandfather, Henry I, had done. His enemies were prepared to believe the worst rumours about Arthur's death, and Philip Augustus saw to it that these rumours were widely publicised.

Philip Augustus was pursuing his life's task of creating the country of France as we know it. When he became king at the age of fifteen in 1180, his realm consisted of an area of a hundred miles long and wide around Paris, stretching from Beauvais and Soissons in the north to Orleans and Troyes in the south, with a small detached enclave further south around Bourges; by the time of his death forty-three years later, he had enlarged his realm more than threefold, and within another thirty years his grandson ruled all modern France except Brittany, Gascony and the Eastern borders. Philip Augustus's consistent policy was to fight the king of England in alliance with the king's heir; when the heir succeeded to the throne, Philip fought against him in his turn. During Henry II's reign, Philip allied himself with Richard

Coeur de Lion against Henry; when Richard became king, John became Philip's ally against Richard; and as soon as John succeeded Richard, Philip began hostilities against John. In 1205 he invade˙ and annexed Normandy, though the Channel Islands, which were in the duchy of Normandy, remained part of the king of England's territories, as they still do today.

The nobles in England blamed John for the loss of Normandy, and the Church had also quarrelled with him. Apart from the murder of Arthur, he had made himself unpopular in many ways. The nobles hated him because he not only seduced their wives but also refused to allow their daughters to marry until they had paid large sums to him as dowry; and though he was entitled, under feudal law, to impose these charges, he demanded enormously excessive sums. He was equally greedy with regard to other feudal dues. He taxed the boroughs and the merchant class as oppressively as he taxed the nobles. Like other medieval kings, he angered his people by protecting the Jews; but in return he required the Jews to pay him large sums as protection money. His cruelty to a Jew in Bristol has been remembered throughout the centuries: he pulled out one of the Jew's teeth every day until the Jews of Bristol paid him 10,000 marks (at least £5 million in terms of today's prices). If he encountered or expected resistance from one of his barons, he seized the baron's family as hostages, and on several occasions he caused the wives and children of noblemen who were opposing him to starve or be hanged.

His quarrel with the Church led him into conflict with a well-meaning English archbishop and an unscrupulous Italian pope. The archbishop was Stephen Langton, an Englishman who had spent most of his life teaching divinity at the University of Paris. The pope was Lotario di Segni, an Italian count who became a learned theologian and in 1198 was chosen as Pope Innocent III two days after he was ordained as a priest. During his pontificate the papal authority in Christendom reached its highest point, for he was as forceful an upholder of papal power as Gregory VII. He was chiefly responsible for launching the crusade to exterminate the Albigensian heretics of Provence; and it was he who first compelled Jews to wear the yellow badge whenever they appeared in public.

Innocent's strategy towards John was cynical in the extreme. The election of the archbishop of Canterbury rested with the canons of the abbey church, but the King's consent to the appointment was necessary. When the see became vacant in 1206, John wished them to choose John de Grey as their archbishop. He made them all swear a secret oath to elect Grey, and then publicly announced that he would approve whomsoever they chose. Innocent summoned the canons to Rome, discovered about their secret oath to John, gave them absolution for breaking it, and put pressure on them to elect Stephen Langton. He then called on John to admit Langton as archbishop, and when John refused, he imposed an interdict on England. This prohibited the clergy from celebrating Mass, from administering the last rites, from officiating at baptisms, weddings and funerals, and even banned the ringing of church bells. It was a terrible experience for a thirteenth-century Christian to be forced to live and die without the solace of the Church and to see himself and his loved ones deprived of all hope of eternal salvation; and the interdict was as effective as the most drastic industrial action in the twentieth century. Innocent rigorously used this weapon against John, while Langton, from the French monastery at Pontigny which had given refuge to Becket, tried unsuccessfully to heal the rift and to persuade John to submit.

As John refused to do so, Innocent proceeded to excommunicate him; and eventually, after the interdict had been in force for six years, he deposed John, and called on Philip Augustus to carry out the judgment of the Church and drive him from his throne. At this juncture, Innocent offered to make a deal with John: if John would do homage to him for England, and agree to hold his kingdom as a feudal fief from the pope, Innocent would not only rescind John's deposition and excommunication and release England from the interdict, but would give him the full support of the papacy against all his enemies. John accepted the offer; and in the house of the Templars at Temple Ewell near Dover, on Ascension Day in 1213, he knelt at the feet of the papal legate, Bishop Pandolfo, surrendered his crown to him, and received it again from his hands as the vassal of the pope. Langton, who had known nothing of Innocent's bargain with John until after it had been carried out, returned to England to perform his duties as archbishop of Canterbury.

John, with Innocent's support, planned a campaign to recover his territories in France by an invasion of Poitou. But when he called on his tenants-in-chief in England to perform their knight service by providing him with soldiers for the war, the northern barons rebelled. Their opposition increased when John's ally, the Emperor Otto IV, was decisively defeated by Philip Augustus at the Battle of Bouvines; and in the spring of 1215 the northern lords marched south to confront John. They insisted that the king should grant the demands for the remedy of their grievances which they expressed in a Great Charter, or, to use the Latin translation, in a Magna Carta.

Stephen Langton had sympathised with the rebels from the start, and had told John that if he refused to negotiate with them he would excommunicate every man in the royal army which marched against them, except the king himself. He and a party of moderate men among the King's advisers, including the justiciar, Hubert de Burgh, were working for a compromise. On 10 May John issued a proclamation granting the main demand which the rebel lords had put forward – that no man should be convicted without due process of law. He also offered to settle his dispute with the barons by arbitration. The barons refused arbitration, and marched on London, where they massacred the Jews and were welcomed by the citizens, while John withdrew to Windsor Castle.

The barons were welcomed on their march by the burghers of many of the boroughs through which they passed, and the corporations of these boroughs, and of London, associated themselves with the rebel cause. They added their own demands to those of the northern lords; and Langton and the king's moderate ministers seem to have put forward others for the welfare of the people as a whole. By the time that the rebels had advanced to Staines in the middle of June 1215, their Magna Carta included sixty-three demands, each favoured by one or other of the groups supporting them.

On Monday 15 June the rebel leaders met the king in a meadow named Runnymede on the south bank of the Thames, half-way between Staines and Windsor. John immediately agreed to all their demands, except the demand of the city of London that he should forgo his right to tax them; and the barons agreed to substitute a more moderate demand of tax benefits for the city. Another four days were spent in hammering out the details and the wording, and in making copies of the document; and on Friday 19 June, John fixed his seal to Magna Carta.

The document issued at Runnymede in 1215 is revered today, perhaps even more in the United States than in Britain, as the foundation-stone of our modern freedoms. This would have surprised the men who drafted it, for they had nothing in common with the leaders of modern revolutionary movements who framed the American Declaration of Independence or the French Rights of Man. The northern nobles and knights who led the revolt of 1215, and the prominent supporters whom they picked up on the way, were selfish and unscrupulous men; several of them had betrayed John during the wars in France by surrendering castles to Philip Augustus in return for French bribes. None of them achieved any reputation as soldiers, statesmen or thinkers. It is not surprising that the propagandists who acclaim them as champions of liberty prefer not to name them as individuals, but leave them hidden under the cloak of anonymity by calling them merely 'the barons'.

The only object of Magna Carta was to satisfy the sectional demands of the groups who supported the revolt against John. Most of the points dealt with the grievances of the tenants-in-chief; John was to promise not to levy excessive charges as death duties or for permitting the marriage of the lords' daughters. But similar protection was given to lesser tenants and to all freemen against excessive charges levied on them by their overlords for the same purposes. If a man died owing money to the Jews, his infant heir was not to be liable to pay interest during his infancy, and his widow's share was to be paid in priority to his Jewish creditors; and Magna Carta added, as an afterthought, that the same provisions should apply in the case of 'debts due to other than Jews'. No excessive taxation was to be levied on the towns; and the tolls, weirs, and other obstacles to navigation on the Thames, the Medway and other rivers were to be removed. The injustices of the forest laws were to be ended, and the pasture land that had been turned into royal forest was to be deforested. The King's officers were not to seize any man's horse, cart, corn or wood without his consent. There were to be no restrictions on the rights of foreign merchants to come to England; and all Englishmen were to be free to travel abroad whenever they wished, except in wartime. Women were to be banned from bringing prosecutions against defendants for any offence except the murder of their husbands. The nobles objected to prosecutions being brought by women, because they thought it unfair that in the ordeal by battle, women, being unable to fight themselves, could choose a particularly skilful fighter to appear as their champion.

Several provisions of the Charter dealt with the administration of justice. No further encroachments were to be made by the king's courts on the jurisdiction of the seigneurial courts; but on the other hand, no attempt was made to suppress the jurisdiction which the king's courts were already exercising as a result of the encroachments made during Henry II's reign, and some of the provisions of the Charter were designed to facilitate and improve the availability of justice in the king's courts.

Magna Carta, like the election manifesto of a modern political party, tried to include something for everybody, or to appear to include something for everybody, except the villeins. Clause after clause of the Charter claims rights for 'every freeman'. Its benefits were thus extended to churls a long way down in the social scale; but the unfree villeins were left out, except in a clause which prohibited the king from impoverishing a lord by levying excessive fines on the land of the lord's villeins. The injustices suffered by the Welsh, who had supported the revolutionary movement, were to be righted; 'the son of Llywelyn and all the hostages of Wales' were to be released, as were the sisters and hostages of King Alexander II of Scotland; and 'the relatives of Gerard of Athée' and 'the whole brood of the same' were not to be employed as government officials anywhere in England.

Only three of the sixty-three demands have any relevance for modern times, and even in these cases the claim that they form the basis of our modern freedom is far-fetched. One clause provided that the king should not levy taxes without the consent of the Great Council of the realm, except to raise money to pay for his ransom when he was a prisoner and for the expenses of conferring knighthood on his eldest son and for the wedding of his eldest daughter. This has been seen as the first enunciation of the principle that there should be no taxation without representation; but though it established the rule that taxes should not be imposed without the consent of the class that was to pay the taxes, it has very little connection with the modern doctrine. The

Great Council of the realm in 1215 was the council of the tenants-in-chief, which became the House of Lords; and it has been an established constitutional convention since 1671, and the law of England since 1911, that the House of Lords have no control over the imposition of taxes, which is to be left to the House of Commons, which did not exist in 1215. The demand that no one should be convicted except by the judgment of his peers has been interpreted as upholding the principle of trial by jury; but trial by jury, in the modern sense, was only beginning to evolve at the time of Magna Carta; and the right of a man to be tried by his peers no longer exists. The last remnants of this right was the privilege of a peer to be tried, in cases of treason or felony, before the House of Lords, which was abolished in 1948.

The principle that no one should be condemned without due process of law did indeed lay down that no one should be arbitrarily imprisoned or fined by despotic government in defiance of the law. This, alone of all the demands in Magna Carta, can be said to have established one of our modern freedoms; for the freedom of the foreign merchant to visit England, and of every Englishman to leave the realm, without paying for an entry visa or a passport is not enjoyed by foreign tourists and British subjects in 1981. It is an irony that the only clause of the Charter which has any relevance in modern times was in fact granted by John a month before Magna Carta was presented to him at Runnymede.

The most remarkable thing about Magna Carta was a clause which authorised revolution. John agreed that the barons should elect a committee of twenty-five members who were entrusted with the duty of ensuring that he observed the Charter; if he did not, a sub-committee of four members were to visit him and give him forty days notice that the committee would call on the people 'to distrain and distress us in all possible ways' by harrying his lands and otherwise making war against him. This legalisation of revolutionary resistance and of civil war may be seen, according to one's point of view, either as an example, or as a violation, of the traditional English respect for the rule of law.

The normal pattern of medieval politics was the alliance between a powerful king and the merchant class in the boroughs against the feudal nobility, in the struggle to curb over-powerful nobles and to enforce law and order. Occasionally there were other alliances; in the rare periods of peasant revolts, the king, the nobles and the merchants united against the peasants; and by the seventeenth century, in the civil war between Charles I and Parliament – in so far as it is possible to describe it in terms of class alignment – the king and the nobles were allied against the merchants and gentry. In 1215 there was an unusual alliance of nobles, merchants and many of the common people against the king. This alliance was not repeated – except perhaps in the reign of Edward II – in England, though it was formed in Scotland at the time of the Protestant Reformation in 1559.

The attitude of the historians and politicians in later times towards Magna Carta has varied from one century to another. During the fifty years which followed 1215, Magna Carta was praised and upheld by the nobility and the people, and it was reluctantly re-issued on several occasions by John's son, Henry III. After the victory of John's grandson, Edward I, the Charter, though not officially repudiated by the king, was evaded in practice by clever legal subterfuges. It was occasionally referred to by rebel lords during the fourteenth and fifteenth centuries; but it was completely forgotten under the rule of the despotic Tudor sovereigns, when King John, after having been regarded as a tyrant for three hundred years, was praised as a national hero who tried, valiantly but unsuccessfully, to uphold the royal authority of the king of England against his rebels and the pope. In Henry VIII's reign, the Protestant bishop, John Bale, wrote a play glorifying John. Shakespeare, sixty years after Bale, was hostile to John; but he makes no reference at all to Magna Carta in his play, though *King John* deals with the revolt of 1215. But a few years after Shakespeare's death, the King's opponents in the House of Commons resurrected Magna Carta as the great Charter of English freedom, a document which had set a precedent for a contract between the king and his people, which the people could enforce, if necessary, by revolution. It has continued for three and a half centuries to be regarded with reverence, though its revolutionary significance has been forgotten.

In modern times, Magna Carta has been less popular with the lawyers than with the politicians. The Charter was not as hostile to the king's courts as many writers have suggested; but the clause which forbade any further encroachments by the king's courts on the jurisdiction of the seigneurial courts held up the development of English law for sixty years, and it was not until the provisions of the Charter were evaded by Edward I's judges that further progress could be made.

In the short run, Magna Carta achieved nothing. A few weeks earlier, John had appealed for help to his new ally and overlord, the pope; and on 18 June, the day before the Charter was sealed, Innocent wrote from Rome to Stephen Langton ordering him to throw the full weight of the Church's authority on John's side and to excommunicate the barons who had risen against him. The archbishop, who had played an active part in drafting the Charter, refused to comply; he was suspended from his functions by the papal legate, and summoned to Rome. Unwilling to disobey the pope's authority, and saddened by the failure of his efforts at compromise, he withdrew to the Continent and for the next five years played no part in English politics.

John immediately prepared for war with the rebels. He was determined to repudiate the Charter, claiming that he was not bound by it, as he had agreed to it under duress. On the other side, the lords wished to drive home their advantage and get rid of John. Some of the more extremist barons had walked out of the meeting at Runnymede before the Charter was sealed, and were already preparing to renew the war; and the twenty-five barons who had been appointed to enforce the Charter soon adopted the same attitude. Under the pretence of holding a great tournament at Staines, they re-assembled their army there; and before John had made any move at all, they proclaimed that he had violated the Charter. They called on the people to exercise their right of revolution; they deposed John, and invited Philip Augustus's son, Louis, the future King Louis VIII of France, to become king of England.

Innocent threatened to excommunicate Philip if he helped the English rebels; but Philip, though he hesitated to intervene himself, allowed his son to accept the offer of the English crown, on the specious grounds that Louis's wife, Blanche of Castile, was the grand-daughter of Henry II of England, and because he falsely claimed that, as John's overlord for Normandy, he had tried and condemned him in his seigneurial court for the murder of Arthur, although in fact no such trial had taken place. John waged a successful winter campaign against the northern lords, and the rebels were in a desperate position when Louis at last responded to their urgent appeals for help and, in defiance of Innocent's prohibition, landed in Thanet with a large army. He was welcomed by the citizens of London, and was soon in control of all south-east England except for Dover Castle and a few other strongpoints which held out against him. John marched into East Anglia, and suffered the disaster of losing his baggage-train, including his treasure and his official documents, while he was crossing the Wash from Norfolk into Lincolnshire.

A few days later, in October 1216, John died at Newark. His contemporaries attributed his death, as they often did when kings died suddenly, to a combination of excessive eating and drinking with the grief caused by the recent disaster in the Wash; but if medical science had been more advanced, the doctors would probably have made a better diagnosis of the cause of his death at the age of forty-eight.

Neither the contemporary chroniclers nor the modern historians give the wholly fictitious version of his death which was accepted by all the Protestant writers of the sixteenth century – that he was poisoned by a wicked monk at the monastery of Swineshead in Lincolnshire. According to the story, the monk, carrying out the orders that he had received from the pope, offered John a poisoned cup of wine, and induced the king to take it by first drinking half of it himself, sacrificing his own life in his fanatical zeal to assassinate an enemy of the papacy. The Tudor writers ignored the fact that John had become the pope's ally before his death.

CHAPTER 5

EDWARD I
AND
ROBERT BRUCE
(1216–1329)

John's nine-year-old son was at Corfe Castle in Dorset when his father died. He was taken to Gloucester by John's supporters and crowned there as King Henry III. The boy was a better figure-head than the unpopular John in the struggle against the French invader and the excommunicated rebels, and under the leader-ship of the justiciar, Hubert de Burgh, the little king's army won several successes against Louis; the naval battle off Sandwich, which Hubert won by throwing powdered lime into the eyes of the French sailors, has long been remembered as a great national victory. In September 1217 Hubert forced Louis to accept peace terms by which, in return for the payment by Henry of 10,000 marks, more than a fifth of the king of England's total revenue, Louis agreed not only to waive his claim to the throne of England but also to restore Normandy; but though he left England with his army, he did not perform his undertaking about Normandy.

Henry III reigned for fifty-six years, longer than any sovereign in all English history except for Queen Victoria and George III.*

---

* But James I of England reigned in Scotland as James VI for fifty-eight years.

After the expulsion of the French, order was maintained comparatively satisfactorily during the king's infancy by the firm rule of Hubert de Burgh. Stephen Langton returned to England and resumed his duties as archbishop of Canterbury. On 7 July 1220, the anniversary of the whipping of Henry II by the monks of Canterbury in 1174, he officiated at a great ceremony in Canterbury when the relics of St Thomas Becket were laid in a splendid tomb which for three hundred years was visited by pilgrims from all over England and Europe and was adorned with priceless gifts. St Thomas of Canterbury's day, 7 July, became one of the major holy days in England.

In 1232 Henry's nobles persuaded him to get rid of Hubert de Burgh, who capped his popularity with the people, the historians and the story-tellers by a sensational escape from prison and a successful invocation of the right of sanctuary when he took refuge from his pursuers in the parish church at Devizes. He was dragged from the church and returned to his prison cell; but the indignant bishop of Salisbury forced the government to take him back to the sanctuary of the church, which was surrounded by soldiers to prevent his escape until Hubert's supporters drove off the soldiers and rescued him.

The virtues and the faults of medieval Christianity reached their fullest development during the thirteenth century. Richard Coeur de Lion's Crusade had failed to recover Jerusalem, and during the next seventy years five crusades were launched. Crusading enthusiasm was stronger than at any earlier time. A great movement developed for the reformation of the abuses in Church life. At the beginning of the thirteenth century St Francis and St Dominic founded their orders of preaching and mendicant friars who, unlike the corrupted monks living in comfort and self-indulgence in the monasteries, travelled in poverty through the country preaching and practising the virtues of Christian self-abasement.

There was an expansion of learning. Universities were founded at Oxford and Cambridge. As in the older universities of Paris and the Italian cities, divinity was considered to be much the most important subject at Oxford and Cambridge; but medicine was also taught, and there were opportunities for scientists like Roger Bacon to pursue their studies. His work on optics contributed to the invention of the telescope and of spectacles, which were being worn for reading by men with failing eyesight before the end of the thirteenth century. Like the work of scientists in later centuries, Bacon's researches were used for military as well as for peaceful purposes, and led to the use of gunpowder as a weapon in the fourteenth century. England was behind Italy in intellectual development; but English scholars read and discussed the works of St Thomas Aquinas, and Scotland produced John Duns, who, though he was afterwards ridiculed by the sixteenth-century Protestants, was considered by his contemporaries to be an important theologian.

The evil aspects of the prevailing religion increased during the thirteenth century. At the height of its power the papacy engaged in a ferocious struggle with the Holy Roman Emperor Frederick II, which led to far greater horrors than the earlier wars against the Emperor Henry IV and Frederick Barbarossa and destroyed the unity of Church and State at the international summit of feudal society, which had been based on the theory that the Holy Roman Emperor was the highest protector of the Church and that the pope was the supreme spiritual upholder of the emperor's secular rule. This struggle led to the most manifest hypocrisy, when Pope Gregory IX not only excommunicated Frederick II for going on a Crusade and recovering Jerusalem without the papal authority but even gave financial aid to the Saracens who were resisting the Crusade. Religion among the people became more hysterical, with manifestations like St Vitus's Dance and the Children's Crusade.

The hatred of Jews increased. The story that the Jews assembled at Easter in order to torture and crucify a little Christian boy whom they had kidnapped, was first believed in England in the case of the child at Norwich in 1144; the chief responsibility for spreading it rests on Thomas Becket's friend and supporter, Bishop William of Norwich. But a similar case at Lincoln in 1255, when a nine-year-old boy, Hugh, was said to have been the victim of the Jews, had worse repercussions. The local judiciary were a little sceptical about the story; but the people of Lincoln were convinced of its truth, and after they had petitioned Henry III when he passed through the city, eighteen Jews of Lincoln were executed for the murder. Another ninety-one Jews were arrested and sentenced to death in London as accessories to Hugh's murder, but were pardoned and set free after the Jews had paid a large sum of money to the king's uncle, Richard, earl of Cornwall.

Henry III was unsuccessful in his wars in France, and by the treaty of 1254 he relinquished his claim to Normandy, Maine, Anjou and Poitou, but retained Gascony from the Charente to the Pyrenees. His attempt to impose his son Edmund as king of Sicily was also a failure. His incompetence, his defeats in France, the Sicilian fiasco, and the resentment aroused by heavy taxation produced a revival of the alliance of John's reign between the nobles, the boroughs and the common people. The king's opponents were led by Simon de Montfort, a French nobleman who had inherited lands in England and the title of earl of Leicester, and who had married Henry's sister Eleanor. Simon set himself up, incongruously but sincerely, as a leader of Englishmen against French and foreign influence, and put forward demands for the abolition of the excessive feudal dues levied on the tenants-in-chief, for the relief of the taxation of the people, for the dismissal of the king's foreign advisers, for the expulsion of the Jews, or at least a restriction on their money-lending rights, and for the defence of the privileges of the boroughs.

In 1258, Simon and the nobles compelled the king to agree to appoint a council of twenty-four members, twelve of whom were to be members of the King's Council and twelve nominated by the nobles, to draft a constitution to limit the royal power. The Council of Twenty-four met at Oxford and decided that Henry should govern with the advice of a council of fifteen nobles and bishops to be chosen by four members of the Council of Twenty-four. They also appointed a number of knights of the shires and city dignitaries to supervise the government administration in the counties. These steps went far beyond anything in Magna Carta, and Henry III, who had only agreed to them under duress, thought they were a violation of his royal privileges; for though it had long been recognised that Kings needed the consent of their nobility before they could impose taxes or make certain legislative changes, it had never been suggested that the nobles of an adult king could usurp his executive powers. Both the pope and St Louis, the king of France, condemned the Provisions of Oxford, and Henry prepared for civil war.

He now had the assistance of his son Edward, who afterwards

succeeded him as King Edward I. Edward was the perfect feudal prince and king – not, like Richard Coeur de Lion, the chivalrous ideal of feudalism, but the reality of a popular and successful king in the thirteenth century. As a young man, according to the chronicler Matthew Paris, he displayed all the worst vices of the feudal nobility; on one occasion, he and his bodyguard seized and mutilated a peasant whom they passed on the highway merely for the pleasure of torturing him. But one must have some reservation about accepting this story, for Matthew Paris, who gives no explanation of Edward's cruelty, was a supporter of Simon de Montfort. At any rate, Edward shed his vicious habits as he grew older, and became a conscientious and Christian ruler.

He was physically impressive, being six foot tall, and his frugal eating and drinking habits kept him slim all his life. His appearance was a real advantage, because a thirteenth-century king had no popular press or media to present him in a favourable light, and had to rely, for his national image, on the impression that he made on the large numbers of his subjects who turned out to see him as he rode through the local towns and along the country roads on his continual travels through his kingdom. His manner was grave, courteous and frank, and a slight impediment in his speech did not impair his effectiveness as an orator. He was in excellent health throughout his life, even in his last years, to a most unusual extent for a man of the thirteenth century. In the 950 years between Penda and Elizabeth I, only five English sovereigns, or six if Matilda is included, lived beyond the age of sixty. Edward the Confessor, Henry III, Edward III, and even Henry I, are remembered in their last years as aged kings; but no one has ever thought of Edward I as an old man, though he lived longer than any of them to reach the age of sixty-eight.

He sometimes suppressed rebellion with great cruelty, but he was never devious, and lived up to his motto *Pactum serva* (Keep faith). He excelled in tournaments; he fought bravely on the battlefield; and he shared the hardships of his men on campaigns even when he was over sixty. He was a faithful husband, and seems never to have had a mistress. He was a devout Christian, keeping the feasts and observances of the Church, and he went on a crusade. He disapproved of the Jews, and eventually expelled them from his realm, but protected them against the illegal violence of the people, and hanged a ship's master who had thrown some Jews overboard and had called on them to pray for the sea to open and save them, as the Red Sea had opened for Moses.

He was wise in counsel, as well as valiant in battle, and played a greater part than even Henry I and Henry II in the development of English law. He was successful against foreign enemies; he conquered Wales; he nearly held his own against his powerful enemy, King Philippe le Bel of France; and the defeat of his plans in Scotland did not come until after his death. His greatest attribute as a statesman was his knowledge of when to stand firm and when to give way, and how to yield to superior power without appearing to do so and without loss of face.

When the civil war broke out in England, he took the field with his father and his uncle Richard of Cornwall in defence of Henry's kingly privileges against Simon de Montfort and the rebels. Simon's army was composed of the citizens of London and of the boroughs as well as of the feudal levies of his supporters among the tenants-in-chief; the royal forces were supported by a few of the nobles, but consisted largely of foreign mercenaries.

The armies marched into Sussex and met at Lewes on 14 May 1264. The battle was fought on the Downs nearby at the place known today as Mount Harry because of Henry III's presence at the foot of the hill during the engagement. Edward, on the right of the royal army, routed the Londoners who faced him and, filled with fury against the low-born citizens, pursued them for many miles and killed many of them; but when he returned to the battlefield he found that Simon had won the day and had captured Richard of Cornwall, while the king had taken sanctuary in Lewes Priory. After a desperate resistance in the streets of Lewes, Edward too was forced to seek sanctuary, and he and his father capitulated next day.

Simon kept Henry and Edward prisoners while he summoned the Great Council of the realm to meet at Westminster in January 1265. He directed every shire and most of the larger towns to send two representatives to attend the Great Council. This innovation has rightly been considered to be the forerunner of the House of Commons, though it did not become an established practice for representatives from the counties and boroughs to attend Parliament until Edward I summoned them to do so ten years later. Simon was threatened with a foreign invasion from France, where Henry's queen and other English royalist refugees were backed to the full by St Louis and by the pope, who believed that the English revolution threatened the fabric of Christendom. More dangerous for Simon was the fact that several of the lords in England were planning to desert him and to rebel on the king's behalf.

Roger Mortimer, baron of Wigmore, who had formerly been one of Simon's leading supporters, entered into secret negotiations with Edward, who was being held prisoner at Hereford. One day in Whitsun week in May 1265 Edward went out riding with the officers who were guarding him. He suggested to the officers that he should try out which of their horses was the speediest. After he had galloped round and round on each of their horses, he suddenly rode off on his own horse and escaped, knowing that they could not catch him, as his horse was fresh and theirs were exhausted. He made his way to Wigmore and to Ludlow and, joining with Mortimer, attacked Simon's forces in the west Midlands. Simon still held the king prisoner, and took him on his campaign, riding at his side and purporting to be acting in the king's name as leader of the royal army.

The decisive battle between Edward and Simon was fought at Evesham on 4 August. It was the first of three battles in English history which ended a civil war on the banks of the Severn; and as at Tewkesbury in 1471 and at Worcester in 1651, the victors made skilful tactical use of the river. Simon, who with his leading nobles formed a ring around the king, was killed there in fierce fighting in which Henry himself was wounded in the mêlée by his son's rescuing soldiers. The rebel cause was lost, though Edward continued mopping up operations for some time.

Edward now ruled the country on his father's behalf. By the standards of the time, he was considered to have acted harshly in confiscating the lands of many of Simon's defeated followers, because the feudal nobility had come to believe that they could revolt when they wished with impunity; but there were no executions. All the laws which had been enacted in the king's name while he was Simon's prisoner were annulled on the grounds that Henry had acted under duress; but at a meeting of the Great Council at Marlborough in 1267 the King voluntarily reissued Magna Carta without it having been demanded.

Preparations were in progress for the Eighth Crusade under the leadership of St Louis, for the Muslims had again recaptured Jerusalem. Edward took the cross, and the nobles and the people voluntarily contributed to the cost of the Crusade with an enthusiasm which showed both the extent to which the royal authority had been restored and the strength of the crusading fervour of the people. St Louis died at Tunis on the voyage, but Edward reached Acre and won a number of battles in Palestine.

One day the envoy of a Saracen emir arrived at Edward's camp and said that his master wished to negotiate peace. Edward received the envoy in his tent, but while he was reading the Emir's letter the envoy stabbed at him with a poisoned dagger and wounded him in the arm. Edward killed the envoy, either with the dagger or with a stool – there are two conflicting contemporary accounts – and his own life was saved by his doctors who cut out the poisoned flesh from his arm. Edward endured the painful operation without a murmur. The story that his wife, Eleanor of Castile, saved him by sucking out the poison from his wound was first told by a chronicler seventy years later and is apparently an invention.

Henry III died at Westminster on 16 November 1272. Edward, who had heard about his illness, was on his way home from the Crusade and was in Sicily when he received the news of his death. Knowing that his realm was in safe hands, he did not hurry home but travelled slowly through Italy and France, visiting the pope in Orvieto, distinguishing himself in a tournament at Chalon, paying homage to the king of France in Paris for his French lands, and visiting his province of Gascony. He landed at Dover in August 1274. The realm of England, where civil war had raged less than ten years before, remained perfectly peaceful during the absence of its new king, who had been directing the administration of the kingdom throughout his stay in Europe by an efficient system of couriers.

His first task was to introduce legislation for the reform and development of English law. At meetings of the Great Council at Westminster in 1275 and 1285, and at Gloucester in 1278, while taking care not to violate Magna Carta openly, he persuaded the lords to pass statutes which enabled the royal judges to resume their encroachments on the jurisdiction of the seigneurial courts.

Magna Carta forbade the king's courts to exercise jurisdiction in cases of a kind which they were not already dealing with in 1215. The Statute *In consimili casu* of 1285 allowed the king's courts to hear cases *in consimili casu* (in similar cases) to those which they already heard; and, by the action of 'trespass on the case', which extended the law of trespass to cover cases ranging from assault and false imprisonment to unauthorised entry on land or stealing another man's goods, all kinds of torts were brought within the jurisdiction of the king's courts.

The rest of Edward's law reform legislation was a pragmatic attempt to remedy legal abuses and to please various influential classes. He pleased the tenants-in-chief by the Statute of Quia Emptores of 1289 which prevented further subinfeudation by enacting that if any tenant granted part of his land to a sub-tenant, the sub-tenant should pay homage not to the tenant but to the tenant's overlord. The Acts which regulated markets, weights and measures, and which provided for the imprisonment of defaulting debtors, pleased the merchants; and the statute which prohibited the courts from sitting on Sundays pleased the Church.

The measures against the Jews pleased the Church, the tenants-in-chief and the common people, for both great and small freeholders were in debt to the Jews and resented having to pay them interest. After legislation had restricted the Jews from practising usury, had prohibited them from employing Christian servants and from eating with Christians, and had forced them to wear a distinguishing badge in public, Edward expelled them from England in 1290. This satisfied Edward's sense of Christian propriety; but it cost him dear, although the lords and merchants of the Great Council voted him a subsidy to mark their gratitude; for the Jews had formerly paid large sums to the king to protect them from massacre. This system of paying protection money could be justified, a little speciously, by the feudal principle that an overlord protected his tenants in return for their services, which was often commuted into money payments. By expelling the Jews, Edward lost a source of revenue which the crown had enjoyed for two centuries; but he allowed the Jews to take their money with them when they left England.

In 1275 Edward began the practice, which he continued throughout his reign, of summoning the boroughs and the knights of the shires to send two representatives from each borough and shire to the meetings of the Great Council. He thus adopted, without acknowledgments, the system introduced by Simon de Montfort in 1265. As with most of his other actions, Edward's motive was practical, not theoretical: as the merchants in the towns and the gentry in the counties would have to pay the taxes which the Great Council imposed, it seemed sensible to consult their representatives as to the best way of raising the money. Partly for this reason, the representatives were very reluctant to attend, and could only be induced to come by the threat of being fined for non-attendance.

Edward did not hesitate to enforce his authority against influential groups. When disorders occurred in London in 1285, he suspended the city authorities from exercising their functions, and sent a royal official to govern London for thirteen years. In 1289 he imprisoned several of the royal judges for corruption. But if the opposition was too formidable, he saved the situation by a timely surrender, as he did in 1297 when, for the only time in his reign, he was confronted with the threat of a rebellion from his tenants-in-chief who refused to assist him in his war in Gascony against the king of France. It was on this occasion that the well-known conversation took place between Edward and Roger Bigod, earl of Norfolk, who refused to serve in France. 'By God, Earl', said Edward, 'you will either go or hang!' 'By God, O King', replied Bigod, 'I will neither go nor hang!' He did not go and he did not hang.

In 1290, Queen Eleanor died at Harby in Nottinghamshire. Edward, who was with her on her deathbed, was deeply affected by the loss of his wife, and carried her body in great state to Westminster for burial in the Abbey. The journey from Harby took twelve days, and Edward ordered that an ornamental stone cross should be erected in the twelve towns where her body rested for the night on the journey, at Lincoln, Grantham, Stamford, Geddington, Northampton, Stony Stratford, Woburn, Dunstable, St Albans, Waltham, West Cheap and the monastery of Charing in the fields between London and Westminster, at the place which became known as Charing Cross. Two of the crosses still survive today.

Edward's conquest of Wales did not originally stem from a calculated policy; but he seized the opportunity offered by circumstances which suddenly arose. Wales was never penetrated by the Anglo-Saxons, but continued throughout the centuries divided into separate Celtic states inhabited by the Welsh-speaking descendants of the Britons who had withdrawn into isolation there in Roman times. At certain periods, for example under Rhodri Mawr (the Great) in the middle of the ninth century, one prince succeeded in making himself ruler of nearly the whole of Wales; at other times the country was fragmented into several small units. By the eleventh century Wales was divided into three independent principalities – Deheubarth in the south, Powys in the centre, and Gwynedd in the north.

After the Norman conquest of England, enterprising Norman lords and knights seized lands for themselves in Wales. Robert FitzHamon, earl of Gloucester, seized a large part of Deheubarth, building a castle at Cardiff and becoming overlord of the modern county of Glamorgan; and in the north, Hugh of Avranches, earl of Chester – whose ferocity, despite his friendship with St Anselm, earned him the nickname of Hugh the Wolf – won a series of campaigns against the Welsh in Gwynedd. The Welsh princes fought against the Normans, but never united with the other rulers of their race against the invader. Even Hugh the Wolf's great adversary, the national hero Gruffudd ap Cynan, who became prince of Gwynedd after winning a civil war in 1079 and ruled there for fifty-eight years, did not hesitate to try to capture and hand over to the English government another Welsh prince, Gruffudd ap Rhys of Deheubarth, who had taken refuge in Gwynedd and was being entertained by him as a guest.

At the beginning of the thirteenth century, the prince of Gwynedd, Llywelyn ap Iorwerth the Great, became ruler of Powys and most of Deheubarth. His grandson, Llywelyn ap Gruffudd, who took the title of prince of Wales, increased his territories by participating in the wars between Henry III and his barons and seizing lands in the English border counties. In 1267 Llywelyn met Henry III at Montgomery and paid homage to him for Wales; but soon afterwards he quarrelled with his brother Davydd, who fled to England. Llywelyn, believing that Edward I was encouraging Davydd's plots against him, refused to renew his homage to Edward; and he alarmed Edward by planning to marry Simon de Montfort's daughter. Eleanor de Montfort was captured by an English ship on her journey from France to Wales, and Edward refused to release her until Llywelyn had paid homage for Wales.

The dispute led to war in 1277. Edward marched against Llywelyn with a large army of 16,000 men, of whom 9,000 were Welsh, and defeated him in a summer campaign. He forced him to do homage and accept humiliating terms. A reconciliation took place between Llywelyn and Edward, who attended, and paid the costs of, the wedding of Llywelyn and Eleanor de Montfort at Windsor; but Edward had now decided to annex Wales, and found an excuse to provoke a second war in 1282 in which Llywelyn was killed. Next year Llywelyn's brother Davydd, who had betrayed both Llywelyn and Edward, was tried as a traitor by Edward's Great Council of the tenants-in-chief at Shrewsbury and sentenced to be hanged, drawn and quartered.

Edward did not entirely destroy Welsh native life, but he reorganised the country on English lines. He granted lands in Wales to his English barons, and introduced the feudal system in place of the tribal organisation which existed there. The English criminal law was enforced, but civil disputes continued to be settled by the old Welsh law which had been laid down by the Welsh prince Howel Dda (the Good) in the middle of the tenth century; and the Welsh language continued in use. Resentment against the Anglicisation of the country caused a serious revolt throughout Wales in 1294–5; but after Edward had suppressed it, there was no further organised resistance. Six years later, Edward conferred Llywelyn's title of prince of Wales on his son Edward, who by a happy coincidence had been born soon after the conquest in the newly built castle at Caernarvon, though there is no truth in the sixteenth-century legend that on that occasion the king showed the baby to the people and told them that he would be their prince. Since 1301 the title of prince of Wales has been borne by the eldest sons of English sovereigns.

Having conquered Wales, Edward turned his attention to Scotland. Once again, as in the case of Wales, he did not act on a premeditated plan, but seized an opportunity which presented itself. The death of King Alexander III of Scotland and of his infant grand-daughter, Queen Margaret, left the throne of Scotland vacant in 1290. There was no close relative of Alexander III, but twelve Scottish noblemen claimed the crown because of their distant relationship to him. They included John Balliol,

Robert Bruce and John Comyn. Edward I asserted that as he was overlord of Scotland, the question of the succession should be decided in his seigneurial court. His claim depended on the controversial interpretations of the oaths of fealty taken by Malcolm Canmore to William the Conqueror, by William the Lion to Henry II and to King John, and by Alexander II to Henry III, and was further complicated by the fact that Richard Coeur de Lion had released William the Lion from his homage in return for his contribution to the cost of the Third Crusade. But when the twelve competitors for the crown and their lawyers came before Edward at Norham on the Tweed to argue that they were the rightful king, they all agreed, before the proceedings began, to acknowledge Edward as overlord of Scotland. Edward's judges, after lengthy hearings, gave judgment for Balliol, whose right was unquestionably established by the feudal principle of primogeniture, though by Scottish law and custom the case was more doubtful; and Balliol, after doing homage for Scotland to Edward, became king.

The Lowlands of Scotland had been reorganised on Anglo-Saxon lines by Malcolm Canmore and his English wife, St Margaret; and their son, David I, had taken steps to introduce the feudal system and Norman and European practices, though the manorial system was never introduced into Scotland. In Lothian and the south-east, the population was largely descended from the early English settlers who had come there from Schleswig-Holstein in the sixth century; and the nobles, many of whom held lands in England as well as in Scotland, had the outlook of the feudal barons in England and throughout Christendom. North of the Tay, in the Highlands, the old tribal system still continued, and was to do so for another four and a half centuries, quite unaffected by feudalism or by any English, Norman or continental customs.

Edward had decided to subjugate Scotland, as he had subjugated Wales. His assertion of overlordship would not, in itself, have entailed anything more than the right to homage, which would have left Balliol as much an independent ruler in Scotland as the Norman kings had been in Normandy and as Edward I was in Gascony, despite his homage for the territory to the king of France. But Edward insisted on hearing appeals from the Scottish law courts; and when Balliol refused to agree, Edward treated him as a rebellious vassal. He invaded Scotland, marching as far north as Elgin, and forced Balliol to submit.

When Edward returned to England, he took with him the Stone of Destiny on which the kings of Scotland were always crowned at Scone, near Perth; according to legend, it was the stone which Jacob, in the book of Genesis, had used as a pillow when he saw, in his dream, the ladder leading to Heaven, and which had been brought to Ireland by a Greek prince many years before the birth of Christ, and to Scotland from Ireland at the time of the Scots' invasion in the sixth century. Edward placed the stone under the throne in Westminster Abbey, and ever since the kings of England have sat above it on their throne at their coronation, being thus crowned king of Scots in the old way. The stone has remained in Westminster Abbey for nearly seven hundred years, apart from four months in 1950-1, when it was stolen by Scottish Nationalists and taken to Scotland before being returned. As well as removing the Stone of Scone, Edward ordered the destruction and obliteration of the ancient Scottish archives and monuments, so as to eradicate the memory of Scotland as an independent kingdom.

Edward deposed and banished Balliol, and took over the direct government of Scotland through English officials, though his authority did not extend north of the Tay. Within a year, a serious revolt broke out in south-west Scotland under the leadership of William Wallace, a country gentleman of Lanarkshire, who attacked and killed Edward's sheriffs and judges. Edward, who was campaigning in France, sent an army to suppress the rising; but Wallace defeated it at the Battle of Stirling Bridge, and proceeded to invade and ravage Northumberland and Durham. Edward himself then invaded Scotland. He was fifty-nine; but though he was injured when his ribs were broken by a kick from his horse, he led his army into battle against Wallace at Falkirk on 22 July 1298. The Scottish army was routed by the English archers. Wallace became an outlaw, harrying the English army of occupation in guerrilla warfare.

The resistance to the English was carried on by two of the claimants to the Scottish throne, John Comyn and Robert Bruce the younger; but after several campaigns Edward forced both Bruce and Comyn to surrender. Bruce came over to Edward's side, and helped suppress the Scottish resistance in Galloway.

Only Wallace still held out. He was eventually captured by a treacherous Scottish gentleman and handed over to Edward; and after being tried at Westminster Hall as a traitor to his overlord, the king of England, he was hanged, drawn and quartered at Tyburn in August 1305. It seemed as if the Scottish resistance was over.

But six months later, another revolt broke out. It began when Bruce met Comyn in the Friars' Church at Dumfries. There is some doubt as to what precisely occurred, but it is certain that Bruce stabbed Comyn as they talked in the church, and that Comyn was finished off by Bruce's followers. According to the account which reached Edward I, and was generally believed at the time, Bruce arranged to meet Comyn in the church in order to propose to him that they should together lead a revolt against Edward, that they should postpone for the moment the question as to which of them should become king of Scotland if they were successful, and that whichever of them ultimately became king should compensate the other by granting him his ancestral lands. Comyn indignantly repudiated the proposal, denounced Bruce as a traitor to his overlord, and threatened to reveal his proposal to Edward. Bruce then decided, on the spur of the moment, to kill Comyn. There is more reason to accept this version than the alternative explanation, more discreditable to Bruce, that, having decided to lead a national revolt against Edward, he thought it best to avoid the possibility of a split in the movement by getting rid at the outset of his rival for the leadership, and invited Comyn to Dumfries with the intention of assassinating him.

The murder of Comyn was followed within a few days by the outbreak of a revolt which had obviously been secretly prepared in advance. It may well have been organised by Lamberton, the Bishop of St Andrews, who was a friend of Bruce, and by Wishart, the Bishop of Glasgow; for the Scottish Bishops resented Edward's policy of packing the Scottish benefices with English priests. But it was considered to be a heinous sin to kill a man in the sanctuary of a church, where even the officers of the law were not allowed to arrest him. Edward had no difficulty in persuading the pope to excommunicate Bruce, and he used the crime as an additional reason, apart from his treason to his overlord, to justify the severest measures against him and his supporters.

Bruce, who was thirty-one in February 1306, had recently succeeded to his father's title of earl of Annandale. He was a feudal nobleman holding large estates in south-west Scotland and in Yorkshire and Huntingdonshire as a tenant-in-chief of the king of Scots and the king of England. His aged grandfather had been one of the competitors for the Scottish crown who had pleaded his cause before Edward, being descended from David I; and one of his sisters had married King Eric II of Norway. He had changed sides several times during Edward I's campaigns against the Scots; but in 1306 he decided to place himself at the head of a popular national movement of the Scottish people, and to win the crown for himself and national independence for his countrymen at the same time.

Popular national uprisings against foreign domination were a new phenomenon which first arose almost simultaneously in several countries of Europe at the end of the thirteenth century. In 1282 the people of Sicily rose against the Norman garrison of their French ruler, Charles of Anjou, and massacred them on the day which became known as the Sicilian Vespers. In 1291 the people of the Swiss cantons of Schwyz, Uri and Unterwalden rebelled against their ruler, the duke of Austria – a revolt in which the participation of William Tell is unfortunately pure invention – and finally won their independence twenty-four years later after annihilating the Austrian feudal army at Morgarten. The Welsh revolt against Edward I in 1294–5, unlike Llywelyn's earlier wars against him, had been an unsuccessful national rising. Scotland, under Wallace, followed suit in 1297. In 1302 the townsmen of Flanders freed their country from French rule by defeating the French feudal army at Courtrai.

The Scottish movement was ultimately victorious under Bruce's leadership. There is no doubt that selfish motives played an important part in the decision of this somewhat unscrupulous feudal noble to become a nationalist leader; but this is not unusual with leaders of popular revolutions. Once he had taken his daring decision in 1306, he knew that there was no going back, and showed extraordinary courage and tenacity. During the struggle he revealed himself as a great military commander and a brilliant political propagandist.

After the death of Comyn, he went to Scone, and had himself crowned king of Scots in the traditional place, though the Stone of Scone was not there. In 1057 Malcome Canmore, after his victory over Macbeth, had been crowned king of Scotland by his ally, Macduff, the thane of Fife; and since that time Macduff's descendants had had the right to place the crown on the king's head at the coronation after the anointing by the bishop. The only available descendant of Macduff was the young countess of Buchan. Her husband, John Comyn, earl of Buchan, was the cousin of the Comyn whom Bruce had killed in the church at Dumfries. He had sworn vengeance on Bruce and was supporting Edward I; but the countess rode to Scone to crown Bruce. He had already been crowned two days earlier by Lamberton; but the romantic and traditional value of a coronation by the countess could not be wasted, and he was crowned again by her at a second ceremony.

Edward sent an army into Scotland, determined to punish the rebels with a savagery which he had never shown before in his long experience of suppressing rebellion. His army was supported by many Scottish collaborators, especially by members of the Comyn family; for, like most other wars of national liberation, Scotland's fight for freedom was in its earlier stages also a civil war. The English defeated Bruce at Methven near Perth. After the battle, the English commander summarily hanged nearly all Bruce's soldiers who were taken prisoner; and Edward revenged himself on Bruce's family. Bruce's wife repudiated her husband's activities, and Edward held her in honourable captivity; but he hanged three of Bruce's brothers and his brother-in-law, and ordered that the countess of Buchan should be imprisoned in a wooden cage at the top of Berwick Castle, where she was held for several years before being released.

Bruce retreated into Argyllshire, where he was again defeated by the Comyns, and fled with a few followers into the hills and forests. After many adventures and escapes he took refuge in the Western Isles and perhaps in the Orkneys and the island of Rachlin off the north coast of Ireland. It was there, according to later legend, that, when he was despairing of his prospects in Scotland, he saw a spider repeatedly trying to weave a web, persevering and starting again after constant failures, and ultimately succeeding. He decided to imitate the spider and try again. The story is not mentioned by any of the contemporary chroniclers.

In February 1307 Bruce landed in south-west Scotland, and was joined by many supporters. Edward I, who had spent the winter at Carlisle, was seriously ill; but when he heard of Bruce's landing, he assembled a new army. He insisted on riding at the head of his men, but was so weak that he could travel only two miles a day. He did not cross the border into Scotland, for he died at Burgh-upon-the-Sands, the last village in England, on 7 July 1307. He ordered his officials to inscribe on his tombstone, in addition to his motto *Pactum serva*, the words *Scotorum malleus* (the hammer of the Scots).

The new king was Edward's twenty-three-year-old son, the prince of Wales, who became King Edward II. He led the army into Scotland as far as Dumfries, but then abandoned the campaign against Bruce. He had for some years been despised by his father and the nobles as a weak and pleasure-loving homosexual who was much too friendly with a young Gascon gentleman, Piers Gaveston. Apart from his other vices, the nobles were particularly shocked by the fact that he took part, with Gaveston and other favourites, in amateur theatricals, which they thought was very improper for a king. He married the king of France's daughter Isabel, a strong, passionate woman, to whom he had been betrothed in his father's lifetime. She found him most unsatisfactory as a husband, although he fathered her four children.

Edward I, shortly before his death, had forced the prince of Wales to send Gaveston away from court; but as soon as the old king died, Edward II recalled Gaveston, and created him earl of Cornwall. The nobles threatened a revolt, and the king was compelled to agree to send Gaveston into exile in Ireland.

Edward soon recalled Gaveston again, and the lords rose in rebellion. Edward and Gaveston organised an army to resist them; but Gaveston was besieged in Scarborough Castle and surrendered to the earl of Pembroke, one of the leading rebels, after Pembroke had promised that his life should be spared. Pembroke took Gaveston under escort towards his castle at Wallingford; but when they reached Deddington in Oxfordshire, Pembroke rode off to visit his wife, leaving Gaveston at the local rectory with only a small escort to guard him. During Pembroke's absence, the earl of Warwick, another of the rebel leaders, arrived with a band of men, seized Gaveston, and took him to

Warwick. After a summary trial before some of the rebel lords, he was hanged on Blacklow Hill in Warwickshire. Edward II was broken-hearted, but was forced to submit to the lords, to pardon them for their rebellion and for Gaveston's death, and to agree to appoint their leaders as his ministers.

In the meantime, Bruce had not wasted his opportunities in Scotland. After waging partisan warfare against the English garrisons for five years, and establishing his control over the north by a successful campaign against the earl of Buchan in Aberdeenshire, he felt strong enough by 1312 to attack the great castles from which the English had hoped to rule the conquered country. Dundee was the first of the English fortresses to fall. An attack on Berwick was repulsed; but Bruce himself captured Perth by storm on a freezing night in January 1313, and Dumfries and the castles of the south-west were seized soon afterwards. The local peasantry captured Linlithgow Castle, after a farmer, delivering hay to the castle, had placed his hay-cart at the castle entrance in a position which prevented the garrison from closing the gate or lowering the portcullis. Bruce's chief lieutenant, Sir James Douglas (the 'Black Douglas') took Roxburgh Castle; the English sentries mistook his men for cattle as they crept up to the walls in black cloaks under cover of darkness. Bruce's nephew Thomas Randolph, earl of Moray, who at one time had fought for the English against him, captured Edinburgh Castle by a daring night attack. Meanwhile Bruce not only raided the north of England but, striking where the enemy least expected, led a successful invasion of the Isle of Man, which he captured from the English.

Bruce's brother made an agreement with the English commander at Stirling for the conditional surrender of the castle on terms which were often granted in medieval warfare: the castle was to be surrendered on 24 June 1314 if by that day, Midsummer Day, Edward II had not sent an army to relieve it; in the meantime, Bruce's forces would leave the defenders in peace. When news of the agreement reached the English court, Edward II raised a great army and led it into Scotland in a supreme attempt to save Stirling, to defeat Bruce, to retrieve English honour and to reconquer Scotland. Modern historians have no hesitation in rejecting as a propaganda exaggeration the statement of the fourteenth-century Scottish chroniclers that the

English host numbered 190,000 men; but the most reliable estimates are that Edward led more than 20,000 soldiers into Scotland, outnumbering Bruce's forces by nearly three to one.

On Sunday 23 June 1314, one day before Stirling Castle was due to surrender, Edward's army met Bruce's at Bannockburn, a few miles south of Stirling. Bruce's 8,000 men, unlike their 20,000 opponents, were not a feudal fighting force, for Bruce himself and a few of his top generals were the only feudal nobles among them. They were peasants who were inspired by national hatred of the foreign oppressor. After a preliminary skirmish on the Sunday afternoon, in which Bruce killed the leader of an English reconnaissance party who had recognised him and charged him, the main battle was fought next day.

Bruce completely out-generalled Edward II. Having safe-guarded his men against a cavalry attack on their flank by digging hidden pits as traps for the horses, he provoked the English knights into launching repeated and costly cavalry charges against the wall of spears presented by his infantry formations; while the English archers, who so often won battles for their Kings, were unable to shoot at the Scots because their own horsemen were in the way. The archers and the English infantry were then dispersed and driven into the marshes by Bruce's horsemen. In the midst of the confusion, Bruce's camp servants, who had been told to keep out of the way in the rear, came up over the brow of the hill to see what was happening. The demoralised English thought that a new relieving army was approaching, and turned and fled in panic. Edward II himself led the way. The commander of the English garrison in Stirling Castle refused to admit him, so he rode to Dunbar and took ship to Berwick. His losses were heavy, but most of his defeated army managed to make their way home to England.

Bannockburn not only won Scottish independence; coming twelve years after the battle of Courtrai, and a year before Morgarten, it shook the military power of feudalism. An English monk, writing in about 1325, thought that Courtrai and Bannock-burn presaged the collapse of the social fabric of Christendom. In Scotland, Bruce summoned the nobles and representatives of the commons to a Parliament at Ayr in 1315, where they accepted him as king. Having gained his throne by popular support, he worked to retain his popularity by introducing legal and administrative reforms which in many respects followed the principles laid down in England in Magna Carta. He obtained international recognition with some difficulty. In 1320 his Parliament at Arbroath sent a message to the pope justifying his position and their support of him. It is an interesting historical document, for while it barely refers to Bruce's hereditary right to the throne, and not at all to feudal rights, it acclaimed 'our lord and sovereign Robert' as 'another Joshua or Judas Maccabeus' who had saved his people, and declared: 'While there exist a hundred of us we will never submit to England.'

After Bannockburn, Bruce took the offensive against the English. His invasion of Ireland achieved nothing; but his forces repeatedly raided the north of England, and in 1318 he led an invasion which devastated Northumberland and Durham, and Yorkshire as far south as Ripon. Four years later, Edward II led another army into Scotland and devastated Lothian; this time Bruce refused to give battle, waited until the English were forced by famine to withdraw, and then pursued them far into Yorkshire, where he nearly took Edward prisoner.

The reverses suffered at the hands of the Scots increased the dissatisfaction of the English nobility with Edward II; and they were also incensed that he had replaced Gaveston with two new favourites, Hugh le Despencer and his son Hugh. In 1322 the nobles revolted; but Edward and the Despencers defeated the rebels at Boroughbridge in Yorkshire. The earl of Lancaster, who had been chiefly responsible for the execution of Gaveston, was taken prisoner and beheaded. Some years later, Edward's queen, Isabel, who sympathised with the rebels, defected while on a diplomatic mission to her native France, where she became the mistress of the rebel exile, Roger Mortimer, baron of Wigmore.

Queen Isabel and Mortimer plotted with their supporters in England to overthrow Edward II. They landed in Suffolk with a small army of Flemish mercenaries. The nobles, the gentry and the people of London rose in their support, and after a short civil war they defeated the king's forces and captured Edward and the two Despencers. The Despencers were hanged, and in January 1327 Edward was forced to abdicate in favour of his fourteen-year-old son. Later in the year he was murdered in Berkeley Castle in Gloucestershire; if tradition is correct, he was killed in a horrible manner in mockery of his homosexuality. Mortimer ruled England in the name of the young Edward III.

Mortimer renewed the war with Scotland, and sent the young king to lead his armies in the north; but the Scots invaded Northumberland, and nearly captured Edward. Mortimer then opened peace negotiations with Bruce which at last brought the long war to an end. Bruce was dying of leprosy, but he settled the peace terms in preliminary negotiations carried on with the English representatives at Holyrood Abbey in Edinburgh. Considering the unbroken successes of the Scots in the fighting of the previous twenty years, the English obtained very advantageous terms. They recognised the independence of Scotland and Bruce as its king; in return, the Scots agreed to pay £20,000 in compensation for the loss of the rights of the English king and landowners in Scotland; and Bruce's four-year-old son David was to marry Edward III's sister Joanna.

Bruce showed his statesmanship by not insisting on more favourable terms. He realised that his recent successes had been won in circumstances which would not always prevail; that militarily England was a stronger power than Scotland; that he was dying, leaving an infant son; and that it was to the advantage of Scotland to have peace. The treaty was ratified at Northampton in May 1328. Five months later, the pope released Bruce from excommunication and his realm from the interdict which the king, the Church and the people of Scotland had happily ignored for more than twenty years.

Bruce died on 7 June 1329, a month before his fifty-fifth birthday. His foresight could not save his country from disasters after his death.

CHAPTER 6

THE TWILIGHT OF
CHIVALRY
AND THE
PEASANTS'
REVOLT
(1329–81)

The nobles who had helped Mortimer depose Edward II soon became alarmed at his ambition. He even struck at the king's uncle, Edmund of Woodstock, earl of Kent, tricking him into believing that his brother Edward II was still alive and into planning his escape from prison. He then had Kent convicted and executed for high treason. Some officers of the king's household persuaded Edward III, who was now seventeen, that his own life would be in danger unless he destroyed Mortimer.

In October 1330 they carried out a well-planned *coup d'état* while the court was at Nottingham. The castle in which Edward was residing with his mother and Mortimer was guarded by Mortimer's followers; but Edward's supporters entered the castle at night by a secret passage and met Edward in the courtyard. He himself then led them to Mortimer's room, where they overpowered the guards and arrested Mortimer, despite the entreaties of Queen Isabel. He was taken to London, put on trial for high treason, and executed. Edward allowed his mother to retire in peace to a country house.

Edward III, like Richard Coeur de Lion, was viewed very

differently by his contemporaries and by later generations. The historians knew that his wars were pointless, costly, and achieved nothing in the long run; his contemporaries saw only his gallantry in love and war, and his victories. After the moral collapse of Edward II's reign, they hailed the accession of the young king as the dawn of a new age of glory. Feudal chivalry, which had been discredited by the humiliations of Courtrai, Bannockburn and Morgarten, was regenerated, and flourished for the last time, under Edward III. The chroniclers wrote admiringly of the gallant king who pursued women but respected those who were too virtuous to become his mistress, and who defeated foreign kings but treated them with the greatest honour as his prisoners-of-war.

Edward turned his attention first to Scotland, where the death of Bruce and the infancy of his son David II opened up fresh opportunities for conquest. Bruce had appointed his nephew and general, Randolph, earl of Moray, as regent for his son. But after three years Randolph died in mysterious circumstances; there were rumours that he had been poisoned. It has been suggested that the old ballad *Lord Randal* referred, in its original form, to Randolph's death.

Edward III hesitated to break the Treaty of Northampton and make war on his brother-in-law; but he allowed John Balliol's son, Edward Balliol, to fit out an expedition from England for the purpose of seizing the throne of Scotland from David Bruce. Balliol was successful, and, having become king, did homage to Edward III for Scotland. David Bruce's supporters drove out Balliol, and by a process which would today be called 'escalation' Edward III became directly involved in the fighting. He won a great victory over the Scots at Halidon Hill near Berwick in July 1333 and captured the town and castle. The English retained Berwick as a valuable bridgehead across the Tweed; and though it was more than once recaptured by the Scots, the English finally acquired it in 1482. The county town was thus separated from its shire, and for 500 years Berwick has remained an English town whereas Berwickshire is a Scottish county.

At this point, Edward had no wish to be involved in war with France; but King David and Queen Joanna took refuge in France, and the French king, Philip VI, gave an increasing amount of aid to David's supporters in Scotland against Balliol and the English.

Edward retaliated by helping Philip's rebel, Robert of Artois, to raid France. Eventually, in 1337, Philip VI declared that Edward, as a rebellious tenant-in-chief, had forfeited Gascony, and the Hundred Years War between France and England began.

It was only after war became inevitable that Edward seriously pressed his claim to the French throne. By the usual feudal law of succession, under which females succeeded in the absence of males of the same degree, Edward was the lawful heir through his mother Isabel, the daughter of King Philippe le Bel. Philip VI argued that succession to the French crown was governed by the Salic Law which excluded all females and those claiming through them. The dynastic claim was always an excuse for Edward III, and not the cause of the Hundred Years War. Apart from the Scottish conflict, he was anxious to help the cities of Flanders, whose independence was threatened by the king of France, for the wool trade with Flanders was an increasingly important source of England's economic wealth. He was also conscious, as were all feudal kings, that a foreign war was the best way of keeping his tenants-in-chief and their knights too busy to have the time to engage in rebellion against him.

The war began with an English naval victory at Sluys, and after a few setbacks Edward was able to follow this with a successful invasion of France. In August 1346 he won a great victory at Crecy near Calais. It was the first battle in which an English army used gunpowder and cannon as a weapon; but a far more decisive role was played by the English bowmen, who established their reputation throughout Christendom as an almost invincible body. King John of Bohemia was fighting on the French side, and, although completely blind, charged with his men and was killed in the battle. Edward III treated his body with great honour, placing it in his own tent.

Edward, prince of Wales, who became known as the Black Prince, led the main attack at Crecy, though he was aged only sixteen. After the battle he assumed the crest of the three feathers and the motto 'Ich dien' of his fallen enemy, the king of Bohemia. They have remained ever since the crest and motto of the princes of Wales.

Edward III followed up his victory by besieging Calais, which surrendered next year and remained in English hands for more than two hundred years. He at first announced that he would hang the garrison to punish the town for its acts of piracy against English shipping; but he spared them all at the intercession of his queen, Philippa of Hainault. During his absence in France, David II invaded England in support of his French ally, but was defeated and captured at Neville's Cross in Durham by the local forces that Edward had left behind to guard the northern frontier.

This year of victories was followed nine years later by another double success. Edward invaded Scotland in January 1356 and devastated Lothian in the campaign which became known as the 'Burnt Candlemas'; and in September the Black Prince defeated King John of France at the Battle of Poitiers and took him prisoner. The hopes which the English people had placed in their gallant king had been more than fulfilled. He had been victorious in all his campaigns in France and Scotland, and held both the king of France and the king of Scots as his prisoners in England.

In 1360, after twenty-three years of war, the peace treaty was signed at Brétigny. The terms showed that Edward, despite his image as a romantic king, was a hard-headed statesman who was more interested in material advantage than in dynastic claims. The French recognised him as ruler of Gascony, and also of Aquitaine, which the kings of England had lost more than a hundred years before, so that he held all south-west France from the Loire to the Pyrenees. They also ceded Calais and a small surrounding area; and he received a large ransom for the release of Kings John and David II. In return, he waived his claim to the crown of France, and abandoned Balliol in Scotland.

The war was resumed a few years later, and spread to Spain; but though the Black Prince was usually victorious, no decisive result was achieved.

Edward III's prestige was very high, both in England and in Europe. In 1363 the Lord Mayor of London entertained five kings at a banquet in the city; Edward was present with his four guests, the kings of France, Scotland, Denmark and Cyprus. The whole population, as well as the merchants of the city, were proud of their king and country; and it was said that every woman in England owned at least one trinket which she had been given as her share of the spoils won in France.

Edward III developed early and faded early. At the age of

fourteen he became king and led his army against the Scots; at sixteen, he married; at seventeen he fathered a son and overthrew Mortimer; at twenty he won Halidon Hill and captured Berwick; at twenty-four he began the Hundred Years War. But after the age of fifty his physical and mental powers rapidly declined. He sat in his palace at Sheen, doting over an unscrupulous young mistress, Alice Perrers, while his eldest son, the Black Prince, won the battles in France and his fourth son, John of Gaunt, duke of Lancaster, governed the kingdom. When he died at the age of sixty-four, he was succeeded by his ten-year-old grandson, Richard II, for the Black Prince, Richard's father, had died a year before.

The revival of chivalry and military glory under Edward III led to a cult of a chivalrous hero, the King Arthur of medieval legend. Geoffrey of Monmouth, in 1136, had translated into Latin the Welsh legends about Arthur in his book *The History of the Kingdom of Britain*; but his Arthur lived in the world of Celtic magic, not of medieval chivalry. The fourteenth-century King Arthur sat at his Round Table, where no one could occupy a higher position than another, surrounded by valiant knights who fought for the right against evil, served God and their king, obeyed the precepts of the Christian religion, and never yielded to the foe but only to the commands of beautiful women. Edward was fascinated by the Round Table legend, and we now know, from the analysis of the timber, that the Round Table at Winchester was made in the first years of his reign.

In 1344 he took a vow to inaugurate a new order of knights as brave and pure as the Knights of the Round Table; but the Order of the Garter acquired its name from the well-known incident which was first recorded in writing by Polydore Vergil at the beginning of the sixteenth century, was rejected as an invention by Victorian scholars, and is now generally accepted as authentic by modern historians. Edward's cousin Joan, the daughter of Edmund, earl of Kent, was aged two when her father was executed; she was brought up at court, and became a lady-in-waiting to Queen Philippa. She married the earl of Salisbury, but was in love with his steward, with whom she had contracted a secret marriage before she married Salisbury; and she was firm in resisting the advances of the king, who was infatuated with her. In 1348 Edward gave a ball at Calais to celebrate the capture of the town. As Joan danced at the ball, she dropped her garter, and when the king picked it up for her, some of the courtiers sniggered. Edward thereupon fastened it to his own leg, saying: *'Honi soit qui mal y pense'* (Let him be ashamed who sees evil in it). This became the motto of the Order of the Garter; and Joan, after the death of Salisbury and her steward, became the daughter-in-law of the importunate king, for she married his son, the Black Prince.

While the cult of King Arthur was spreading among the aristocracy, the people were worshipping their own plebeian hero, Robin Hood. The story told of his adventures in Sherwood Forest in Nottinghamshire, where Robin and his band of merry men – the very tall man incongruously named Little John, Will Scarlock, and the fat and jovial Friar Tuck – lived as outlaws, defied the authority of the sheriff of Nottingham, and stole from the rich to give to the poor, but never robbed a poor man or raped a woman. The story expressed the feelings and desires of those popular groups who did not, like the ecclesiastical chroniclers, the merchants and many sections of the common people, extol the merits of law and order, but hated the officers of the law who enforced the forest laws, and preferred to opt out of feudal society by living as hunters and outlaws in the forest, rather than as villeins working on the land. Apart from being an enemy of the rich and a champion of the poor, Robin Hood also accomplished great feats, not with the sword and lance of the nobles and knights, but with the longbow, the weapon of the common people. He shot an arrow from Robin Hood Hill into the roof of Ludlow Church, a distance of a mile and a half, and accomplished a similar feat near Dublin.

The Robin Hood legend reached the height of its popularity in the fifteenth and early sixteenth centuries, when it was constantly sung and acted, to the annoyance of the authorities, by Morris dancers and strolling players, especially on May Day. But the stories were already very popular by the middle of the fourteenth century. The Victorian historians did not believe that Robin Hood ever existed; but an entry in the records of the Sheriff of Yorkshire refers to the seizure of chattels worth 32s. 6d. belonging to 'Robert (or Robin) Hood, fugitive', in 1230. This outlaw was probably almost as far removed from the Robin Hood of legend as was the British leader Arthur in 500 from Edward

III's hero. The stories are more likely to be of fourteenth- than of thirteenth-century origin, for they contain no reference to Jewish moneylenders, whereas corrupt and jovial friars are often mentioned.

Later writers placed Robin Hood's adventures in the reign of Richard Coeur de Lion, during Richard's absence on the crusade and his imprisonment in Austria, while his usurping brother John was misgoverning England. This was later followed by Sir Walter Scott in his novel *Ivanhoe*; but it is certainly wrong, and was undoubtedly an attempt by the sixteenth-century writers to placate the authorities by making Robin not an outlaw defying the laws of his rightful king but a loyal subject resisting a rebellious usurper. These writers went even further in their efforts to make Robin respectable by stating that he was an aristocrat, the earl of Huntingdon, who had been deprived of his lands by the usurper for his devotion to his king. This is complete fiction.

England underwent important economic and social changes during the fifty-year reign of Edward III. The Hundred Years War not only revived the feudal ideal of chivalry, it also weakened the military, economic and social structure of feudalism. Edward could not fight the long war with just the feudal levies, but also engaged mercenaries; and many English peasants enlisted in the army for wages and became full-time professional soldiers. When their services were dispensed with, some of them, not wishing to return to their labour in the fields in England, followed Sir John Hawkwood and other English mercenary leaders to fight in the wars in Italy.

The feeling of national solidarity, of hatred of the French and the foreigner, also weakened feudal ways of thinking. In 1351 Edward's Parliament passed the Statute of Treasons, most of which is still in force today and regulates the present law of high treason. The Act limited high treason to seven types of offence: attempting to kill the king; raping or seducing the king's wife, his eldest daughter before her marriage, or the wife of the king's eldest son; waging war against the king in his realm; giving aid to the king's enemies either in his realm or abroad; killing the Lord Chancellor or other high officers of state; forging the king's seal; and making or circulating false coins. Treason was therefore restricted to offences against the king and his royal authority, and the old feudal concept of treason against an overlord was finally abolished.

Edward III, unlike his grandfather Edward I, has never been remembered as a lawgiver; but another important piece of legislation was enacted in 1363. It set up the Courts of Quarter Sessions which were not abolished until 1971. The Statute *In consimili casu* of 1285 had enabled the king's judges to resume their encroachments on the jurisdiction of the seigneurial courts which had been halted by Magna Carta, and by the middle of the fourteenth century this had progressed so far that the seigneurial courts had virtually ceased to function. As the king's courts were unable to cope with all the criminal cases in the country, it was necessary to establish new courts to deal with petty and moderately grave offences. The duty was entrusted to the justices of the peace.

The office of justice of the peace had originated in 1195, when the knights and gentlemen in the counties were appointed to carry out certain executive and judicial functions in their districts, including military duties in time of war and rebellion. Their judicial activities increased in the fourteenth century. The Act of 1363 enacted that all the justices of the peace in the shire were to meet four times a year to deal with those crimes which were not sufficiently serious to be tried before the king's itinerant judges at Assizes. Most of the JPs were lords of the manor in their districts; but this criminal jurisdiction for the whole shire, which they exercised at Quarter Sessions, had nothing in common with their decaying seigneurial jurisdiction over their tenants. The JPs also sat in their own localities in courts which became unofficially known as Courts of Petty Sessions.

The Act of 1363 accelerated the process of transforming the local gentry from feudal lords of the manor into the country gentlemen who as JPs ruled England until the beginning of the twentieth century. Until 1888 they were the only form of local government in the rural areas, and carried out important executive duties, in connection with local defence in wartime, road repairs, and the Poor Law administration, though today their power to regulate the opening hours of inns and drinking establishments is their only remaining executive function. The local knights and squires controlling the village constables, supervising the administration of their parishes, and sitting in judgment on malefactors who poached in their woods, brawled in the inns and at the fairs, and committed crimes against the king's law and authority, became one of the most important features of English life, and continued long after such duties in other countries were being performed by paid officials of the king or central government.

The growth of international trade during the fourteenth century, particularly the wool trade with Flanders, had increased the importance of the towns; and this had accelerated the circulation of money and the breakdown of feudal society. The commutation of feudal services into money rents, which had been increasing continually since the eleventh century, had by the fourteenth century reached a stage where the prevailing relationship on the land was that of large landowners, of tenant farmers who paid them rent, and of landless agricultural labourers who, in return for money wages, worked for the tenant farmers or occasionally for the large landowners themselves. But many peasants were still unfree villeins, and they became increasingly dissatisfied as more and more of their fellows became free.

The process had been facilitated by the Black Death, the plague which struck Europe in the middle of the century. It reached England in the summer of 1348, and during the next eighteen months spread from Dorset to nearly every region in the country. Some historians have estimated that between one-third and half the population died from the Black Death; but recent research suggests that this figure was reached only in certain areas and in specific occupational groups, and that the national deathrate was no higher than 20 per cent. The Black Death was followed by later outbreaks of plague, and it seems likely that the population of England, having risen from two million in 1066 to four million in 1348, had fallen to two-and-a-half million by the end of the fourteenth century.

The fall in the population, and consequently in the labour force, immediately led to a sharp rise in wages. The government tried to check this by the Statute of Labourers of 1351, which made it a criminal offence for labourers to demand, or for employers to pay, more than the maximum wages fixed by the justices of the peace in the district. But the statute was very largely evaded, as the bargaining position of the labourers was strong enough to induce the employers to pay higher wages than were allowed by law. The growing prosperity of the paid labourers increased the dissatisfaction of the villeins. During the twenty-five years after the Black Death there were constant complaints from the lords of the manor of villeins deserting the land and refusing to perform their feudal obligations to their lords.

The social discontent was undoubtedly responsible for the Peasant Revolt which broke out in 1381; but the rising might not have occurred had it not been for the political and religious discontent which spread during the minority of Richard II. The Parliament which met in 1376 denounced the government of John of Gaunt, and great resentment was felt at the poll tax of 1380, which was imposed on every inhabitant of the realm over the age of fifteen. At Oxford, John Wycliffe was teaching heretical doctrine, attacking the power of the priesthood at its most vital point by denying the Real Presence of Christ's body in the consecrated bread and wine of the Eucharist. A much more Radical monk, John Ball, preached the doctrines of social equality which throughout the Middle Ages were expounded from time to time, in every country of Christendom, by a small minority of priests who believed that true Christianity demanded the establishment of a classless society. John Ball entered a monastery at York, but soon left it and moved to Colchester. He travelled through Essex and Kent, standing in front of the churches and preaching to the people, as they came out, that all men were equal and that villeins should not serve and obey their masters. He was excommunicated, and on three occasions was sentenced to short terms of imprisonment by the archbishop of Canterbury.

In the summer of 1381 the peasants rose in south-east England. The Kentish peasants were led by Wat Tyler. Nothing definite is known about his earlier career, but he is said to have served in the army in France. The peasants went first to Maidstone, where they released John Ball from the county jail; then, after entering Canterbury, where they were welcomed by the urban population, they marched on London. On the road they met the king's mother, Joan of Kent, returning from a pilgrimage to Becket's shrine at Canterbury; but they let her go unharmed after taking a few kisses from her and her ladies. At Blackheath they were joined by the Essex peasants. John Ball preached to them in the fields at Blackheath, taking as his text the rhyming jingle which he had composed:

> When Adam delved and Eve span,
> Who was then a gentleman?

If the hostile chroniclers are to be believed, he called on the peasants to kill the lords who opposed them.

The peasants, who were now about 20,000 strong, demanded to see the king and present their petition to him. Their chief demand was that all villeins should be set free; but they also denounced lawyers, foreigners, and some prominent individuals like Sudbury, the archbishop of Canterbury, who was also Lord Chancellor. They entered London, burned John of Gaunt's palace of the Savoy, and broke into the Tower of London. Joan of Kent again escaped unharmed when they entered her bedroom and rumpled the sheets around her; but Sudbury, the Lord Treasurer Sir Robert Hales, and other officials were taken out and beheaded. The peasants also killed several lawyers in the city, and released prisoners from the jails; but Tyler, who exercised a strict discipline over his followers, forbade looting, and executed a man who looted.

Richard II was only fourteen years of age, but he rode out to meet the peasants at Mile End. They cheered him, and told him that they demanded their freedom from villeinage, the reform of the Church by a reorganisation which would leave only one bishop in England, and the establishment of a society in which there should be no class distinction and all men should be equal except the king. He promised to grant their demands, and issued a pardon to everyone who went home in peace. About half the peasants then went home; but the rest stayed with Tyler, and again met the king at Smithfield on 15 June. Tyler apparently adopted a threatening attitude which alarmed the king's retinue, and he was suddenly stabbed by William Walworth, the Lord Mayor of London, who was with the king. He fell from his horse and was killed by the king's men as he lay wounded on the ground. As the infuriated peasants prepared to avenge their leader's death, Richard rode into their midst, told them that he would be their leader, and again promised them pardon and charters of manumission ending villeinage. They dispersed, and returned to their homes.

The peasants also rose in several other parts of England. In Hertfordshire they ransacked the abbey at St Albans. The leader of the Norfolk peasants was Litster, who captured Norwich and established himself there in state, perhaps intending to make himself ruler of a peasant republic.

As soon as the Kent and Essex peasants had dispersed, Richard II revoked the pardons and the charters of manumission that he had granted, and sent his soldiers to round up the rebels, and his judges to try them at the county assizes. When he was reminded of his promises to end villeinage, he replied: 'Villeins you are, and villeins you will remain.' The leading rebels, including John Ball and Litster, were executed, the king himself being present to see Ball hanged, drawn and quartered for high treason at St Albans. The bishop of Norwich, Henry Despencer, carried out a number of executions of the Norfolk peasants, giving absolution to his victims before hanging them.

But after the first batch of death sentences had been carried out, an amnesty was granted to the other rebels; and the vengeance of the government and the ruling classes was mild compared with those which followed the peasant revolts in France in 1358 and in Hungary and Germany in 1514 and 1525, when the feudal nobility are said to have exterminated in each case about 100,000 peasants, and certainly inflicted the most barbarous tortures on the rebel leaders. Torture was not used in England in 1381 – apart from those involved in the sentence of hanging, drawing and quartering – and although the contemporary chroniclers stated that 1500 of the rebels were executed, modern research suggests that the correct figure is much lower. This may have been partly due to the fact that the peasants, though they killed the archbishop of Canterbury and several other people, did not commit the atrocities against the families of the nobility which marked the Jacquerie in France and the peasant revolts in other countries. The English in their peasant revolts, and in most of their civil wars, have been relatively – if only relatively – humane on both sides, and have fallen far short of the shocking cruelties practised by the rebels and the authorities in Germany and elsewhere in Europe.

Although the peasants' chief demand in the revolt of 1381 was the abolition of villeinage, their fury was not in practice directed against the feudal nobility or the gentry; and the feudal lords and

111

knights did not play a prominent part in suppressing the revolt and punishing the peasants. The peasants killed priests and lawyers, not lords and gentlemen; they burned the houses of lawyers in the towns, and monasteries in the countryside, but usually not manor houses. It was appropriate that the leading figures in the suppression of the revolt were the bishop of Norwich and the Lord Mayor of London, whose action in murdering Wat Tyler was honoured by the addition of a dagger to the coat-of-arms of the City of London which is still borne on the city's shield today. Traditionally the merchants in the cities and boroughs, for their own reasons, had favoured the abolition of villeinage and had encouraged escaping villeins to take employment in the towns; but after Wat Tyler's men had stormed into London and set fire to buildings there, the city authorities were the rebels' most determined enemies.

The unsuccessful revolt seems to have had little effect on the conditions of the villeins. All the charters of manumission were revoked, and many lords hardened their attitude towards the peasants and became more reluctant to set them free; but others hastened to do so before another outbreak occurred. The economic and social forces which had been gradually bringing about the abolition of villeinage continued to operate after 1381, and within a generation it was almost extinct.

CHAPTER 7

AGINCOURT
AND THE
WARS OF
THE ROSES
(1381–1501)

Although there was relatively little cruelty in the suppression of the Peasants' Revolt, there was a great deal of duplicity. It is not uncommon for rulers to argue that their promises to rebels are void, having been given under duress; but few of them have equalled the deceit of Richard II in promising to pardon the rebels and grant all their demands, and proclaiming himself their leader, and then, immediately they had dispersed, revoking both the pardon and the promises. The boy of fourteen has often been praised for his courage at Smithfield; but his perjury equalled his courage.

He continued to show the same duplicity in later life. When he grew to manhood he disgusted his nobility by his luxurious and effeminate way of life, by choosing low-born favourites as his ministers, and by ending the war with France. In 1388 the nobles led a revolt, which gained much popular support, and arrested and executed his favourites. He never forgave them, but bided his time and plotted their ruin.

The leaders of the revolt of 1388 were Richard's uncle, the duke of Gloucester; Thomas Mowbray, duke of Norfolk; the earl of

Arundel; and Henry Bolingbroke, earl of Derby, John of Gaunt's son. Within ten years Richard had executed Arundel, organised the assassination of Gloucester, and contrived to start a quarrel between Mowbray and Bolingbroke, who accused each other of treason against the king. They were summoned to prove the charges by the ordeal of battle, and met for a deadly tournament near Coventry in the presence of the king. Just as the fight was about to begin, Richard stopped it and banished both the combatants from England, Mowbray for life and Bolingbroke for six years. A few months later, John of Gaunt died, and Richard seized his lands, which would otherwise have been inherited by Bolingbroke.

Richard, who did not realise the strength of the opposition which he had aroused in England, led an expedition to complete the conquest of Ireland. During his absence, Bolingbroke landed in Yorkshire, and was joined by nearly all the English nobility. When Richard returned from Ireland he was trapped by Boling-broke's forces in Flint Castle, and surrendered. He was taken to London and compelled to abdicate, and next year was murdered in his prison at Pontefract Castle. Bolingbroke succeeded him as King Henry IV.

Henry's fourteen-year reign was almost entirely occupied with suppressing rebellions. The nobles who had placed him on the throne were dissatisfied with the rewards which he granted them, and rebelled against him, as they had rebelled against Richard on his behalf; but he succeeded with difficulty in defeating them and retaining his crown. His most formidable rebel was the Welsh leader, Owain Glyndwr. Apart from the rising of 1294–5, Glyndwr's revolt is the only national movement which has united the whole of Wales.

Glyndwr was a very different person from the bombastic buffoon, 'Owen Glendower', in Shakespeare's *Henry IV* Part I. He was a gentleman from Merioneth, owning several large estates, and after studying at Oxford University became a lawyer in London. He led the people of Wales against Bolingbroke, ostensibly on Richard II's behalf, but really in order to win their national freedom. He won several battles against Henry IV's armies and became ruler of Wales; but he was eventually defeated, and ended his life as a hunted fugitive, though we do not know when, where, or how he died.

At the death of Henry IV in 1413, his son Henry V began his short and glorious reign. According to the later chroniclers, whose stories were inserted by Shakespeare in his plays, Henry V in his youth, before he became king, associated with robbers and other criminals, and on one occasion, when he was summoned before the Lord Chief Justice to answer for his misconduct, he struck the Chief Justice in the face, and was thereupon sent to prison for contempt of court. But, according to the story, he became a reformed character as soon as he came to the throne; he immediately broke with his criminal associates, and retained the Lord Chief Justice in office. The story of his committal to prison, which was first recorded by Sir Thomas Elyot in 1531, is almost certainly untrue; and the other stories of his riotous youth may well be an invention of his enemies, the Beaufort family, for he certainly distinguished himself as a military leader in his father's armies in the wars against the rebel lords and Glyndwr. There is, however, contemporary authority for the story that when his father was dying, he prematurely placed the crown on his head when the old king had only temporarily lost consciousness.

As king he became a national hero, which he still is today. He reasserted Edward III's claim to the throne of France, and renewed the Hundred Years War. His success was complete. He won one of the greatest victories in European history, conquered half France, was accepted as king of France by the French king and nobility, and finally ensured his posthumous glory by dying at the age of thirty-five before things began to go wrong.

He invaded France in 1415, but after besieging and capturing the port of Harfleur he was unable to continue the campaign, because he had lost one-third of his army of 9,000 men from dysentery during the siege. He therefore marched towards Calais, intending to embark for England. The French decided to intercept him and destroy him at Agincourt. His men were outnumbered by at least seven to one, but thanks to their superior morale and discipline, and above all to their bowmen, they won a great victory. The French cavalry was shot to pieces by the archers. Nearly 7,000 French were killed. Henry's chaplain, who was with him at Agincourt, wrote that only 13 Englishmen died; and even modern historians, while rejecting the chaplain's figures, agree that Henry's losses did not exceed 300.

Henry was therefore able to return to England in triumph, and in new campaigns during the next five years he conquered France. He was greatly helped by the deadly feuds among the French nobility. The French king, Charles VI, had been insane for more than twenty years, and could do nothing except pass the time playing cards, which were first invented for him. The authority of his son, the Dauphin, to act on his behalf was challenged by the nobility, who had divided into the two great warring factions, the Burgundians and the Armagnacs. Henry V made an alliance with the duke of Burgundy, the most powerful of the French king's tenants-in-chief, whose territories extended from the Lake of Geneva to the Zuyder Zee and included most of modern Belgium and Holland. The English and the Burgundians conquered all northern and western France, and Charles VI and most of the French nobility submitted to Henry, though the Dauphin still resisted in the south-east.

By the Treaty of Troyes in 1420 it was agreed that Henry should marry Charles's daughter Catherine; that Charles should remain king of France for the rest of his life, with Henry as his regent; and that at his death Henry should succeed him as king of France, which he would govern through a council composed of Frenchmen. Normandy was immediately ceded to Henry, but was to be reunited to France when Henry succeeded to the French throne. The treaty declared that by these means the crowns of England and France 'shall for perpetual future time remain and be in one and the same person'. As usual when politicians boast that a state of affairs will endure for ever – or for a thousand years – it did not last even for a generation.

Henry V was a very different character from his great-grandfather Edward III. He was a cold, virtuous, abstemious fanatic, who wished to conquer France, not from a desire for both glory and commercial gain, but because he believed that it was his religious duty to Christendom to unite England and France. He waged the Hundred Years War in a much less gentlemanly fashion than Edward III and the Black Prince. At Agincourt he ordered his soldiers to kill their French prisoners-of-war who had surrendered during the battle, when he wrongly thought that the French reserves were about to launch a new attack. His men were indignant at this, not for humanitarian reasons, but because it lost them the opportunity to obtain a ransom for the prisoners in the usual way; but Henry insisted that only nobles of the highest rank, whose ransom would be very large, should be spared. At Agincourt he had at least the excuse that his army was so greatly outnumbered that it would have been impossible to guard the prisoners. This did not apply on a later occasion when, to the anger of his Burgundian allies, he killed prisoners who had surrendered after the Burgundians had promised them their lives. He often hanged the garrisons of the towns that he captured.

He justified his savagery by his belief in his mission to end the long era of warfare between England and France by uniting the two nations under one king – himself. The French respected him, and many of them welcomed him as their king. They appreciated the way in which he maintained discipline in his army and prevented his troops from looting and raping; and they believed that he would bring law and order to France.

Apart from war, Henry had a cruel streak in his nature. He accused his stepmother, Queen Joan, of witchcraft, and imprisoned her. His worst act of cruelty was committed with the best intentions. He was present, when he was prince of Wales, at the execution of the Lollard martyr, the artisan John Badby, who was burned for heresy in 1410. When Badby was half-burned, Henry ordered the flames to be put out, and Badby to be pulled out of the fire. Henry tried unsuccessfully for some time to persuade him to recant before the fire was rekindled and he was finally burned to death. As king, he intensified the persecution of the Lollards, and executed several of them as rebels and heretics.

Henry V did not live to become king of France. Two years after the Treaty of ·Troyes and three weeks after his thirty-fifth birthday, he died of dysentery at Vincennes on 31 August 1422. Charles VI survived him by fifty-one days, and was therefore succeeded, not by his conqueror, but by Henry's nine-month-old son, Henry VI, whose uncle, the duke of Bedford, acted as regent during his childhood.

In France, Bedford made little headway against the Dauphin's forces in south-east France, and suffered a series of reverses after the Dauphin was helped by Jeanne Darc (incorrectly called Jeanne d'Arc and Joan of Arc), a seventeen-year-old peasant girl from Lorraine, who believed that she had been sent by God to liberate France from the English, and persuaded the Dauphin to

117

put her in command of his armies. Her religious and nationalist zeal inspired the French soldiers, and transformed the Dauphin's supporters from a selfish, quarrelling faction into enthusiastic patriots; but she did not arouse the people and lead a national war of independence like Wallace and Bruce, Glyndwr, the Flemish merchants and the Swiss peasants had done in their countries. She merely added her own charismatic personality to the Dauphin's feudal levies and mercenaries.

Joan successfully relieved the town of Orleans, which the English were besieging, and crowned the Dauphin as King Charles VII at Rheims; but soon afterwards she was defeated and taken prisoner at Compiègne by the Burgundian allies of the English. Bedford bought her from the duke of Burgundy for the enormous sum of £80,000, and arranged for Cauchon, the bishop of Beauvais, who was one of his French supporters, to condemn her for witchcraft. She was burned at Rouen on 30 May 1431, when she was nineteen years of age. Bedford celebrated his success by taking Henry VI, who had attended one of the sessions of Joan's trial, to Paris, where he was crowned king of France in Notre Dame a week after his tenth birthday.

Later generations of Englishmen have had a guilty conscience about Joan of Arc, though Shakespeare, 160 years after her death, still regarded her as a harlot and sorceress who had been rightly condemned. She became in due course a French national heroine, and has at times been the symbol of anti-English hatred in France, as well as being canonised as a saint in the twentieth century by the Catholic Church; but it was French Catholic churchmen who sent her to the stake.

Henry VI grew up to be a deeply religious man and a weak ruler. Like Edward the Confessor, he busied himself with his prayers and with establishing religious and educational foundations, including Eton and King's College Cambridge, while his ministers quarrelled violently and plotted each other's downfall. At times he suffered from insanity and from complete physical paralysis. In France, the nobility rallied behind Charles VII, and were everywhere victorious against the English. In 1453 the Hundred Years War ended when the English forces, thirty years after Henry V's triumph, were driven out of all the English territories in France except for the town of Calais and the countryside for a few miles around. It was the first time since

1153 that the king of England had not been the ruler of at least one French province.

The indignation of the English nobility and people at the humiliating defeats in France gave Richard, duke of York, the opportunity of forming a party among the nobility and enlisting the support of the merchants in the towns in his demands for a reform of Henry VI's government and the removal of his unpopular ministers. After York had incited an unsuccessful popular revolt in Kent under the leadership of a local mercenary, Jack Cade, he himself led a rebellion of part of the nobility and compelled the king to accept him as regent. In due course he put forward his claim to the throne, for as a descendant of the third son of Edward III he had a better right than Henry VI, who was descended from Edward's fourth son, John of Gaunt, duke of Lancaster.

The war between the houses of York and Lancaster began in 1455. The participants adopted various badges, but the most famous emblems were the red rose worn by Henry VI's Lancastrian supporters and the white rose of the followers of the duke of York. Although it has been suggested that the phrase 'the Wars of the Roses' originated with Sir Walter Scott 350 years later, it was occasionally used in the sixteenth century. The contemporaries clearly associated the roses with the two factions, though the story that the badges were first chosen by the party leaders during an argument in the Temple Gardens in London is a picturesque invention by Shakespeare.

There is a conflict of evidence as to how far the people of England were affected by the Wars of the Roses. To judge from the writers of the next century, including Shakespeare, it was a traumatic experience for the population; and foreign ambassadors in England in the reign of Henry VIII believed that it was the memory of the Wars of the Roses, and a fear of the recurrence of civil war, which made the English ready to accept the despotic government of the Tudors. But many contemporary documents suggest that the Wars of the Roses were hardly noticed by most of the inhabitants of England.

The wars were restricted as far as area, time, and the participants were concerned. Battles were fought in only eight of the thirty-nine counties of England – in Hertfordshire, Northamptonshire, Leicestershire, Gloucestershire, Herefordshire, Shropshire, Yorkshire and Northumberland. If we count the Wars of the Roses as lasting from 1455 to 1485, campaigning took place during only fifteen months throughout these thirty years. The armies did not consist of the old feudal levies of the tenants-in-chief and their vassals, but of small forces of paid retainers of the participating noblemen; many of these retainers were soldiers who had been discharged from the wars in France. If it ever occurred in fact, as in Shakespeare's *Henry VI* Part III, that a father killed a son and a son killed a father in battle, this must have been because the father and the son chose voluntarily to take service in the households of different lords, and that these lords fought on different sides.

There is therefore some reason to believe that the accounts of the sixteenth-century writers were part of a propaganda exercise by the supporters of the Tudor monarchy to exaggerate the miseries of civil war in order to justify the ruthless royal autocracy. It seems clear that the Wars of the Roses were a much less horrifying experience for the people of England than the civil war between Stephen and Matilda had been for their ancestors three hundred years before. But the people, or at least the thinking and vocal part of them, were shocked at the sight of the aristocracy fighting and exterminating each other, even if they themselves were not personally involved. Their reaction was probably like the attitude of the ordinary citizen of Chicago to the gang warfare of the 1920s; they never saw anyone killed, but thought it disgraceful that the killing was taking place.

The nobles were more affected than the people by the Wars of the Roses. From the outset, it was the practice of the victors after every battle immediately to execute their aristocratic prisoners-of-war on the battlefield, even though the victims were often their cousins. Twenty-six of the sixty-four English peerages became extinct during the Wars of the Roses.

After Richard duke of York had fallen at the Battle of Wakefield, the leadership of the Yorkists passed to his son Edward, who defeated the Lancastrians in a battle fought in a snowstorm at Towton in Yorkshire in March 1461, and was proclaimed King Edward IV. On the Lancastrian side, the leading figure was the formidable and ruthless Queen Margaret of Anjou, whose peace-loving husband Henry VI deplored the war and the slaughter. Despised by his wife and his warlike nobles, he was revered as a saint by the common people, who both during his lifetime and after his death believed that he, or his corpse, could perform miracles.

After Towton, Henry and Margaret fled to Scotland, but returned to Northumberland to organise an insurrection against Edward IV. The revolt failed, and Margaret and her nine-year-old son, the prince of Wales, were nearly captured by the Yorkists. The well-known story of their escape was being told by chroniclers within a few years of the incident: in their flight they met a fierce robber in the forest, but he did not harm them after Margaret had told him that the child was his future king.

In 1464 Henry and Margaret again invaded Northumberland, but were defeated at Hexham. Margaret and the prince of Wales escaped to France. Henry lived happily for a time as a wandering beggar in the monasteries in the hills of Furness and Yorkshire; but he was recognised, captured, and imprisoned in the Tower of London.

The most powerful noble on the Yorkist side was Richard Neville, earl of Warwick. He quarrelled with Edward IV after the Yorkist victory. Edward, who was very susceptible to beautiful women, fell in love with Elizabeth Woodville when she visited him after her husband had been killed fighting for the Lancastrians, to beg him to permit her to retain her husband's forfeited lands. Soon afterwards Edward married her, and placed her relatives in positions of influence. Warwick resented being ousted by the queen's upstart relatives. He transferred his allegiance to the Lancastrian side, and with the help of troops sent by King Louis XI of France he deposed Edward, who fled to Holland, and replaced Henry VI on the throne.

Within six months, Edward had received aid from Louis XI's great enemy, Charles the Bold, duke of Burgundy. He landed with an army in Yorkshire; entered London, where he captured Henry VI; defeated and killed Warwick at Barnet; and won a decisive victory over Margaret's forces at Tewkesbury. Henry VI's son, the prince of Wales, was taken prisoner and put to death at Tewkesbury, and a few days later Henry VI died in the Tower. It was generally believed that he had been murdered by Edward IV's brother, Richard, duke of Gloucester.

The victory of the Yorkists in 1471 was welcomed by the merchants of London and the boroughs, for they remembered the failure of Henry VI's government to maintain law and order, and the Yorkists had been much more successful than the Lancastrians in maintaining discipline among their soldiers and preventing them from looting. Throughout the war the White Rose had been strongest in the south-east, and the Red Rose in the north and west. This is undoubtedly the reason why the nineteenth-century historians, who inherited their view of history, through the Whigs, from the middle classes of earlier times, tended to be on the side of the Yorkists against the Lancastrians. The reign of Edward IV was a period of optimism and growing prosperity. Freehold and copyhold tenures were increasingly replaced by leasehold tenure – by tenancies granted for a fixed term of years, or from year to year, from quarter to quarter, from month to month, or from week to week, and terminable by notice on either side, with no security of tenure. Villeinage had completely disappeared. The wool trade between England and the Yorkists' ally, Burgundy, was flourishing; and the towns were slowly growing in size.

The new economic and social situation led to a further development of English law. Littleton, one of Edward IV's judges, gave judicial decisions, and enunciated legal principles in a book, which have established him as one of the leading authorities on the common law. Henry VI's Chief Justice, Fortescue, who, unlike Littleton, was a prominent Lancastrian supporter, also made an important contribution to the development of constitutional and legal doctrines.

The optimism of Edward IV's reign suffered a shock when the king died in 1483. His son, Edward V, was aged twelve, and his uncle Richard, duke of Gloucester, carried out a *coup d'état*. Richard was a vigorous man of thirty, with an excellent military record during the Wars of the Roses; he was only very mildly disfigured by the slight humpback of which his enemies, the future chroniclers, and Shakespeare made so much. With the support of the duke of Buckingham, one of the most powerful Yorkist nobles, he secured the custody of Edward V and his younger brother, the eleven-year-old duke of York; executed the relatives of the queen mother, Elizabeth Woodville, who had been in power under Edward IV; beheaded another powerful nobleman, Lord Hastings; and had himself proclaimed king Richard III, at the invitation of the Lord Mayor and city corporation of London, and of Parliament, after he had produced very questionable evidence that Edward V and his brother were illegitimate. The two children were imprisoned in the Tower of London, and were never seen again. Within a few weeks, rumours were circulating all over London that Richard III had murdered them.

Richard's guilt of the death of the 'Princes in the Tower' was accepted by his contemporaries, by the chroniclers, by Shakespeare, and by most historians and the general public ever since; but since the beginning of the seventeenth century his champions have repeatedly asserted his innocence. The case against him is weakened by the fact that many of the assertions of the Tudor historians are certainly untrue; but though Richard's guilt cannot be conclusively proved, the case against him is much stronger than the case against Henry VII, who is usually accused of the murder by Richard's supporters, though Buckingham is occasionally held responsible. Richard had a stronger motive than Henry VII, because, though the princes were rival claimants to the throne against both Richard and Henry, Richard's position was less secure in 1483 than Henry's in 1485. In the weeks before the princes were last seen, Richard had been executing every nobleman who was a real or potential danger to him, whereas Henry VII, at least in the early years of his reign, was more merciful and less inclined to put his enemies to death than most other kings of England. The strongest argument against Richard is that, although it was being rumoured on all sides in the autumn of 1483, and publicly proclaimed in France, that he had assassinated the princes, he never exhibited them by making them ride through the streets of London, which was the accepted practice when kings were wrongly accused of having killed prisoners who were in their custody.

Richard III's executions aroused resentment and anxiety among the new Yorkist nobility, though the king was popular with many of the merchants. His chief ally, Buckingham, entered into secret negotiations with Henry Tudor, earl of Richmond, who was in exile in France. Richmond was the grandson of a Welsh gentleman of the bodyguard of the infant King Henry VI, who had become the lover of Henry V's widow, Queen Catherine, and had perhaps secretly married her; but on his mother's side he was descended from John of Gaunt. He was the only surviving Lancastrian claimant to the crown. He planned to invade England with mercenaries from Brittany, while Buckingham launched a rebellion in England; but Buckingham was defeated and executed by Richard's officers, and Richmond called off his planned invasion.

He tried again less than two years later, and in August 1485 landed at Milford Haven with an army of 2,000 Breton mercenaries. He marched into the Midlands and met Richard's forces at Bosworth. A few days before the battle he left his army, at considerable personal risk, and had a secret meeting with his stepfather, Lord Stanley, whose brother William had already joined him. Lord Stanley's retainers formed an important element in Richard's army. By agreement with Richmond, Lord Stanley deserted Richard on the eve of the battle and remained neutral. Richard was defeated and killed at Bosworth. As he fell, the crown on his helmet rolled under a bush, where it was found by Richmond's men; and Lord Stanley placed it on Richmond's head on the battlefield.

Richmond became King Henry VII, and married Edward IV's daughter, Elizabeth, thus uniting the Lancastrian and Yorkist royal houses, which he symbolised by adopting as his badge a blended red and white rose. But the fighting was not over. In the next year the Yorkists fomented a rebellion in Ireland and England, putting forward a young boy, Lambert Simnel, whom they pretended was the earl of Warwick, the son of Edward IV's brother, the duke of Clarence. Simnel was in fact the son of a working man of Oxford, and Warwick was being held a prisoner by Henry VII in the Tower. Henry defeated the rebels at Stoke-on-Trent, and instead of executing Simnel for treason, he exposed the falsity of his claim to be a Yorkist prince by giving him employment as a scullion in his kitchens. Simnel was later promoted to be a falconer, and was still living nearly fifty years later.

An even more serious revolt broke out when a Flemish lad, Perkin Warbeck, was put forward by the Yorkists as being Richard, duke of York, who had been murdered with his brother, Edward V, in the Tower. He was received at the courts of the Holy Roman Emperor, the king of France and the king of Scots; but after waging a vigorous campaign in Northumberland, he launched another attack in Devon, and was captured by Henry's forces at Taunton. Henry had been too alarmed by Perkin Warbeck's revolt to be as lenient to him as he had been to Lambert Simnel. He executed both Warbeck and Warwick, though Warwick had committed no offence except to try to escape from the Tower.

There were other plots and risings during Henry VII's reign, and other executions. One of the plotters whom he beheaded was his stepfather's brother, Sir William Stanley, who had fought for him at Bosworth. Sir William, like the lords who had made Bolingbroke king a century earlier, found that it was easier to put a rebellious nobleman on the throne than to remove him by a second rebellion.

CHAPTER 8

HENRY VIII
AND THE
RELIGIOUS
REVOLUTION
(1501–58)

The year 1485 is commonly accepted today as the beginning of a new historical era. No one who lived in 1485 can have seen it in this light. All that had happened was that another round had been fought in the Wars of the Roses, another claimant had killed the king and seized his crown; the most optimistic people could look forward to a few years of peace before Henry Tudor, in his turn, was defeated and put to death by a new rival. But changes in government and in the people's way of life had been taking place in the years before 1485, and more startling changes were about to occur in the new century.

The reduction of the nobility caused by the Wars of the Roses, and by Henry VII's policy of refusing to create new peerages, had left the king with no serious rival to challenge his power, and this led to an extension of central government control over the king's subjects. The supreme governing body was the Privy Council, so called because, unlike the Great Council of the realm, which had become the House of Lords, it was the king's private council, and consisted, not of all his lords, but only of those advisers whom he invited to attend its meetings. By the sixteenth century 'the

Council' consisted of some fifteen or twenty men, of whom about half were noblemen holding the great offices of state, and the other half were the leading bishops. They sat several times a week, and advised the king on the important decisions of internal and foreign policy. They also exercised legislative and judicial powers. They issued proclamations in which they promulgated new laws, and summoned before them offenders accused or suspected of political offences, interrogating the suspect, and punishing him.

The Council exercised these judicial powers not only over powerful nobles and prominent political leaders, but also over obscure artisans and labourers in the remotest parts of the realm. A husbandman or blacksmith who grumbled about the king's policy, or made jokes about his ministers, in an inn in Cornwall or Lincoln-shire, might find, if his words had been overheard and reported by a spiteful neighbour, that he received a summons to appear on a given date before the Council in London, Greenwich or Richmond. In most cases he would be let off with a warning; but sometimes he was sentenced to a few months' imprisonment, or occasionally to have his ears cut off. If the suspect was a great nobleman or wealthy man, the Council might fine him, or bind him over to be of good behaviour, giving security of an enormous sum of money – perhaps half his total assets – which he would forfeit to the king if he committed another offence. North of the Trent, the Council's powers were exercised by the Council of the North in York.

The Council never imposed the death penalty. Any offence punishable by death was sent by the Council for trial in the king's common law courts, unless the offender was sentenced to death without trial by an Act of Attainder, which was enacted, like any other Act of Parliament, by a bill passing the House of Commons and the House of Lords and receiving the royal assent.

Occasionally the Council ordered a suspect to be interrogated under torture, though in England, unlike any other country in Europe, the use of torture was unknown in ordinary legal proceedings. The English common law provided for cruel punishments, such as the hanging, drawing and quartering of male traitors, and the burning alive of women guilty of high treason or of murdering their husbands; but it did not permit suspects to be tortured before their trial in order to force them to confess their guilt, which was the regular practice on the Continent, and in Scotland, because under the English system the defendant's guilt was proved, not by his confession, but by the evidence of witnesses for the prosecution. But the Council, when exercising their judicial powers, did not adopt the procedures of the English common law. The churchmen who sat on the Council, and their secretaries and assistants, had nearly always been trained in the canon law of the Church and the Roman civil law of Continental Europe which was closely connected with it. Their experience as civil lawyers, and the argument of political necessity, led them to resort to torture whenever it was essential to obtain a confession. The King's Council ordered torture for the first time as early as the reign of Henry II; but it was used in only a few isolated cases until the fifteenth century, when it began to be regularly resorted to under Henry VI; and it became much more common in the next century under Henry VIII.

The prosperity of Edward IV's reign continued after 1485, and tempted Henry VII and his Council to increase taxation. This enabled the king to build up financial reserves from which he could pay for more government officials and for soldiers in times of rebellion and foreign wars, for the old feudal system of raising an army by knight-service had ceased to operate. The archbishop of Canterbury and Lord Chancellor, Cardinal Morton, became notorious for his method of sending out commissioners to interrogate landowners and merchants about their income and assets and to assess a suitable tax contribution from them. This method has been known since the seventeenth century as 'Morton's Fork', though it was probably invented, not by Morton, but by another of Henry VII's ministers, Richard Foxe, bishop of Winchester. The taxpayer was impaled on one or other prong of the fork: if he claimed that he had heavy expenditure, the commissioners said that he was obviously a wealthy man and could therefore afford to pay a large tax contribution; if he showed that he lived frugally and economically, he was told that as he spent so little, he must have accumulated a great deal of money through his savings, and should therefore pay a large amount of tax.

The reign of Edward IV saw the development in England of a new invention which was to have a decisive political influence.

Printing, which began in Holland and Germany in the middle of the fifteenth century, had been introduced into England by Caxton in 1478. It made possible the distribution of ideas and propaganda which would have been impossible when only handwritten manuscripts could be produced. The great revolutionary movement of the sixteenth century, the Protestant Reformation, could not have occurred if printing had not been invented. Although only a minority of the population could read, a substantial part of the people, including the lower classes, were reading printed propaganda tracts by the first half of the sixteenth century, and those who could read often read them aloud to those who could not. Masters read aloud to their families and servants, and men read aloud to their friends in taverns. The government was well aware of the potential danger from the dissemination of printed revolutionary publications, and instituted a strict censorship. No printer was permitted to publish any document without a licence from the Council; those who broke this regulation, or distributed books and pamphlets, were frequently summoned before the Council and punished.

In Europe, new nations and alliances were being created. At the end of the fifteenth century France, which sixty years before had been a conquered country under English domination, became the most powerful state in Europe, and her armies overran northern Italy. The great duchy of Burgundy, stretching from Savoy to Friesland, had been linked by marriage to the Austrian territories of the Habsburg family, and passed under the rule of the Holy Roman Emperor, Maximilian I, who established the precedent that the emperor, though still in theory elected by the seven electors of the empire, was in practice the hereditary heir of the house of Habsburg. Spain became one realm in the last years of the fifteenth century, when King Ferdinand of Aragon and Queen Isabel of Castile united their two kingdoms by their marriage, and then conquered the Moorish kingdom of Granada. Twenty years later, Ferdinand annexed Navarre, leaving Portugal as the only state in the peninsula which was independent from Spain.

Henry VII, like the Emperor Maximilian and Ferdinand and Isabel in Spain, was afraid of the power of France, and not only maintained the traditional English friendship with Burgundy, but married his son Arthur, prince of Wales, to Ferdinand and

Isabel's daughter, Catherine of Aragon. The bride and bride-groom were both only fifteen when the wedding took place in 1501, and four-and-a-half months later Arthur died. King Henry, who was unwilling to waste the results of his diplomacy or to return the dowry which Catherine had brought, arranged for her to marry his second son, Henry. By the laws of the Church a widow was not permitted to marry her deceased husband's brother; but Pope Julius II granted a dispensation for Prince Henry's marriage to Catherine to take place. This dispensation was to have profound historical consequences thirty years later.

The international situation had also been transformed by the discovery of a new world. Portugal had taken the lead in new geographical discoveries in the middle of the fifteenth century when Prince Henry the Navigator sent his sea captains to sail down the west coast of Africa. By the end of the century Bartholomeu Diaz had sailed round the Cape of Good Hope, and in 1510 the Portuguese established a colony in Goa in India which lasted for 450 years. In 1492 the Genoese sailor, Christopher Columbus, sailed from Palos under the auspices of the king and queen of Spain and discovered the American continent, which was acquired for Spain. Columbus had previously failed to persuade either the king of Portugal or Henry VII to finance his expedition. This was an error of judgment on Henry's part, but one for which he can hardly be blamed in the circumstances. His subsequent attempt to retrieve the mistake by sending another Italian sailor, John Cabot, to explore the north-west Atlantic led to the discovery of Newfoundland, but brought no advantage to England.

Henry VII died at the age of fifty-two in 1509. He was succeeded by his second son, Henry VIII, who was two months short of his eighteenth birthday. The handsome young king was welcomed by his subjects as the very opposite of his dour, cautious father. His first act was to put to death Edmund Dudley and Richard Empson, two lawyers who had been especially hated for their part in enforcing Henry VII's high taxation. In their place he appointed as his chief minister Thomas Wolsey. He was the son of a butcher of Ipswich, and had entered the Church and become dean of Lincoln. Wolsey, the supreme example of the corruption of the Church in the early sixteenth century, was at the same time Lord Chancellor, archbishop of York, bishop of

Durham, abbot of St Albans, and the papal legate in England. He amassed a large fortune for himself and his illegitimate son, and made himself hated by both the nobility and the people. He also showed the qualities of a great statesman, especially of a great Foreign Minister, and directed English diplomacy with outstanding skill for eighteen years.

Henry VIII spent the money which his father – and Dudley and Empson – had amassed for the Crown, in lavish fêtes, tournaments and banquets on New Year's Day, St George's Day, May Day, and on all the major feasts of the Church, when he distinguished himself by the splendour of his dress and his prowess on horseback. As these peaceful exploits were not enough to establish a reputation for gallantry, he invaded France in alliance with the emperor, and won a battle and a short campaign. But Wolsey's policy was to switch from war to peace, and from alliance with the emperor to friendship with France. He arranged for Henry to have several personal meetings with the Emperor Charles V and with the king of France; his interview with Francis I of France in English territory near Calais in 1520 became known as the Field of Cloth-of-Gold because of the splendour of the occasion. Henry was the last English sovereign for nearly two hundred years to meet a foreign king.

The image which Henry VIII established was largely a fake. His sombre father had fought in the thick of the battle at Bosworth, cutting his way to within a few yards of Richard III before Richard fell; the glamorous Henry VIII took good care to remain in a place of safety in every battle in which he took part. He had a number of love affairs as a young man, but the reputation for sexual virility which he established with his contemporaries and with future generations by having six wives was another fake; already by the time he was in his early forties his second wife, Anne Boleyn, was complaining that he was almost impotent. On the other hand, his reputation for gluttony was well-deserved; he had an enormous appetite, and in his last years measured 54 inches round the waist.

He was a very intelligent and cultured man. He patronised the arts, and made England the intellectual centre of Europe. He played the lute well, and composed music. He was a learned theologian, writing books on matters of theological controversy, and holding his own in argument with the most learned divines.

He was also cruel. Henry VII occasionally put to death a rival unjustly for reasons of political expediency, but he was often merciful. There is hardly a single case on record of Henry VIII exercising mercy. Again and again, whether in cases of political offences by an important statesman or trifling crimes committed by a household servant, the decision of subordinate officers or of the Council to treat the matter comparatively leniently was overruled by the king, who insisted on the severest punishment. Undoubtedly one of the reasons for the savagery of the political repression during his reign, and the cruelty of the methods employed, was the strong element of sadism in Henry's character.

This formidable and frightful ruler was destined to face the greatest political and intellectual upheaval which had ever confronted an English sovereign, and to play a vital part in its development, often by acting in a way which he did not approve of, and producing results which he did not intend. The Protestant Reformation not only gave to the countries of northern Europe a new form of the Christian religion, but led first to the establishment of absolute monarchy, then to the growth of democratic ideas, and finally to liberalism, radicalism and socialism. The man who first set this tremendous process in motion, John Wycliffe, was born in the unlikely place and time of the North Riding of Yorkshire in about 1330. He became a professor of divinity at Oxford, where he put forward the ideas which after his death were developed by Jan Hus and his followers in Bohemia, and a century later by Luther, Calvin and other great Protestant theologians in Germany and Switzerland.

The Protestants, disgusted at the corruption, immorality and cynicism which pervaded the ecclesiastical hierarchy, the parish clergy, and the monasteries throughout Western Europe, claimed that they wished to reform the Church by purging it of the abuses which had crept in during recent centuries and restoring the doctrines and practice of the early Church in the time of Christ's Apostles and their immediate successors. In fact, the essence of Protestantism was to weaken the authority of the clergy and their function as the intermediary between man and God. In every dispute over doctrine or practice in the Church between Catholics and Protestants, and between the more moderate and the more extreme Protestants – over private masses, the administration of the Sacrament in both kinds, the language of the Church services, confession, the marriage of priests – the effect of the Protestant, or the more extreme Protestant, doctrine was to reduce the importance of the priesthood until, in the case of the most extreme Protestant sects, it was virtually abolished altogether, and man was urged to communicate direct with God without the intervention of a priest.

The Protestants appealed to the authority of the Bible, the Word of God, against the authority of the Church. They urged the people to read the Bible, and to argue about the interpretation of the text; so the Catholics made it a criminal offence for the ordinary layman to read the Bible. The Catholics taught that a man would be saved, and go to Heaven, if he performed good works, which in practice meant paying money to priests and monks to celebrate masses and to pray for his soul; the Protestants put forward the doctrine of salvation by faith, believing that masses and the prayers of monks made no difference at all as to whether a man's soul went to heaven or hell. The Catholics believed that the clergy should not marry, but should remain a separate and holier caste; the Protestants believed that they should marry like anyone else. The Catholics believed that by performing Mass, the priest performed the miracle of the trans-substantiation of the bread and wine into the body and blood of Christ. The Protestants denied that the priest had this power, and that a transubstantiation took place.

The first reaction of the kings of Europe was to condemn Protestantism as a subversive doctrine which, by attacking the authority of the Church and the clergy, weakened all authority. They therefore used all the power of the State to suppress it as a heresy, and burned alive the men and women whom the ecclesiastical courts condemned as heretics. But the persecuted Protestant theologians, realising that royal authority was the only force which was strong enough to break the power of the Church, put forward the doctrine that the kings in their realms were appointed by God to regulate religion as well as all other aspects of their subjects' lives. They advocated the absolute power of 'the Prince', by which they meant the emperor, king, prince or duke who was the ruler in any independent sovereign state. They taught the doctrine of passive obedience – that it was the duty of the Christians to obey the Prince in all things, whether the Prince was just or unjust, unless the Prince ordered him to offend against God – that is to say, to become a Catholic. In that case, the Christian must disobey and suffer martyrdom, though even then he must not rebel, or actively resist the Prince and his government. The doctrine was most fully expressed by the English Protestant, William Tyndale, in his book *The Obedience of a Christian Man* in 1528: the subject must obey the king, even if he 'be the greatest tyrant in the world'.

In 1517, Luther in Germany denounced the papal corruption, and was protected by the independent sovereign princes of Germany who wished to free themselves from the domination of the pope and the emperor. Henry VIII wrote a book attacking Luther, and the appreciative pope granted him, as a reward, the title of 'Defender of the Faith', which his successors have borne ever since. But while Henry burned Lutherans in England, he was impressed by Tyndale's *Obedience of a Christian Man*, and its doctrine of obedience to tyrants, and commented: 'This book is for me and all Kings to read.'

It was probably inevitable that England, like all the kingdoms and principalities of northern Europe, should eventually become Protestant; but the immediate cause of the Reformation in England had nothing to do with religious principles. Henry was worried that Catherine of Aragon had been unable to give him a male heir, and he had fallen in love with Anne Boleyn, the daughter of a gentleman of Kent. He came to believe that his marriage to Catherine was displeasing to God, because he had offended in marrying his brother's widow. He decided to divorce Catherine and marry Anne, and asked the pope to nullify his marriage to Catherine on the grounds that the papal dispensation of 1503, permitting him to marry his brother's widow, had been invalid.

Pope Clement VII, a member of the reigning Medici family of Florence, was a pliant politician without any strong principles. He would have been very willing to comply with Henry's wishes had it not been for the fact that he was afraid of Catherine's nephew, the Emperor Charles V, whose armies were in control of Italy. He therefore tried to avoid giving a decision for as long as possible, and managed to delay doing so for seven years. But the Protestant theologians all over Europe were suggesting another way out for Henry: if the pope refused to find reasons for invalidating the dispensation of 1503, Henry could claim that no pope had power to grant a dispensation to break the laws of God, and that as a text in the Bible forbade a man to marry his brother's widow, Henry's marriage to Catherine was void, whatever any pope might have said.

Henry was very reluctant to adopt this attitude, which meant a rejection of the pope's authority and a reliance on a seditious Protestant argument. He therefore tried for six years to find another way out, and to induce the pope, by diplomatic pressure, to grant the divorce. Meanwhile he summoned a Parliament in 1529 which remained in session for seven years and during this time enacted far-reaching legislation which changed the religious, political and social system in England. The House of Lords consisted of 49 lords spiritual (2 archbishops, 17 bishops, 28 abbots and 2 priors) and 51 peers, nearly all of whom held peerages which had been created in the previous forty years. The members of the House of Commons were country gentlemen from the rural constituencies and merchants representing the towns, and included a large contingent of lawyers. Nearly all these members were Catholics; but they knew that many priests and monks were corrupt; they resented the domination of Cardinal Wolsey; and they shared the English national resentment of the interference of papal officials in Rome with the English Church, of the expense and long delays of legal proceedings in Rome, and of the annual contribution paid by the English Church to the pope. They were loyal to their king, and admired his energy and pugnacity and his ruthlessness in dealing with Papist and Protestant trouble-makers and with criminals, vagrants and gipsies, though the contemporary chroniclers' statement that 72,000 malefactors were hanged in his reign is probably an exaggeration.

As soon as Parliament met, Henry dismissed Wolsey, who had become very unpopular in the country, from his office of Lord Chancellor; and only Wolsey's death in the following year saved him from being tried and executed for high treason. The king persuaded the willing MPs to enact legislation against the clergy, and imposed a heavy fine on the English Church for having collaborated in Wolsey's misgovernment. Acts were passed which restricted the papal rights in England. He still hesitated to take the final step and repudiate the pope's supremacy over the Church; but his hand was forced in January 1533 when he discovered that Anne Boleyn was pregnant by him, and might give birth to a son who could be his long awaited male heir. He quickly married her secretly; and as the archbishop of Canterbury had recently died, he appointed as his successor Thomas Cranmer, a middle-aged Cambridge don who had never held any important post in the Church, but was mildly Protestant and had written a book in favour of Henry's divorce. He then ordered Cranmer to sit as a judge to try his divorce action against Catherine.

Cranmer held his court in the abbey at the quiet Bedfordshire town of Dunstable in order to avoid the risk of riots by Catherine's sympathisers in London, where many sections of the people, especially the women, supported her. He gave judgment that Henry's marriage to Catherine had been invalid, and within ten days the news of the marriage to Anne was made public, and she was crowned as queen of England. Her child was born in September. To the bitter disappointment of Henry, and to the joy of the pope and Catherine's supporters, it was a girl – the future Queen Elizabeth I.

The break with Rome was now completed. In December 1533 Henry repudiated papal supremacy over the English Church. Parliament passed an Act which enacted that the king was 'next under Christ the Supreme Head of this Church of England', and made it a criminal offence to use the term 'the pope', who was to be referred to as 'the bishop of Rome'.

An extensive propaganda campaign was launched throughout the country. In every town and village the people, who were compelled by law to go to church every Sunday and holy day, listened week after week to sermons which complied with the orders sent by the Council to the bishops and passed on by them to their parish priests. The theme of all these sermons was well summarised in a passage from the book by one of Henry's leading propagandists, Sampson, the future bishop of Chichester: 'The word of God is, to obey the king and not the bishop of Rome.' The bishops and officials wrote about Henry in more fulsome and obsequious language than had ever been used about an English monarch. Cranmer inserted eulogies of Henry in many of his religious writings. When he wrote to Henry, in a letter intended for publication, that he was 'beseeching Your Highness most humbly upon my knees', Henry altered this passage in his draft to read: 'Prostrate at the feet of Your Majesty, beseeching. . . .'

An Act of Parliament made it high treason to deny the king's right to any of his titles, which meant that anyone who denied that he was Supreme Head of the Church of England would be hanged, drawn and quartered as a traitor. Another Act provided that the king's officers could require anyone to swear an oath that he believed that the king was Supreme Head of the Church. Anyone who refused to take the oath when required to do so was guilty of an offence punishable by imprisonment for life. The oath was put to everyone in authority in the kingdom. The Council administered it to prominent officers of the State and to eminent public figures; the bishops administered it to their clergy; the mayors to the aldermen; the sheriffs to the justices of the peace; the JPs to many gentlemen and householders in their districts; and many householders to their families and servants.

The repudiation of papal supremacy and the break with the religious traditions of centuries were accepted with enthusiasm by many of the country gentlemen and the merchants in the towns, and with some bewilderment by most of the common people. Only a handful of individuals resisted the pressure of the propaganda and the duress. John Fisher, bishop of Rochester, refused to take the Oath of Supremacy; so did Sir Thomas More, a former Lord Chancellor, a personal friend of the king, and an internationally famous author. The abbot and monks of the Charterhouse in London also refused to take the oath. They were hanged, drawn and quartered, and Fisher and More were beheaded, in the summer of 1535. Catherine of Aragon and her daughter Mary, who also refused to comply, were held under house arrest until Catherine died in January 1536, after which Mary at last capitulated and took the oath. There was hardly any other opposition.

The Catholic kings of Europe were shocked at Henry's proceedings, but took no action beyond occasional protests. They respected his right, as a sovereign prince, to do what he wished in his own realm, and they also respected his power and welcomed him as an ally. A few of the leading English Catholics, including Princess Mary and Bishop Fisher, made secret approaches to Charles V, urging him to invade England in order to save the English people from Henry's tyranny and to prevent the heretic king from separating England from the international Church. But Charles ruled out armed intervention as too risky, and as he thought that economic sanctions would achieve nothing, he decided to confine himself to urging the pope to impose 'ecclesiastical censures'. This meant that Henry, despite occasional anxieties about foreign intervention, could proceed without hindrance with his designs in England.

In the years that followed the repudiation of papal supremacy, Henry was still burning Protestant heretics, especially those who denied transubstantiation; but other heretics were taken into the king's service, and, taking care not to go too far, introduced a few Protestant reforms into Church doctrine and practice. Cranmer and several other bishops, though they were sentencing the more extreme Protestants to be burned, were sympathetic to Protestant doctrines; but the rest of the bishops, under the leadership of Stephen Gardiner, bishop of Winchester, were zealous adherents of traditional Catholic doctrine, while being as active as Cranmer and his colleagues in upholding royal supremacy over the Church and persecuting the pope's supporters. In 1533 Henry appointed as his secretary and chief minister, not a leading churchman, but a layman, Thomas Cromwell, a blacksmith's son who had become a merchant and a solicitor and had risen in Wolsey's service. Henry made Cromwell a peer, appointed him Lord Privy Seal, and created for him a new post, that of the King's Vicegerent in Church affairs. This gave Cromwell, a layman, precedence over all the bishops and archbishops, and supreme authority over the Church, subject only to the king himself.

Nearly every year a Commission of bishops sat to discuss some new innovation in the Church services or to draft new Articles of Faith. At numerous and lengthy sessions in private, the bishops argued over nearly every word in their drafts and amended drafts, with Cranmer and the Protestant bishops advocating a change, or the insertion of a word, which would sanction a Protestant practice or imply a Protestant interpretation on some disputed point of doctrine, while Gardiner and the Catholic bishops opposed it. The dispute was sometimes ended by a decision by Cromwell in favour of the Protestant position, but more often by one by the king in favour of the Catholics. Once the decision had been taken, the edict was repeatedly read out in the pulpits in the parish churches throughout England, and vigorously enforced by all the bishops, including those who had opposed it in the privacy of the Commissioners' meetings. They all unquestioningly accepted the king's decision. When the bishops in 1540 submitted to Henry their opinions on the subtle theological issues of the number and nature of the Sacraments and the ordination of bishops, they all added a postscript in which they stated that though this was their opinion at the moment, they would alter it and say the reverse if the king preferred.*

Henry willingly agreed to the demand of his Protestant advisers for the suppression of the monasteries in which monks, in contravention of Protestant doctrine, prayed for the souls of the dead; because, by suppressing the monasteries, he could seize their great wealth for himself. To provide an excuse for suppressing them, he sent Commissioners to visit every monastery in England. There was undoubtedly a considerable amount of good living in the monasteries, with much gluttony and occasional homsexuality; but the Commissioners exaggerated every irregularity and impropriety which they found, and produced the damaging report which was expected of them, though sometimes they found nothing worse to say than that a monk working in the kitchen had dipped his finger in meat grease and licked it on a fast day.

The Commissioners' report on vice in the monasteries was read out in the House of Commons, where the indignant MPs greeted it with outcries against the monasteries and shouts of 'Down with them!' The monasteries were duly suppressed. This caused much dissatisfaction among the conservative and Catholic population of the north, where the monasteries, which often stood in isolated parts of the countryside, served a useful purpose as a house of refuge for travellers and paupers in the district; and it was one of the causes of a Catholic rebellion, the Pilgrimage of Grace, which broke out in Lincolnshire and Yorkshire in the autumn of 1536. The strength of the insurrection forced Henry to parley and play for time before suppressing it in due course and executing the ringleaders. In other parts of the kingdom, there

---

* 'This is mine opinion and sentence at this present, which I do not temerariously define, and do remit the judgment thereof wholly unto Your Majesty.'

was probably a good deal of satisfaction at the dissolution of the monasteries, because, whatever other sins the monks may or may not have committed, they had a reputation for being grasping and oppressive landlords.

The king seized the property of the monasteries without compensation, though he paid yearly pensions to the monks for the rest of their lives. In a few cases, he gave the monastery's lands to his favourite ministers and courtiers; he is said, in one case, to have gambled it away in a game of dice. Usually the property was sold to the local gentry, or to speculators, who in many cases were the former land agents or solicitors of the monks. The speculators then resold it at a profit to the local gentry. The result was that the gentry acquired a vested interest in the dissolution of the monasteries, and had no wish to see the return of a papist government which would take the land away from them and restore it to the monks.

Henry also agreed to the suggestion of his Protestant advisers that he should suppress the shrines where relics were exhibited and so-called miracles performed. Here again Commissioners were sent to expose the frauds by which, in some shrines, the monks faked miracles by pulling levers and by other tricks. The valuable gifts which pilgrims had given to the shrines were seized by the king. The richest loot came from Thomas Becket's shrine in Canterbury cathedral, to which pilgrims had come from all over England and Europe for over three hundred years. A court of law gave judgment that Becket had been a traitor to his king, Henry II; his bones were disinterred and burned, and the priceless ornaments on the tomb were taken to the royal treasury in London. Twenty carts piled high with the valuables were needed to take them away.

The suppression of the papist supporters was intensified, and several prominent Catholic nobles and prelates were executed, among them the abbot of Glastonbury, who was hanged on Glastonbury Tor. The victims were in many cases condemned without any form of trial by Act of Attainder; and where trials were held, the verdict was a foregone conclusion. As soon as the abbot of Reading was arrested, Cromwell made a note on those scraps of paper which he used as a memo pad: 'The abbot of Reading to be sent down to be tried and executed at Reading.'

Three years after his marriage to Anne Boleyn, Henry discovered that she had lovers, and she was beheaded; but contrary to the hopes of the Catholics, this did not put an end to the Reformation. Henry's third wife, Jane Seymour, was the daughter of a knight of Wiltshire; she gave Henry the son he needed, and died twelve days later.

In 1538 Henry became alarmed when the Emperor Charles V and Francis I of France made peace and had a friendly meeting at Aiguesmortes. For twenty-five years he had utilised the hatred between the Habsburg and Valois dynasties and had played them off against each other. Now there was a danger that they would unite against him and lead a joint Catholic crusade to reconquer his schismatical realm for the Church. Cromwell advised him to counter the threat by an alliance with the German Lutheran princes, and to cement it by marrying Anne, the sister of the duke of Cleves. Henry was reluctant to adopt this policy. He considered the German Lutherans to be heretics and rebels against their emperor; and he was very displeased when, after marrying Anne of Cleves as his fourth wife, he found her physically unattractive. He was also conscious that the majority of his subjects were disturbed by the increasing Protestant innovations in religion, and that they blamed Cromwell for this.

He therefore initiated a sharp turn of policy in 1540. He beheaded Cromwell, burned one of his leading Protestant advisers, and vigorously enforced a recent statute, the Act of the Six Articles, which punished with death by burning or hanging all who questioned the traditional Catholic doctrines. In the last six years of his reign, more Protestants were burned than Catholics were executed; while in foreign policy, he resumed his traditional alliance with the emperor against France. On the King's Council, the two factions watched each other, and denounced their opponents' less eminent supporters. After Henry's fifth queen, Katherine Howard, whom he had met at Gardiner's house, was found to have committed adultery and was beheaded, Henry married Katherine Parr, who, though the widow of a Catholic nobleman, was a Protestant bluestocking; but she had little influence over Henry's policy, and was once denounced to him as a heretic.

Cranmer too was accused of heresy, but was protected by the king. When he told Henry that he was ready to go to the Tower and stand trial as a heretic, as he was sure that he could vindicate himself, Henry would not hear of it; and his reply, as told by Cranmer to his secretary, Ralph Morice, and later written down by Morice, is very revealing of the nature of Henry's regime and of how well Henry himself understood it. 'O Lord God!', he said to Cranmer, 'What fond simplicity have you, so to permit yourself to be imprisoned, that every enemy of yours may take vantage against you. Do not you think that if they have you once in prison, three or four false knaves will be soon procured to witness against you and to condemn you, which else now being at your liberty dare not once open their lips or appear before your face? No, not so, my Lord, I have better regard unto you than to permit your enemies so to overthrow you.' In this basic respect, totalitarian regimes have not changed throughout the centuries.

In August 1546, six weeks after a Protestant gentlewoman from Lincolnshire, Anne Askew, had been burned for denying transubstantiation, Henry casually said to Cranmer and a few other courtiers at an evening party that he intended to abolish the Mass and repudiate the doctrine of transubstantiation. He died five months later, before he had done so, but after he had made a Will in which he appointed a Regency Council for his nine-year-old son, Edward VI, consisting almost entirely of the Protestant faction on the Council. The leading Catholic nobleman, the duke of Norfolk, who had been one of Henry's closest advisers for twenty years and had arrested Cromwell, was imprisoned in December 1546 together with his son, the earl of Surrey, on a charge of high treason. Surrey was beheaded, but Norfolk was spared because Henry died during the night of 27 January 1547, forty-eight hours before the date fixed for Norfolk's execution.

Power passed into the hands of Jane Seymour's brother, Edward Seymour, duke of Somerset, who collaborated closely with Cranmer in pressing ahead with a Protestant Reformation of the Church. They re-emphasised the absolutism of royal authority and the Christian duty of obedience to the prince, hailing Edward VI as the new Josias, who in the Old Testament had become king at the age of nine; but there was an immediate relaxation in the rigour of Henry VIII's dictatorship.

Somerset and Cranmer promulgated a new liturgy, the Book of Common Prayer, which laid down that the service of the Mass should henceforth be held in English, not in Latin, and made certain changes in ritual which by implication could be interpreted as denying transubstantiation. The Prayer Book did not go nearly far enough to satisfy the Protestant extremists, but it provoked an insurrection by indignant Catholics in several parts of England in the summer of 1549. The most formidable one was in Devon and Cornwall, which coincided with an equally serious rising in Norfolk under Robert Kett, whose followers were not Catholic opponents of the Prayer Book but Protestants who were angry at the enclosures of common land.

All the rebels were defeated. The rising in Norfolk was suppressed by John Dudley, earl of Warwick. A few weeks later, he overthrew the government of Somerset and eventually beheaded him. He took the title of duke of Northumberland, and became the most powerful man in the realm. He continued the Protestant innovations and in 1552 introduced a much more radical Church service in the Second Book of Common Prayer. Every advance towards Protestantism was made an excuse for his own enrichment. No one was more indignant than the Protestant preachers at the corruption of the nobles who had taken over the leadership of the Protestant cause; and they were forced to admit that, though the monks had been harsh landlords, the gentlemen who had acquired their lands treated their tenants even worse than the monks had done. A few of the more outspoken Protestant preachers, like Latimer and the Scottish refugee, John Knox, denounced the covetousness of the Protestant nobles, but they were powerless to prevent it.

The hopes of all the Protestants turned on the young king, who was a very intelligent boy and an enthusiastic Protestant; but when he reached the age of fifteen he contracted consumption, and by the summer of 1553 he was dying. At his death he would be succeeded by his Catholic sister Mary, who was known to be a bitter enemy of the Reformation. The dying young king therefore planned with Northumberland to oust Mary from the succession and give the crown to his distant relative, Jane Grey, the daughter of Northumberland's closest ally, the Protestant duke of Suffolk. Jane Grey had just married Northumberland's son, Guilford Dudley. The scheme was originally thought out by Northumberland; but Edward VI approved of it enthusiastically, and used all his energies on his deathbed to persuade his reluctant Council to support the grant of the crown to Jane.

Edward died on 6 July 1553. Mary, who had been living in

retirement in Norfolk and Essex during the last years of her brother's reign, was summoned by the Council to come to the king at Greenwich a few days before his death, the intention being to arrest her when she arrived. She set out on her journey, but when she reached Hoddesdon she was met on the road by a well-wisher who warned her of the Council's plans. She turned her horse's head and rode without pausing to the house of her Catholic supporter, Mr Huddleston, at Sawston Hall in Cambridgeshire; and after staying there for the night, she reached her house at Kenninghall in Norfolk next day. In London, Queen Jane was proclaimed, and all opposition was suppressed. The emperor's ambassador, and Charles V himself, warned Mary that resistance would be hopeless, and urged her to escape from England while there was still time; but she rejected their advice, and called on the people to join her at Framlingham Castle in Suffolk and fight for her as their lawful queen.

The nobility, the gentry and the people flocked to her support. Northumberland assembled an army of foreign mercenaries and marched against her; but when he reached Cambridge he was informed that 40,000 men had joined her at Framlingham – the correct number was about 15,000 – and he hesitated to advance further. Meanwhile in London four of the lords of the Council, the earls of Arundel, Shrewsbury and Pembroke, and Lord Paget, had decided to go over to Mary. On 19 July they persuaded the Lord Mayor to proclaim Mary as queen in London, and the whole city went mad for joy. The people lit bonfires in the streets, the church bells rang, and the fountains ran with wine, the traditional way of celebrating a joyous event. Suffolk sadly told his daughter that she was no longer queen, and Northumberland himself proclaimed Mary as queen in Cambridge and threw himself on her mercy.

Mary granted no mercy to Northumberland, but he and two of his closest collaborators were the only persons put to death for supporting Jane; for though Jane herself, with her husband and Cranmer, were sentenced to die for high treason, the sentence was not carried out. Charles V and his ambassador in London, Renard, were worried at Mary's leniency. The emperor was delighted that Mary had not followed his advice and had stayed in England to fight and triumph over her enemies; and he now reaped the reward for the diplomatic support which he had always given her, and won the greatest political triumph of his reign when his son Philip, Prince of Spain, married Mary in Winchester cathedral in July 1554 and took the title of king of England. Through Philip and Mary, Charles V held Dover and Calais and controlled the English Channel, the sea route through which his treasure-ships from Mexico and Peru sailed with their cargo of silver to the money market at Antwerp; and he had virtually encircled his greatest enemy, France.

King Henry II of France was a zealous Catholic who had instituted a particularly savage persecution of Protestants in his kingdom; but he was alarmed at the prospect of the marriage of Philip and Mary, and in January 1554 tried to forestall it by encouraging a Protestant revolt in Kent under the leadership of Sir Thomas Wyatt. Wyatt and his followers hoped to prevent the Spanish marriage; but his revolt failed, with disastrous results for the English Protestants. Renard now managed to convince Mary that her mercy to Jane Grey's supporters had been misplaced, and she swung to the other extreme. The death sentence on Jane Grey was carried out; Wyatt and many of his supporters were executed; and during the rest of her reign, Mary was a more cruel persecutor of her opponents than even her father Henry VIII had been.

Her half-sister Elizabeth had lived quietly in the country during Edward VI's reign; but she had joined Mary and had ridden into London at her side after the victory over Jane. She was known to be a Protestant. When Mary urged her to become a Catholic, she at first refused, and eventually agreed, hoping that her conversion would turn away the queen's anger and that the reluctance which she had shown would convince the Protestants that she was still a Protestant at heart. It was a dangerous game to play. The result was that Wyatt and his rebels were known to be in favour of putting her on the throne in Mary's place, while Renard and Gardiner, who had become Mary's Lord Chancellor, were convinced that she should be executed to prevent her succeeding to the throne and making England a Protestant state again if Mary died childless. They persuaded Mary to arrest her and send her to the Tower on a charge of high treason; but though her life was in great danger, she was not brought to trial or attainted. She refused to make any confession, or let slip any word which could have incriminated her; and her popularity with the gentry and the people made it very problematical for Mary and her Council whether they could persuade the MPs in the House of Commons to pass an Act of Attainder sentencing her to death. Eventually Mary, Gardiner and Renard reluctantly agreed to spare her life.

Mary restored the Catholic Mass as it had existed under Henry VIII, acknowledged papal supremacy over the Church of England, and launched an intensive persecution of Protestant heretics. The gentlemen and merchants in the House of Commons had no great objection to this; but they were worried that Mary would restore the monastic lands for which they had paid good money in Henry VIII's time. Chiefly for this reason, they made difficulties about re-enacting the law for the burning of heretics which the Protestants had repealed when Edward VI became king. Eventually an unofficial bargain was struck. Mary, though she reopened a few monasteries and gave back to them the Crown lands which Henry VIII had taken, agreed not to restore the other monasteries and not to deprive the gentry of their monastic lands; and the Act reuniting the realm to Rome was enacted.

Henry VIII's great critic, Cardinal Pole, returned to England as papal legate after twenty years of exile – the Act of Attainder sentencing him to death as a traitor was repealed while he was travelling through Kent – and at a great ceremony at Westminster on 30 November 1554 absolved the nation from the sin of schism and proclaimed that 30 November should be celebrated each year as a new holy day, the Feast of the Reconciliation. Three weeks later Parliament passed the Act for the Burning of Heretics, and the first of the new batch of Protestant martyrs, the famous preacher John Rogers, was burned at Smithfield on 4 February 1555.

The number of victims of Mary's persecution was small compared with those who were executed by Charles V and Philip II in the Netherlands, to say nothing of the 100,000 Protestants killed in the massacres in France; but they were far more numerous than in any previous reign in England. Whereas 10 heretics had been burned in the 24 years of Henry VII's reign, 81 in the 38 years of Henry VIII's reign, and two in the six years of Edward VI, Mary burned 283 heretics in the three-and-three-quarter years between February 1555 and her death in November 1558. Nearly all of them were burned in south-east England, the greatest number in London, Essex and Kent; there was one burning in the diocese of Exeter (Devon and Cornwall), but none north of Chester.

The victims, like the earlier Protestant martyrs of Henry VIII's reign, came from all classes except the nobility. There were theologians from the universities, lawyers, gentlemen, merchants, artisans, craftsmen and labourers; and a substantial minority among them were women. But for the first time they also included a few men who had held the highest positions in the Church under Henry VIII and Edward VI, including five bishops – Hooper of Worcester and Gloucester, Ferrar of St David's, Ridley of London, Latimer of Worcester, and Cranmer, archbishop of Canterbury.

Cranmer, unlike the other bishops, recanted his Protestant opinions, signing no less than eight separate recantations; but Mary nevertheless decided to burn him, though it was contrary to all precedent in England to burn a heretic who had recanted. At the last moment, he repudiated his recantations; and as the flames were lit, he held his right hand in the fire for it to be burned first, because it had offended by signing the recantations. His admirers have often suggested that he recanted because of ill-treatment or pressure, while his critics think that he did so in the hope of saving his life. But a reliable account, written a few months after his death by a man who was in close contact with him during the last weeks of his life, indicates that he repeatedly recanted and repudiated his recantations because of sincere doubts as to which doctrine was the truth that would ensure his salvation and which was the false doctrine that would send him to hell; and he was influenced, at every stage, by intimate personal recollections and experiences.

Although it is not easy to assess the feelings of the mass of the people in the sixteenth century, there is good reason to believe that the burnings of Mary's reign caused a good deal of resentment – far more than had been caused by those of the Protestant martyrs twenty years before. The burnings, as always, took place in public in the market towns of the district, and in Smithfield in London; the people came to watch, lifting their children on their shoulders to enable them to see; when a heretic was burned at Dartford in July 1555, the local fruiterers did good business selling cherries to the spectators. Increasingly during the years

1555-8, the burnings were the occasion for demonstrations of sympathy for the martyrs and of opposition to the government. Sometimes these demonstrators were arrested and flogged.

The resentment was partly due to the fact that the heretics in Mary's reign, unlike those burned by Henry VIII, were put to death under the authority of an Italian pope and a Spanish king. The sixteenth-century Englishman hated foreigners. In Edward VI's reign, this hatred was directed against the foreign Protestant refugees who had been granted asylum by the English government; under Mary, it was aimed at the Spanish courtiers and their retinues who had come to London with King Philip. Mary's government also became unpopular because of the inflation which had begun in the last years of Henry VIII and which continued under Edward VI and Mary as a result of the influx of silver into Europe from the Spanish colonies in America. For many decades prices had remained stable, with a labourer's wages at about 4d. (1½p) a day. In the 1540s it had risen within a few years to 7d. a day, and prices rose faster. The Protestant refugee, John Ponet, the former bishop of Winchester, put the position forcefully, if unfairly, in the book that he wrote in Strasburg and smuggled illegally into England: 'When were ever things so dear in England as in this time of the Popish Mass and other idolatry restored? Whoever heard or read before that a pound of beef was at fourpence? A sheep twenty shillings. A pound of candles at fourpence. A bound of butter at fourpence. A pound of cheese at fourpence. Two eggs a penny.'

To make matters worse, Mary committed the unpardonable fault in a ruler of getting involved in an unsuccessful war. She went to war with France in alliance with Philip's Spanish kingdom; and though a joint Spanish and English force under Philip's personal command won a great victory at St Quentin in August 1557, in January 1558 the French captured Calais, which the English had held for 210 years. After five years Mary had lost nearly all the enthusiastic support which she had had when she won her crown in 1553; and not only the persecuted Protestants were eagerly awaiting the day when she would be succeeded by Elizabeth.

In the spring of 1555 the government had announced that Mary was pregnant; but it was a hallucination on her part, and the heir, who would preserve England as a Catholic state after her death, did not come. Soon afterwards, at Philip's insistence, Elizabeth was invited to live at court, and treated with full honour as the queen's sister. Having decided not to put her to death when they had the opportunity to do so in 1554, the Spaniards believed that they had no choice now except to try to win her friendship. Although they strongly suspected her of being a secret heretic, the only alternative to Elizabeth was worse from their point of view. If Elizabeth was excluded from the succession, the next in line was the grand-daughter of Henry VIII's sister Margaret, who had married King James IV of Scotland. This was Mary, Queen of Scots. Apart from being the reigning queen of Scotland, she was engaged to marry the French Dauphin, the heir to the throne of France, and since her childhood had lived at the French court. If she became queen of England, then England as well as Scotland would be united with France. Philip preferred to see England ruled by a heretic queen than by a French queen.

Queen Mary Tudor was only forty-two in the autumn of 1558, but she was a broken-hearted and dying woman. She was devoted to Philip, and deeply saddened by the fact that he spent nearly all his time abroad in the other territories which he ruled. She was conscious that, despite all her efforts, she had not succeeded in extirpating heresy in England; and, like all her subjects, she was humiliated by the loss of Calais. A few days before her death, she told two of her ladies-in-waiting that 'when I am dead and opened, you will find Calais lying in my heart'.

She died at St James's Palace in the early morning of 17 November 1558. Her Privy Councillors rode at once to Hatfield to inform Elizabeth that she was queen. The burning of heretics stopped immediately. The last martyrs had suffered at Canterbury on 10 November. Two men who had been sentenced to be burned at Smithfield were reprieved by Elizabeth, and lived to a great age before dying in their beds.

149

CHAPTER 9

ELIZABETH I:
THE
PROTESTANT
VICTORY
(1558–1603)

The new Queen was aged twenty-five. She came to the throne in very difficult circumstances. England had lost a war, the government was bankrupt, and the army and navy had been run down to a dangerously low level. France was a powerful enemy, and controlled Scotland through the French-born Mary of Guise, the mother of Mary, Queen of Scots, who ruled there as regent for her daughter in France. Philip of Spain, who had succeeded Charles V as ruler of the Netherlands as well as Spain, and was the most powerful sovereign in Europe, was still England's ally; but religious differences might make him reluctant to help a Protestant queen. At home, Mary's bishops were very hostile to Elizabeth. Under Henry VIII, a powerful section of the Church hierarchy had been willing to co-operate in an anti-papal policy while defending the Catholic orthodoxy of the Church of England against the heretics; but these bishops had accepted papal supremacy in Mary's reign, when the issue had been simplified as being between the pope and the heretics. The Catholic bishops were not prepared to recognise Elizabeth as Supreme Head of the Church of England as they had recognised Henry VIII.

Elizabeth immediately appointed William Cecil (afterwards Lord Burghley) as her secretary and chief minister. He was a country gentleman from Northamptonshire who had been secretary to the Privy Council in the reign of Edward VI, when he had skilfully furthered his career by shifting his loyalty at the right time from the duke of Somerset to the duke of Northumberland. He was not the stuff of which martyrs are made, but he was a sincere Protestant. He had become a Catholic and gone to Mass in Mary's reign, but had held only minor posts in the government service, and for most of the time had lived quietly at Wimbledon. Now, at the age of thirty-eight, he became Elizabeth's chief minister, and continued in this office for forty years until his death.

He was an exceptionally able man, with remarkable clarity of thought. Whenever he and the queen had to take an important policy decision, he was in the habit of writing down on a few sheets of paper the pros and cons of adopting either of the two alternative policies. Early in 1559 he drew up for Elizabeth a document in which he clearly set down the dangers which would result if the queen and the realm converted to Protestantism: it would arouse the antagonism of the bishops and of many members of the Establishment, and would give the king of France and the Scots a convenient excuse for attacking England. He nevertheless advised Elizabeth to take the risk and comply with the Will of God, especially as she could counter the hostility of the foreign Catholic sovereigns by stirring up their Protestant subjects to rebel. She followed his advice. She was crowned at a Protestant coronation ceremony by the bishop of Carlisle, as the see of Canterbury was vacant and the archbishop of York refused to crown her.

Her Parliament passed the necessary legislation to abolish the papal supremacy over the Church, and gave Elizabeth all the powers over the Church which her father had held, though with the more modest title of 'Supreme Governor' of the Church of England instead of 'Supreme Head'. The Catholic Mass was abolished, and the Thirty-nine Articles of Religion and the Third Book of Common Prayer repudiated transubstantiation, thus proclaiming the doctrine which had been accepted under Edward VI and for which the martyrs had gone to the stake under Henry VIII and Mary.

Unlike the bishops, the country gentlemen accepted the change to Protestantism. The JPs who in the reign of Henry VIII had burned heretics for denying transubstantiation, who under Edward VI had fined and imprisoned Catholics for witnessing it at Mass, and under Mary had again burned the Protestants for denying it, now changed for the fourth time in twelve years and fined and imprisoned the Catholics. They could justify their actions by the convenient doctrine of passive obedience – that the duty of a Christian was to obey the prince and burn and imprison either Protestants or Catholics as the king and his Council ordered. Elizabeth encouraged this attitude. None of Mary's Bishops, JPs or other officials was punished for having obeyed his queen and persecuted Protestants in Mary's reign, provided that he now obeyed his new queen and upheld Protestantism. Those who refused were punished; and, to the delight of the Protestants, two of the most savage of persecutors under Mary, 'Bloody' Bonner, the Bishop of London, and Nicholas Harpsfield, the archdeacon of Canterbury, were imprisoned for many years, Bonner dying in prison, and Harpsfield being released on bail only a few months before his death.

The Protestants did not forget the sufferings of their colleagues during the four terrible years between 1555 and 1558. They were powerfully described by John Foxe in his book, *Acts and Monuments of these latter and perilous days touching matters of the Church*, which became popularly known as 'Foxe's Book of Martyrs'. It is the longest book that has ever been written by a single author in the English language, running to four million words, or five times the length of the Bible; and like the Bible, Harriet Beecher Stowe's *Uncle Tom's Cabin*, and Karl Marx's *Capital*, it is one of the few books which has had a profound effect on world history. Foxe was a divinity scholar from Lincolnshire who became a secret Protestant in the last years of Henry VIII's reign. When England became Protestant under Edward VI, he began writing a book which was to be an account of the sufferings of all the Protestant martyrs in England and Europe from the first persecution of the Lollards at the end of the fourteenth century to the last victim of Henry VIII.

He had nearly finished the book when Mary became queen, and he fled abroad, taking his manuscript with him. While living as a refugee in Switzerland he wrote an account of the per-

secution of the Christian martyrs by the Roman emperors in the
first centuries after Christ, so as to link these persecutions in the
reader's mind with those of the Protestants in his own time.
While he was writing, his co-religionists in England, including
some of his personal friends, were being burned in a more
intensive persecution than any which he had so far described;
and when he returned home after Elizabeth's accession, he
travelled all over England interviewing people who had known
the martyrs and had witnessed their executions, as well as
consulting the official records and transcripts of their trials.

The first English edition of the *Book of Martyrs* was published in
1563; but Foxe continued his researches, and in the second
edition of 1570 added a great deal of new material as well as
correcting a few mistakes in the first edition. The book was very
widely read. Convocation ordered that a chained copy of it, along
with the English Bible, should be placed in every cathedral in
England, and most parish churches also had a copy. The 1570
edition was often reprinted. As the younger generation, and
their children and grandchildren in the seventeenth century,
read of Hooper's three-quarters of an hour's ordeal in the fire, of
the blind girl burned at Derby, and of the new-born baby thrown
back into the flames in Guernsey, they were filled with a bitter
hatred of popery which continued from one generation to
another for over three hundred years.

Elizabeth, like her father and sister, ruled as an absolute
monarch; but her regime, at least in the early years, was much
more lenient than theirs. This has been largely overlooked, both
by the critics and the defenders of 'Tudor despotism'; but the
contemporaries were well aware that not all Tudors were equally
despotic. In about 1565 Cranmer's secretary, Ralph Morice,
trying to excuse Cranmer from the accusation of having been too
compliant in Henry VIII's reign, hoped that his successors 'in this
mild and quiet time' would be as resolute as he had been 'in a
most dangerous world'. Elizabeth was eager to conciliate the
loyal Catholics as far as possible. They were forbidden to celebrate
Mass, but those who did so were punished, not by death, but
only by fines and imprisonment; and if they were content to
celebrate it in the privacy of their homes they were usually left in
peace.

In the first year of her reign, the young queen was confronted with a major problem of foreign policy, and took the most important decision of her long reign – one of the most important which has ever been taken by an English statesman. In the summer of 1559 a Protestant revolution broke out in Scotland. This northern kingdom, with a population of about half a million, with a capital city of only 15,000 inhabitants, and only six towns with a population of more than 2,000, was a far poorer country than England. Its soil was so poor that the smallholders, who often held only a few acres of land on an unfertile hillside, were unable to earn a living, as only fish was plentiful; and many Scots emigrated to France, Norway, Germany and Poland in search of a livelihood. Only exceptionally, under the rule of a few powerful kings like Robert Bruce, James I and James IV, did an effective government enforce its authority over the kingdom; usually the power of the local nobility was stronger in the district than the king's.

The corruption of the Church before the Reformation had gone much farther in Scotland than in England. Despite all the abuses of the English monasteries and the system of pluralities and absentee bishops and priests, religious life continued to function, under a curate if not a vicar, in every parish in England; in Scotland, the practice of granting benefices to the great monasteries, to aristocratic laymen, and to the king's infant bastards, had produced a state of affairs in which there were no religious services held, or any local clergyman to be found, in the majority of the parishes of Scotland.

In 1542 Mary, Queen of Scots, succeeded to the throne at her father's death when she was six days old. Henry VIII had planned to marry her to his son, the future Edward VI, and thus gain control of Scotland; and when the Scottish government refused to agree, he repeatedly sent his armies to invade Scotland, where they devastated the farms in the Border regions and burned Edinburgh to the ground. The Scots sent Mary to safety in France.

Protestantism had appeared in Scotland, chiefly in Dundee and Ayrshire. The Scottish Protestants, in the absence of a strong central government and with the national traditions of lawlessness, never accepted Tyndale's doctrine of passive obedience to the king, and from the beginning took the path of revolutionary violence. They produced a very forceful spokes-

154

man, John Knox, a priest of Haddington. He became involved with a group of Protestant gentlemen who, at the instigation of Henry VIII, murdered the chancellor of Scotland, Cardinal Beaton, and seized St Andrews Castle. The king of France, who as usual was Scotland's ally against England, sent a fleet to recapture the castle from the rebels, and Knox was put to work as a galley-slave in the French navy until Edward VI's government obtained his release in exchange for French prisoners-of-war in England. He became an influential preacher in England in Edward VI's reign, but escaped abroad when Mary became queen, and settled in Calvin's Geneva.

The experiences of Mary's reign persuaded many of the younger English Protestant refugees to abandon their belief in Tyndale's doctrine of Christian obedience; and Knox, with his lawless Scottish background, went further than any of them in advocating the doctrine that it was justifiable for Protestants to revolt against Catholic rulers. In a series of pamphlets, he called on the Scottish nobility and, failing them, on the common people, to overthrow the Catholic government by revolution; and in another book, aimed especially at Queen Mary of England, he put forward the view that no woman was permitted by God's law to govern a kingdom. Mary's Parliament enacted that anyone found in possession of Knox's books was to suffer death.

In the summer of 1559 Knox returned to Scotland, and the first sermon that he preached at Perth started a riot which quickly developed into a revolution. Most of the nobles joined it, and within seven weeks nearly the whole of the Lowlands, including Edinburgh, was in the hands of the rebels. The French government prepared to send troops to crush the rebellion; the rebels appealed to Elizabeth for aid. Elizabeth was indignant at Knox's book against the government of women, though he hastened to assure her that she herself was an exception to the rule, a Deborah sent by God to lead His people. She disapproved even more of Knox's theory of revolution, and of the practical example that he had set in Scotland of inciting the people to revolt against their sovereign. But Cecil believed that this was a great opportunity to make Scotland Protestant, to destroy French influence there, and to transform Scotland from a French into an English satellite state. He recommended that the Scottish Protestants should be helped first with money, then with arms, and finally with men.

The money and the arms proved insufficient to ensure the triumph of the Scottish Protestants, and in November 1559 they were driven out of Edinburgh by a French garrison. Elizabeth now had to take the fateful decision. Intervention meant risking war with France at a time when she had only a few thousand soldiers and less than twenty warships available to fight one of the strongest armies in Europe. She knew that she could not rely on the help of Philip of Spain, though she also knew that the French Protestants were threatening to start a civil war in France. She took the decision at a Council meeting at Greenwich on 12 December to send her admiral William Winter to the Forth at mid-winter with a fleet of fourteen ships to bring military aid to the Scottish Protestants, and he sailed on 27 December from Gillingham. His journey took nearly a month, for there were fierce gales in the North Sea, and he was forced to take refuge in Yarmouth and Hull. Six of his ships were lost in the gales, but he reached the Forth with the other eight on 22 January 1560, just in time to rally the Scottish Protestants. The French ships bringing reinforcements from France to the queen regent were scattered by the storms, and those that escaped destruction had to turn back to France.

In the spring, Elizabeth sent an army of 11,000 men, nearly all her available forces, across the Scottish border. They marched to Edinburgh and besieged the French garrison in Leith. Cecil himself went to Edinburgh and negotiated a peace treaty with the French representatives, while the French government was hamstrung by a Protestant conspiracy in France. Under the terms of the treaty, all French troops were withdrawn from Scotland and the Scottish Protestants were left free to settle the religious issue. On 15 August 1560 Scotland became a Protestant state with Knox's Church established as almost an independent power in the realm, with a fully Calvinist doctrine and governed by local congregations and an elected General Assembly, without bishops. Any Catholic who attended Mass was punished for the third offence by death.

Philip of Spain remained inactive during the events in Scotland. After Mary Tudor's death he had offered to marry Elizabeth, after obtaining the necessary papal dispensation, and thus perpetuate the Anglo-Spanish union; and when Elizabeth tactfully declined, he proposed an extension of the alliance on a temporary basis. He did not realise the potential threat of Elizabeth to Spanish power in Europe, though he was repeatedly warned against her by the count (afterwards duke) of Feria, who had been sent to London as ambassador in the last years of Mary's reign and had married Lady Jane Dormer, one of Mary's ladies-in-waiting. Jane Dormer came from a devout English Catholic family; her great-uncle was one of the Carthusian monks who had been executed for refusing to take the Oath of Supremacy to Henry VIII. Later, as Queen Mary's lady-in-waiting, she became utterly devoted to the queen.

Feria was recalled to Spain a few months after Elizabeth's accession, and his wife accompanied him. Their house in Madrid became a refuge for many English Catholics. Prompted by his English wife and guests, Feria became the leading advocate at Philip's court of a tough anti-English policy, urging the king to crush Elizabeth before she became strong enough to menace Spain, and to liberate the oppressed Catholics in England from the heretics. Philip's other Spanish advisers were much less enthusiastic, and the King himself, being very cautious and dilatory by nature, always favoured the more passive alternative. In the summer of 1559 he warned Elizabeth that if she continued to encourage heresy and to help the Protestant rebels in Scotland, he would leave her to her fate and remain neutral in any war in which she became involved with France. This was the worst threat that he made to her, and he so greatly underestimated her power and resolve that he thought it would be enough to bring her to heel.

Philip and his advisers realised that he was in a dilemma about Scotland. His sister Margaret of Parma, the regent of the Netherlands, warned him that if Elizabeth were allowed to ensure the victory of the Scottish Protestants, it would be a great encouragement to heresy and sedition everywhere, but that if the French intervened successfully to crush the revolt, it would be as great a disaster to Philip as the loss of Brussels: if French troops occupied Scotland, they would overrun England, and, holding Dover as well as Calais, would control the English Channel and the sea route from Panama to the money market at Antwerp. She thought that Philip's only course was to intervene himself in Scotland and send Spanish troops to crush the Scottish Protestants. Philip assembled 4,400 troops in the ports of the Netherlands where they were ready to sail for Scotland; but he consulted the duke of Alba, who was soon to become notorious as the persecutor of the Dutch Protestants. Alba hated heretics, but he was over fifty, and did not appreciate the realities of the new power alignment in Europe. He had been fighting the French all his life, and was much too pleased to see them in difficulties in Scotland to worry much about Elizabeth. He strongly advised against intervention in Scotland. At this juncture, Philip heard that the Turks had attacked a Spanish naval base near Tunis. He sent his troops in the ports of the Netherlands, not to Scotland, but to fight the Turks in North Africa. He thus missed his best chance to defeat Elizabeth.

In 1561 Mary, Queen of Scots, returned from France to Scotland, but her position as the Catholic queen of a Protestant kingdom was very difficult. She had to deal with several rebellions from her Protestant nobles. Elizabeth, despite her disapproval of the Scottish Calvinist rebels, was persuaded by Cecil to give them financial and diplomatic support, and asylum in England when Mary defeated their rebellions. The English ambassador in Edinburgh, Thomas Randolph, was discreetly involved in most of the Protestant plots. In March 1566 a band of Protestant lords broke into Mary's room in her palace of Holyrood-house and murdered her secretary, the Italian Riccio, in her presence. Elizabeth ought to have been shocked; in her own realm, any gentleman who even drew his sword in the precincts of the court, in the course of a quarrel with another gentleman or for any other reason, was sentenced to a term of imprisonment. But she refused to extradite the murderers when they fled to Northumberland. Two days before the murder of Riccio, Randolph had written to Cecil that something was about to happen in Edinburgh, but that he and Elizabeth had better not know about it in advance.

A year later, Mary's Catholic husband, Lord Darnley, was murdered when his house at Kirk-o'-Field in Edinburgh was blown up in the night. It was widely believed in Scotland that he had been killed by Mary's lover, the earl of Bothwell, with her connivance; and these suspicions were confirmed when she married Bothwell three months after Darnley's assassination. The Protestants rose again in revolt, and imprisoned Mary on the island in the lake at Lochleven in Kinross-shire, where she was forced to abdicate in favour of her infant son. He was crowned as King James VI at the age of thirteen months, and the government of Scotland was taken over by the Protestant lords.

Elizabeth was indignant that the Scots should imprison their queen and compel her to abdicate, and to the embarrassment of Cecil and her other advisers insisted on making the strongest protest against the action of the Scottish rebels. She went so far as to threaten to send an army to invade Scotland and liberate Mary from captivity unless the lords released her; but she did not carry out her threat when the Scots told her that if English troops crossed the border, Mary would immediately be put to death.

After Mary had been imprisoned for a year at Lochleven, she escaped, and raised an army of her supporters; but she was defeated at Langside near Glasgow. Remembering the stand which Elizabeth had taken against her rebels in the previous year, she fled across the border into England and asked her for asylum and aid against the rebels. Elizabeth's reaction was to hold her as a prisoner for nineteen years in various castles in the north of England and in the Midlands. Officially, she took the line that she could not restore Mary to her throne until she had investigated the accusations of the Scottish lords that Mary had murdered her husband, Darnley. She set up a court of inquiry; but the investigations were lengthy, and were repeatedly adjourned.

For three years Elizabeth encouraged Mary with false hints of support, and induced her to make various concessions which weakened her position in Scotland in the hope of being released from captivity and restored as queen of Scots by English influence. In Scotland, civil war broke out between Mary's supporters – 'the Queen's lords' – and her enemies, 'the King's lords', who had placed her baby son on the throne in her place. Whenever the queen's lords appeared to be winning, Elizabeth persuaded Mary to order them to withdraw. Mary agreed to all Elizabeth's terms for her restoration to the throne; but Elizabeth always suggested new conditions and delays. Meanwhile the king's lords were attacking and hanging the queen's lords in Scotland.

Elizabeth was now showing her teeth to the Spaniards. At Christmas 1568 six Spanish treasure-ships bound for Flanders were attacked by privateers in the Channel; and they put into Falmouth, Plymouth and Southampton without having obtained a formal safe-conduct from the English authorities. While they were there, Elizabeth heard that a Spanish fleet in the port of Vera Cruz in Mexico had attacked the ships of two English sea-captains, John Hawkins and Francis Drake, who had challenged the Spanish monopoly of the slave trade by taking Negroes from Africa to the Spanish colonies in America. Elizabeth thereupon seized and detained four of the Spanish treasure-ships in her harbours, with their cargo, after the other two ships had succeeded in escaping. Philip and his governor of the Netherlands, Alba, retaliated by seizing all the property of English merchants in the Netherlands, to which Elizabeth replied by seizing Spanish property in England, including twenty-six Spanish ships in English ports, and by placing an embargo on trade with Philip's dominions. The dispute, which harmed Spain more than England, continued for nearly four years before a settlement was reached and the property restored on both sides.

The quarrel had not been settled in November 1569, when a Catholic revolt broke out in Northumberland and Cumberland under the leadership of the earls of Northumberland and West-morland. The rebels captured Durham, celebrated Mass in the cathedral, and burned the Book of Common Prayer and the English Bible. They also linked up with Mary's supporters in south-west Scotland. They asked Alba for help. He referred the matter to Philip in Madrid, who asked Alba for further infor-mation, and then dallied over a decision, with the letters passing between Madrid and Brussels taking three weeks in each direction. The Catholic revolt was suppressed before Philip had taken any action.

Elizabeth's forces crushed the rebellion, and after hanging the rebels along the roads in the north, entered Scotland and ravaged the lands of Mary's supporters. Three years later, the last resistance of the queen's lords was crushed when Elizabeth sent an army with cannon to capture their stronghold of Edinburgh Castle. Mary's last chance of release had gone. Cecil had already advised Elizabeth that Mary should never be released from prison, because they had done her so much injury that she would never forgive them, and whatever they might do or she might promise, she would always be their enemy.

The revolt in the north spurred the pope into action. His predecessor, Pius IV, had adopted a conciliatory policy towards Elizabeth, even when she repudiated papal supremacy and scornfully refused his invitation to send delegates to the Ecumenical Council of Trent; but in February 1570 Pius V issued a bull of excommunication against Elizabeth, in which he absolved her subjects from the duty of obedience to her. The bull caused a violent Protestant reaction in England against the Catholics and Mary, which increased next year when Cecil discovered a plot to assassinate Elizabeth in which some of Mary's closest advisers were involved. The House of Commons passed a resolution asking the queen to put the Queen of Scots to death.

The chief reason for their ardour was that Elizabeth had no Protestant heir, and that Mary was the heir to the crown of England. Elizabeth's advisers were therefore eager that Elizabeth should marry and have children; but though marriage negotiations with foreign rulers were often begun, Elizabeth always broke them off. If she had married a foreign sovereign, it would have placed England under his control; and she would have aroused jealousies among the nobility by marrying an English subject. She was thought to be deeply attached to Robert Dudley, earl of Leicester, the son of the duke of Northumberland of Edward VI's reign; but marriage with him would have caused a scandal after his wife died in mysterious circumstances in 1560. So Elizabeth remained unmarried and without an heir.

This was a cause of constant anxiety to Cecil and the Council. When Elizabeth fell dangerously ill in 1562 with smallpox, they made secret plans, in the event of her death, to proclaim her distant relative, the earl of Huntingdon, as king; for although he was an almost unknown young man, he was a Protestant. Cecil and the Protestants would never have agreed to have Mary, Queen of Scots, as their sovereign; but as long as she lived, there was an incentive for the Catholics to assassinate Elizabeth to make her queen of England.

In August 1572 the French king's mother, Catherine de Medici, organised the Massacre of St Bartholomew, when the French Protestants who had come to Paris for the wedding of Catherine's daughter to their leader, King Henry of Navarre, were murdered during the night. The massacre spread throughout France, and about 10,000 Protestants were killed. Public opinion in England was outraged. Elizabeth, who was conscious that Spain, not France, was her greatest enemy, confined herself to a strong diplomatic protest to the French government; she did not break off diplomatic relations, and within a few months was negotiating for an alliance and a possible marriage with the king of France's brother. But hatred of papists was intensified in England.

By this time, English sailors were fighting the Spaniards in the Atlantic and off the coast of Central America. Drake plundered the Spanish treasure-ships as they came with their cargo of silver from the mines of Mexico, and made unexpected attacks on the Spanish ports in the Caribbean. In December 1577 he left Plymouth on a voyage round the world, returning in September 1580 after sailing through the Straits of Magellan, up the west coast of America to California, and across the Pacific and home by the Cape of Good Hope, having plundered many Spanish ships and ports on the journey. To patriotic Englishmen, with their hatred of foreigners, the raids on the Spanish ships and colonies brought national glory for England. It was also a religious war for Protestantism. Many sea-captains took with them on their journeys a copy of Foxe's *Book of Martyrs* and read it aloud to their crews. The gentlemen and seamen of Devon and Cornwall who sailed the Spanish Main were zealous Protestants, though only twenty years earlier these counties had been staunchly Catholic. All over Europe, the Protestants acclaimed Drake and displayed the portrait of the Protestant hero.

The English Catholic refugees in Rome, Spain and Flanders sent secret agents to contact their supporters in England. Several of them were members of the Society of Jesus, which had been founded forty years before by the Spaniard, Ignatius Loyola. Elizabeth's government believed that they were involved in the plots to assassinate the queen, and soon every English Protestant was shuddering at the word 'Jesuit'. The Jesuit missionaries maintained that their only object in England was to celebrate Mass in secret for the English Catholics, who otherwise would be deprived of the opportunity to attend Mass; but the books published in Italy and the Netherlands by Cardinal Allen and the other English Catholic refugees made it clear that they wished to overthrow Elizabeth's government and restore, with Spanish help, the situation which had existed in good Queen Mary's days, when the Mass was openly celebrated in England and heretics were 'most worthily burned with fire and consumed to ashes'. Many of the Catholic missionaries were caught by the agents of Francis Walsingham, who had taken over from Cecil the direction of Elizabeth's counter-espionage service. They were examined under torture by the Council and hanged, drawn and quartered for high treason.

One of the prominent English Catholic refugees was John Story, a learned Oxford theologian and civil lawyer who had been counsel for the prosecution at Cranmer's trial for heresy. After Elizabeth's accession, he fled to Flanders, where Alba entrusted him with the duty of searching ships arriving from England to make sure that they were not bringing heretical literature into Spanish territory. One day in 1570 he went on board an English ship in the harbour at Antwerp to search for heretical writings. The captain seized him, and quickly sailed to England, where Story was tried for high treason and executed.

The Catholics stirred up a revolt in Ireland. The kings of England had been nominal rulers of Ireland since the reign of Henry II, but exercised effective control over only a small part of the country, and governed Ireland through the goodwill of the native Irish nobility. The English regarded the Irish as a barbarian race; Acts of Parliament in the fourteenth and fifteenth centuries prevented racial integration, intermarriage, or fraternal association and social intercourse between Englishmen and Irishmen.

At first the Protestant Reformation made no progress, and aroused no interest, in Ireland. During the reigns of Henry VIII, Edward VI and Mary, the religious strife between Catholics and Protestants in England had no repercussions in Ireland, except among a few English theologians there. The Irish only became ardent Catholics after England had again become Protestant in Elizabeth's reign, when colonisation by the English was speeded up. Catholic missionaries from the Continent succeeded in stirring up revolts of the Irish tribal chiefs against the heretical English oppressors in the name of the Catholic Church. King Philip unofficially sent Spanish soldiers to assist them, but they were defeated by Elizabeth's troops. One of the Catholic agents who took part in the revolt was the English theologian and polemicist, Nicholas Sanders. He had just completed in Madrid his book *The Anglican Schism*, which is the leading contemporary account, from the Catholic point of view, of the religious struggle in England under Henry VIII, Edward VI and Mary. After the defeat of the Irish rebellion, he became a fugitive in the hills of Munster, where he died of cold and starvation.

In 1585 Elizabeth sent an army of 6,000 men under the Earl of Leicester to fight alongside the Dutch Protestants in their war of independence against Spain. The poet and courtier, Sir Philip Sidney, was one of many young English gentlemen who volunteered to fight the Spaniards in the Netherlands for the queen, for England, and for the Protestant religion. He died of a wound which he received at the Battle of Zutphen; after riding back, wounded, with great difficulty to the English camp he ordered that the water which was brought to assuage his thirst should be given to a wounded common soldier whose need was greater than his own. The heroism of Sidney and his fellow-volunteers in the Netherlands stirred the emotions of the people of England when they read and heard of their deeds in the broadsheets and ballads about current events which were sold and sung on the streets of London.

Elizabeth now yielded at last to the demand of her ministers and her Parliament that she should execute Mary, Queen of Scots. There was evidence that Mary had been implicated in two plots to assassinate Elizabeth; some people, then and now, believed that it was forged and planted by Elizabeth's agents. In October 1586 Mary was put on trial in her prison at Fotheringhay in Northamptonshire, and sentenced to death. There was no precedent for the trial, condemnation and execution of a reigning sovereign, which Mary still claimed to be, despite her forced abdication nineteen years earlier; and Elizabeth shrank from taking so revolutionary a step, and one which would so weaken the concept of royal authority and immunity. She delayed for three months before consenting to the execution; but her Council demanded it as the threat of open war with Spain, and a Spanish invasion, loomed larger. In desperation, she tried to persuade Mary's jailers to murder her in prison, for Mary's assassination would certainly cause less indignation among foreign sovereigns than if she were officially executed; but none of the officials was prepared to carry out the murder without a written authority and pardon from Elizabeth, which was out of the question.

Eventually Elizabeth signed the warrant for Mary's execution, but still hesitated to send it to the jailers at Fotheringhay. Her

Under-Secretary of State, Davison, then sent it to Fotheringhay without informing Elizabeth. When she heard that Mary had been beheaded, she claimed that she had not authorised it, and sent Davison as a prisoner to the Tower. He was released two years later, after paying a heavy fine.

There was great indignation among the Catholics in Europe at the crime of regicide which had been committed by the English heretics and their queen who, according to a papal bull of 1570, had forefeited her throne and no longer deserved the loyalty of her subjects. Philip of Spain was more eager to avenge Mary than he had been to liberate her and place this pro-French queen on the English throne. He decided to invade England and overthrow Elizabeth. In the spring of 1587 he began to assemble an invasion fleet, his great Armada, at Cadiz. Drake obtained Elizabeth's permission to attack Cadiz and burn the fleet before it was ready to sail; and although Elizabeth later cancelled the order, the revocation came too late to reach Drake, who successfully carried out the operation. Philip proceeded to assemble another invasion fleet. Drake again urged the queen to allow him to attack it in port and strike a crippling blow at 'God's enemies and Her Majesty's'; but the duke of Parma, Philip's governor in the Netherlands, had opened peace talks with Elizabeth, apparently with the deliberate intention of lulling her into a false sense of security, and in view of the prospects of peace she refused to exacerbate the situation by allowing Drake to attack.

In the summer of 1588 the 'Invincible Armada' sailed from the Spanish ports and made for the English Channel. She carried 8,000 sailors and 18,000 soldiers. The plan was to sail to Calais, which was occupied by Parma's troops, where 34,000 of his men would embark, and then to proceed to Margate, where the 52,000 soldiers would be landed. With the assistance of the English Catholics, who would start an insurrection at the appropriate moment, they would capture London, depose Elizabeth, and Philip would be proclaimed king of England, by virtue of a papal bull which he had obtained, giving him the kingdom of which Elizabeth had been deprived. He would then give it to his daughter.

The Armada was sighted off the Lizard on 19 July 1588.* The

* 29 July by our modern calendar, which the Spaniards had adopted six years before, but which was not introduced into England until 1752.

well-known story that the news was brought to Drake when he was playing bowls on Plymouth Hoe, and that he said: 'There's plenty of time to win this game and thrash the Spaniards too', was first recorded about forty years later, and may, or may not, be a true account passed on by someone who was present. As the Armada sailed slowly up the Channel towards Calais, it was continually harassed and seriously mauled by a flotilla of far smaller English ships; and in the harbour at Calais a large part of the fleet was destroyed by the burning fire-ships which Drake sent into the harbour to ignite the Spanish galleons. The plan to transport Parma's troops to England had to be abandoned; and the Armada, driven out into the open sea by the fire-ships, was battered and scattered by heavy gales and driven north up the east coast of England. Most of the ships were sunk with their crews; a few managed to return to Spain by sailing round the north coast of Scotland and the west coast of Ireland. By the time that Elizabeth addressed her troops at Tilbury on 8 August, where they were waiting to fight the invaders, the danger had passed. She told them that she feared neither Philip nor Parma, and that though she had the body of 'a weak and feeble woman', she had 'the heart and stomach of a king, and of a king of England too'.

After this great English and Protestant victory, the war continued for sixteen years. The English fought the Spaniards in the Atlantic and the Caribbean, in Ireland, and in France, where Elizabeth sent troops as well as money to help King Henry of Navarre, the leader of the Protestants in the French civil war. He eventually defeated the French Catholics and their Spanish allies, and became King Henry IV of France, though not until after he had become a Catholic, because he thought that 'the Crown was well worth a Mass'.* England and Spain finally made peace in 1604, six years after Philip's death and a year after Elizabeth's.

The queen's last years were saddened by the unsuccessful rebellion of her favourite courtier, Robert Devereux, earl of Essex, who wished to seize control of her person and overthrow the influence of her chief minister, William Cecil's son, Robert. She was genuinely fond of Essex, but had no hesitation in consenting

---

* This statement by Henry's minister, Sully, is usually misquoted as 'Paris is well worth a Mass', and attributed to Henry himself.

to his execution for his act of high treason. She urged Henry IV to take note of her example, because royal authority would be fatally weakened if treason and rebellion went unpunished.

She died on 24 March 1603 at the age of sixty-nine. Her forty-four year reign had not only ensured the triumph of Protestantism in Britain and in northern Europe, but had greatly increased the wealth, power and prestige of England. Her navy had triumphed over the great Armada of the king of Spain; her sailors had circumnavigated the world, and had established a colony on the North American continent (in the modern state of North Carolina) which they named Virginia after their virgin queen. At home, the merchants were prosperous; the common people enjoyed a higher standard of living than in most other European countries, though beggars and able-bodied vagrants were becoming an increasingly serious problem; and by the last decade of the reign all classes were smoking the tobacco of Virginia in their clay pipes with the same gusto with which they ate their enormous meals of English roast beef.

A new popular entertainment, the theatre, had developed into something far more stimulating and valuable than the religious morality plays of earlier generations. The theatre produced a number of gifted playwrights; one of them, William Shakespeare, from Stratford-upon-Avon in Warwickshire, has been recognised throughout the world as the greatest dramatist of all time. Though his plays contain a few topical references which are lost on modern playgoers, they are in no sense peculiar to his own age, and are even more popular in the twentieth than in the sixteenth century. Yet if he had been born fifty years earlier, he could never have realised his genius. It is inconceivable that Shakespeare's plays could have been written or produced in the time of Henry VIII or Mary, before English intellectual thought had been freed from the limitations of medieval Christianity and the doctrinal arguments of the early years of the Reformation.

CHAPTER 10

CAVALIERS
AND
ROUNDHEADS
(1603–60)

In the last years of Elizabeth's reign, a new conflict was beginning which would cause even greater political upheavals in the seventeenth than in the sixteenth century. Henry VIII had relied on the support of the Protestants in overthrowing papal supremacy, while at the same time persecuting them for advocating heretical doctrines. The same pattern was repeated, on a more radical level, in Elizabeth I's reign. She repudiated transubstantiation and accepted the Zwinglian position for which heretics had been burned in her father's reign; but she opposed the more extreme doctrines which the English Protestant refugees had learned in Calvin's Geneva, for she thought them subversive of royal authority. She refused to suppress the crucifix in her chapel royal, or to ban ecclesiastical vestments; and, most strongly of all, she rejected the Calvinist demand for the abolition of bishops and the adoption of the Presbyterian system by which the Church was controlled by the local congregation and by their representatives in the General Assembly of the Church.

While Edmund Grindal, who had been a refugee in Geneva in Mary's reign, was Elizabeth's archbishop of Canterbury, the

Calvinists were treated with considerable toleration; but after his death in 1583 Elizabeth appointed Whitgift to succeed him, and strongly supported Whitgift's energetic methods to stamp out extremism. The Protestant extremists who denounced bishops, crucifixes and vestments became known as 'Puritans', because they wished to purify the Church from the 'dregs of Popery'; the word 'puritan' had not yet acquired its later and modern meaning. With the queen's full approval, Whitgift imprisoned several Puritan agitators, though the Puritans were Elizabeth's most enthusiastic champions in the struggle against Rome and Spain and the most vociferous in demanding the execution of Mary, Queen of Scots. In 1588 some Puritans began secretly publishing a number of pamphlets attacking bishops, signed with the pseudonym 'Martin Marprelate'. They were caught and executed in 1593.

The queen was so greatly admired by the Protestants for her leadership in the fight against popery and Spain that they were willing to forgive her for imprisoning and executing Puritans; but things were different when she was succeeded by James VI of Scotland, the Protestant son of Mary, Queen of Scots, and the next in line to the English throne. James had been brought up in Scotland by the Calvinists who had deposed his mother; but he resented the domination of the Presbyterian Church, and when he became old enough to rule himself he was surprisingly successful in limiting its power in Scotland, just as he was more successful than any earlier Scottish king in enforcing law and order and the royal authority in his lawless realm. He became convinced that Calvinism and Presbyterianism were a threat to the royal authority.

He was still only thirty-six when on 26 March 1603 an English gentleman, Sir Robert Carey, rode into the courtyard of Holyrood-house as James was sitting down to supper. Carey, who had ridden from London to Edinburgh in sixty hours, told James that Elizabeth had died at dawn on the 24th and that he had succeeded to her throne as James I. As James rode south on his journey to London, he was amazed, already in the north of England, at the grandeur of the houses of the nobility at which he stayed and at the general prosperity of his new realm; and his wonder increased as he passed through the much more prosperous south of England. He only once returned to Scotland during the remaining twenty-two years of his life, for he much preferred to live in wealthy, orderly England, where, unlike Scotland, royal authority was respected. He was determined not to allow the Church of England to become Presbyterian like the Church of Scotland. When the English Puritans urged him to abolish bishops, he told them: 'No bishop, no king'.

Two years after he came to England, he was the target of an assassination plot when a group of English Catholics planned to kill him by blowing up the House of Lords when he opened Parliament on 5 November 1605. The discovery of the plot and the arrest and execution of the plotters aroused a fresh outburst of Protestant enthusiasm and hatred of popery, and 5 November has been celebrated in England ever since; but this was the last occasion on which James I was acclaimed by the Protestants. The extremists were not prepared to forgive him, as they had forgiven Elizabeth I, for his opposition to Puritanism; and even the more moderate Protestants were indignant when James pursued a friendly policy towards Spain and imprisoned, and later executed, the very popular Protestant, Sir Walter Raleigh, in order to placate the Spanish government. In 1618 the Thirty Years War between Protestants and Catholics broke out in Germany, and led to the invasion of Protestant Bohemia by the armies of the Catholic Holy Roman Emperor. Although the king of Bohemia had married James's daughter Elizabeth, and English volunteers rushed to fight for her and the Protestant cause, James refused to intervene. His policy of neutrality in the Thirty Years War angered the English Protestants.

Royal absolutism, which under Henry VIII and Elizabeth had been an instrument of Protestantism, had become an obstruction to it; and the Protestants began to oppose it. The leadership in this struggle was taken, not by the Puritan theologians who had fallen foul of Elizabeth, but by the lawyers, though many of these were proud to accept the label 'Puritan'. The common lawyers, organised in the four Inns of Court in London, had become an increasingly important group in society with the increase in commerce and with the sales of land which followed the break-down of feudalism, though they had not yet played the leading part in politics which they were to do during the next three centuries. The higher political posts had hitherto usually been filled by the ecclesiastical and civil lawyers who staffed the royal administration. The common lawyers had always felt a professional hostility to the civil and canon lawyers, and disapproved of their Roman law procedure, with its interrogation of defendants and the use of torture instead of proving the guilt of the accused by the evidence of witnesses at a trial by jury. In the eyes of the common lawyers, the use of torture and the civil law procedure by the Council in the exercise of its special jurisdiction in political cases discredited the royal government and associated it with tyrannical and foreign practices. The common lawyers had not voiced their disgust as long as Elizabeth reigned, for their connection with the merchant class and the country gentry, and the laws excluding Catholics from becoming lawyers, had made them firmly Protestant; but it was different under James I.

The leader of the lawyers' opposition to the king was Sir Edward Coke. As Elizabeth's solicitor-general, he had acted as an agent of royal despotism; but when James I appointed him chief justice of the Court of King's Bench, he delivered a number of judgments in which he restricted the extent of the king's prerogative power, and laid down the principle that the king was not above the law. His most far-reaching decision was that the power of the king and his Council to make new laws by royal proclamation, which had so often been exercised in the sixteenth century, was illegal, as the king's prerogative did not extend to the making of new laws, which could only be made by Act of Parliament. James was indignant at Coke's judgments, and eventually dismissed him from his office as chief justice. Coke then became an MP, and the leader of the opposition to the king's policy in the House of Commons. He was chiefly responsible for reviving the memory of Magna Carta, and for interpreting it as the great charter of English freedom.

The merchants were also opposed to the king's policy and his restrictions on freedom of trade. In the sixteenth century, the king's government interfered continually in everybody's daily life. Not only were the people forced to attend church and to worship with exactly the words and gestures prescribed in such detail in the Book of Common Prayer; they were also told which colour of cothes they were allowed to wear – red for the nobility, dark colours for the merchants, lawyers and academics, and so on – and how many different dishes a nobleman, a gentleman, an archbishop, and a bishop were allowed to eat at the same meal. The fasting laws prescribed on which days of the week, and at which hours of the day, the people could eat meat, fish and cheese. These laws were periodically enforced by JPs and the king's officers, who entered private houses at dinner time to see that they were observing the fasting and sumptuary laws.

The merchants objected to the constant government interference and to the practice by which the king granted monopolies in the sale of tobacco and other commodities. Elizabeth had granted monopolies, but only occasionally for she had taken note of the criticism of them in the House of Commons. James I gave many more, especially to his favourite, George Villiers, with whom he had a homosexual relationship, and whom he first knighted and then promoted by degrees through all the ranks of the peerage to be duke of Buckingham by the time he was thirty.

James just managed to stave off a head-on collision with the House of Commons until after his death in 1625, when he left his twenty-four-year-old son Charles I to face the strongest opposition which any sovereign had encountered since the Wars of the Roses. The House of Commons immediately launched a strong attack on Buckingham's corruption and incompetence, for Charles, though he was not a homosexual like his father, retained Buckingham as his chief minister. The House refused to pass the necessary legislation to enable the king to collect taxes until they had prosecuted Buckingham by impeachment proceedings in the House of Lords. The king was forced to dissolve Parliament in order to save his minister, and to forgo the money from the taxes.

After two years of conflict, Charles arrested Sir John Eliot, a Cornish gentleman who had succeeded Coke as his most prominent critic in Parliament, and imprisoned him and other Opposition MPs. Elizabeth and her predecessors had often exercised the power to arrest anyone who displeased them, by virtue of their royal prerogative; but this power was now challenged in the courts by Eliot and his colleagues, who claimed that it was illegal. The court ruled against them; but the widespread resentment in the country, and Charles's need for money, compelled him to give way in 1628 and grant the Petition of Right. This enacted that no one could be arrested by the king's order, but only when charged with a specific offence; that only

Parliament could impose taxes; and that civilians were not to be subjected to martial law. Two months later, Buckingham was assassinated by a Puritan fanatic, who was certainly not in touch with Eliot and the Parliamentary leaders. The murder was celebrated all over England, with bonfires on the village greens and toasts to the assassin in the taverns; Charles blamed Eliot and the Opposition for his friend's death.

In 1629 Charles suddenly dissolved Parliament. The MPs barricaded themselves in the chamber and, holding the Speaker by force in his chair, passed a resolution declaring that anyone who introduced popish innovations in religion, or who levied taxes without the consent of Parliament, would be guilty of high treason. Charles arrested Eliot and the Parliamentary leaders, and determined to rule without Parliament in future. Three years later, Eliot died in prison. His supporters believed that his death had been accelerated by the harsh conditions in his cell, and resented the king's refusal to release his body for burial in his family vault in Cornwall.

Charles ruled without a Parliament for eleven years. He chose as his chief minister a very able Yorkshire gentleman, Thomas Wentworth, who had formerly been one of his active critics in the House of Commons. Wentworth, who was created earl of Strafford, was especially hated by the Opposition for his defection from their ranks. In his ecclesiastical policy, Charles relied on William Laud, the archbishop of Canterbury. Laud was a strong opponent of Puritanism, and though he was certainly not a papist, as the Puritans alleged, he maintained all the 'dregs of popery' – vestments, crucifixes and ritual – to which they objected, and favoured some doctrines which had been rejected as too Catholic even in Elizabeth's reign. Critics of the policies of Strafford and Laud were severely punished by imprisonment, the pillory and mutilation. The Puritan writer, William Prynne, had his ears cut off in public in Palace Yard in Westminster for writing a book against the theatre which by implication criticised Charles's French-born Catholic queen, Henrietta Maria. When John Lilburne protested against Prynne's punishment, he was whipped from Fleet Street to Palace Yard in Westminster, where he was placed in the pillory, and was then imprisoned during the king's pleasure.

Charles, without a Parliament to grant him money, extended to

173

the whole of England the traditional 'ship-money' tax imposed on the coastal counties. John Hampden, who had been one of Eliot's leading supporters in the House of Commons, refused to pay the ship-money imposed on his property in the inland county of Buckinghamshire, and contested the validity of the tax in the Court of Exchequer. His counsel's argument raised the whole question of the king's power to tax his subjects, and though a majority of the judges decided against him, he became a popular hero by his stand against the king.

In 1637 Charles made a disastrous blunder when he tried to extend Laud's High Church despotism over his Scottish subjects. He ordered that a new Church service should be introduced in Scotland in place of the Book of Common Order which John Knox had established in 1560. The new service book did not make very drastic changes, but the Scottish Presbyterians had no doubt that it was the first step by which the king and Laud would destroy the independence and the Presbyterian system of the Scottish Church and impose upon Scotland an Anglican Church with bishops and Catholic ritual. On the first Sunday on which the new service was used in St Giles Church in Edinburgh, there was a riot, which began when a woman named Jenny Geddes, who sold wares in the street market, cried out that the service was 'a Mass' and threw her stool at the dean's head. When Charles threatened to use force to overcome the opposition to the new service, the Scottish Presbyterians organised a National Covenant, as they had done before the revolution of 1559, by which the signatories agreed to fight together to defend the true religion. It was organised by the powerful Scottish nobility under the leadership of the marquis of Argyll. Nearly every man in Scotland signed the Covenant, most of them enthusiastically and a few under duress.

In 1639 Charles sent an army to invade Scotland, but it was defeated. Next year he renewed the war, with even more disastrous results. The Scottish Covenanters invaded England, defeated Charles's army at Newburn near Newcastle, and at Ripon forced him to agree to humiliating peace terms, under which the Scottish army was to remain in occupation of the six northern counties of England at Charles's expense, until they were satisfied that all their demands had been complied with. Charles returned to London, defeated and bankrupt, and was forced to summon a meeting of Parliament and to yield to all the demands of his enemies.

The Parliament which met on 3 November 1640 became known as the Long Parliament, for it was still in existence, in a truncated form, in 1660. Under the leadership of a gentleman from Somerset, John Pym, it began to carry through a far-reaching political revolution. It ordered the immediate release from prison of Prynne, Lilburne and all the victims of Charles's tyranny, and arrested Strafford and Laud, who were impeached in Parliament for high treason. Acts were passed restricting the king's right to dissolve Parliament or to govern for more than three years without a Parliament. The criminal jurisdiction of the Council and its sub-committee, the Star Chamber, was abolished, as was the use of torture, though this continued to be legal in Scotland, to which the statutes of the English Parliament did not extend. The more extreme Puritans now wished to transform the Church of England into a Presbyterian Church. A bill abolishing bishops was passed in the House of Commons, but Pym did not proceed with it, owing to the opposition of his more moderate allies in the House of Lords.

Future generations of constitutional lawyers were taught to regard the acts of the Long Parliament in 1641 as laying the foundations of the rule of law in England; but in fact Parliament acted in a revolutionary, not a legal, spirit. It passed a resolution declaring that the judgment of the Court of Exchequer in Hampden's ship-money case was illegal, and impeached the judges who had given the majority judgment in the case. Finding that the impeachment proceedings against Strafford were running into difficulties because of Strafford's able defence, they abandoned the trial and resorted instead to the procedure of an Act of Attainder. But a bill of attainder, like all other Parliamentary bills, could not become law without the royal assent. Would Charles consent to the bill putting his loyal minister to death?

The House of Commons passed the bill of attainder with enthusiasm; but Pym and his supporters knew that there would be strong opposition in the House of Lords, where a majority of the peers, and all the bishops, supported the king and Strafford. By an arbitrary and unprecedented ruling, Pym insisted that the bishops were not entitled to vote on the issue, and organised demonstrations by his ardent supporters, the apprentices of the

City of London, to overawe the opposition in the Lords. At this juncture, Charles issued an arrogantly worded statement in which he declared that it did not matter how the House of Lords voted on the bill, as he would never give his royal assent to it. The waverers in the Lords then decided that, as the king would in any case veto the bill, they need not brave the anger of the London mob by voting against it, and the bill passed.

Charles at first refused his assent; but he gave way after the apprentices had demonstrated on several days in front of his palace in Whitehall. Strafford himself wrote to the king from the Tower, advising him to consent to the bill, for he believed that Charles's wisest policy in the situation would be to sacrifice him to appease the people's wrath and to gain time. Charles followed his advice, and gave his consent to the bill – a decision of which he was ashamed for the rest of his life.

Strafford was beheaded on Tower Hill on 12 May 1641. As he walked to the place of execution, he passed beneath the window of the cell in which Laud was imprisoned; and seeing the archbishop at the window, he asked and received his blessing. Four years later, Laud was also sentenced to death and executed as a traitor by another Act of Attainder. By this time, Parliament was dispensing with the royal assent to their legislation.

After Strafford's execution, Charles played for time for seven months, and then decided to arrest five of his leading opponents in the House of Commons, including Pym and Hampden. On 4 January 1642 he marched with his bodyguard to the House, entered the chamber, and called on the five members by name. They were not there; they had been warned in advance of the king's plan by Pym's spies in the royal household, and had taken refuge with their supporters in the City of London. When Charles drove to the Guildhall to order the Lord Mayor to arrest and surrender the five members, someone threw a paper into his carriage bearing the words: 'To your tents, O Israel!' – the declaration of war. The people came out on to the streets and erected barricades to prevent the king's soldiers from entering the city to arrest the five members. A few days later, Charles left Whitehall for Oxford, and the five members returned from London to Westminster amid the cheers of the people.

The Civil War began in August, when Charles raised his standard at Nottingham. For the next four years, the war was fought all over England, with fighting taking place in nearly every county. Apart from the Battle of Marston Moor, in which about 45,000 men took part, no army on either side numbered more than 13,000 in any battle. There were many sieges of the walled towns, of medieval castles, and of fortified manor houses, which sometimes changed hands several times. The king's followers called the Parliamentarians 'Roundheads' because their supporters among the London apprentices had short hair, though nearly all the 'Roundhead' leaders wore their hair long. The Roundheads called the king's men 'Cavaliers' from the Spanish word *'caballeros'*, to signify that they were foreign papists.

The nobility for the most part supported the king, and only a handful of them fought for the Parliament. The country gentlemen were about equally divided between Cavaliers and Roundheads. The majority of the merchants supported Parliament, though some of the wealthier merchants, and the City livery companies, supported the king. The yeomen in the countryside formed the backbone of the Roundhead army, and some of the artisans in the towns, especially the young apprentices in London, supported Parliament; but the poorest sections of the population were usually neutral. The Civil War was not a class war, but there were elements of a class war in it, as is shown by the fact that the Cavaliers despised the Roundheads, though often without justification, as base-born fellows.

Geographically, London, the south-east and East Anglia were for Parliament. The north of England and Wales were for the king. The south-west, though it was the home of many of the Roundhead leaders, passed into the control of the king in the early part of the war. As far as religion was concerned, the more extreme a Protestant a man was, the more enthusiastically he supported the Roundheads. The Catholics, realising who was their greatest enemy, fought loyally for the king, though he and they tried to keep this secret in order to avoid causing him political embarrassment.

The first major battle was fought on 23 October 1642 at Edgehill in Warwickshire. It was indecisive. The king's nephew, Prince Rupert – the son of the exiled king and queen of Bohemia – who commanded the right wing of the royal army, scattered the Roundhead left wing with one of the irresistible cavalry charges with which he was to win many battles in the next eighteen months. But the earl of Essex, who had been appointed Commander-in-Chief of the Parliamentary forces because he was one of the few noblemen on the Roundhead side, more than held his own in the centre against the Cavalier infantry commanded by the king himself. After the battle, Essex's army drew back, leaving the road to London open. Rupert led the Cavalier vanguard in a dash for the capital, and on 13 November reached Turnham Green, only seven miles from Westminster; but the Puritan preachers in London roused the people to a pitch of enthusiasm for the cause, and they turned out in strength to block Rupert's advance. He withdrew without fighting from Turnham Green towards Oxford, where the king established his headquarters for the duration of the war. London and the Roundhead cause were saved.

The war went badly for Parliament in 1643. Rupert won a number of victories in the no-man's-land between Oxford and London, in one of which, at Chalgrove, Hampden was killed. In Yorkshire, the Cavaliers defeated the Roundhead leader, Sir Thomas Fairfax, and were masters of all England north of the Humber except for the port of Hull, which held out as a Roundhead pocket of resistance. On the south coast, the Parliamentary general, Sir William Waller, was at first victorious in Sussex and Hampshire; but in the summer of 1643 the Cavalier commander, Sir Ralph Hopton, raised an army for the king in Cornwall, with which he marched eastwards, seizing Devon and Somerset for Charles. The campaign culminated in the rout of Waller's army at Roundway Down in Wiltshire. The Roundheads were successful only in East Anglia, where their commanders, the earl of Manchester and Oliver Cromwell, crushed the Cavalier resistance in Norfolk and Lincolnshire.

In view of the serious military situation, Pym and the Parliamentary leaders turned to the Scots for help. The Scottish Covenanters, having won their own war against the king, at first adopted a policy of neutrality in the English Civil War. When the Roundheads appealed to them for aid, they insisted that in return for their help the Roundheads should make the Church of England a Presbyterian Church. This was not at all to the liking of those moderate Anglicans who supported Parliament; but Pym persuaded them that they had no choice, as they desperately needed the help of the Scots. In September 1643 Parliament passed an Act making the Church of England Presbyterian, and in January an army of Scottish Covenanters crossed the Border and attacked the rear of the Cavaliers in the north of England. In the summer of 1644 the Scottish army linked up with the Roundheads under Manchester and Cromwell marching north from Lincolnshire, and their united forces defeated the hitherto invincible Prince Rupert at Marston Moor near York. The whole of the north of England then passed into Roundhead control.

The Presbyterians were now confronted with a new threat from more extremist Protestant sects. The Calvinists had always been as convinced as the Catholics that they had a duty to God to persecute heretics who denied the true faith; they had not only burned Unitarians who questioned the divinity of Christ, but suppressed any religious worship outside the organisation of the Presbyterian Church. During the Civil War in England, these extremist sects increased, particularly in the districts of East Anglia which were occupied by Cromwell's army. The sects became known as the Independents. They believed that any group of Protestants should be free to meet together for worship without permission from the Anglicans, the Presbyterians or any other authority. Not content, like the Presbyterians, with abolishing bishops, they came close to abolishing the priesthood. Cromwell in Ely encouraged any of his soldiers who felt the urge to do so to go up into the pulpit in the cathedral during the church service and preach to the congregation. He and the Independents demanded religious toleration for all Protestants, though they believed that the Popish mass should be banned and that the adherents of the persecuting religion, of whose activities they had read in Foxe's *Book of Martyrs*, should be severely suppressed. The Independents' demand for religious toleration was anathema to the Presbyterians.

Cromwell was a gentleman who was born and spent his youth in the country town of Huntingdon, though in his early thirties he moved to the neighbouring borough of St Ives. He was brought up as a Puritan, and like many of his colleagues was a deeply religious Calvinist. He was a man of great physical and mental energy, who enjoyed outdoor sports, hunting and riding. He was very fond of music, and was emotional by temperament; he suffered from fits of depression and hypochondria, though at other times he displayed boisterous good spirits, with a liking for practical jokes. He was elected MP for Cambridge in the general election of 1640, and in the Long Parliament in 1641 became a member of the 'Root and Branch' party which demanded the abolition of bishops and the adoption of the most vigorous measures against the king's supporters.

At the outbreak of the Civil War, he raised a troop to fight for Parliament. He put the yeoman farmers in his regiments through an intensive course of military training which made them the finest cavalry units in the Parliamentary army; but he saw them, not only as a fighting force to defeat the Cavaliers, but also as a revolutionary political group who would uphold the cause of the Independents against the Presbyterians and secure religious toleration for all Protestants. He and his supporters in London used his brilliant military successes as propaganda in favour of the Independents and toleration. The meeting of the Long Parliament and the outbreak of the Civil War had led to the appearance of the first newspapers in England. Small printed pamphlets with some four or six pages appeared regularly two or three times a week, giving the news of the stirring events which were occurring and the writer's opinions about them. The Independent newspapers praised Cromwell for his victories, and claimed that at Marston Moor it was he, and not the Presbyterian Scots, who had won the battle. Cromwell himself periodically came to London during a lull in the fighting and advocated the cause of the Independents in the House of Commons.

During the winter of 1644-5 he worked to get rid of Essex and Manchester and the Parliamentary generals of noble birth and moderate opinions who had been given the command because of their rank. He achieved this by persuading Parliament to pass the Self-Denying Ordinance by which all members of either the House of Lords or the House of Commons were to be ineligible to exercise a military command. This forced most of the Roundhead generals to resign, and also applied to Cromwell himself; but at the last moment amending legislation was passed which exempted Cromwell from the provisons of the Self-Denying Ordinance and allowed him to continue leading his regiments. They became known as the New Model Army, for he insisted that they should all be clean-living Puritans who would fight with enthusiasm for the Good Cause.

In June 1645 Cromwell defeated Charles I and Prince Rupert at Naseby in Northamptonshire and then mopped up the Cavalier forces in the south-west; and the war ended a year later with the surrender of Oxford to the Roundhead armies and the collapse of Cavalier resistance. Charles escaped to the north, and surrendered to the Scottish Covenanters at Newark. They had been trying for many months to induce the Parliament in London to pay the expenses of their military operations, and they now agreed to hand over Charles to the Parliament in return for Parliament agreeing to pay them £400,000, half of it in advance. The deal was strongly criticised by the Cavaliers as a Judas-type transaction by which the Scots sold their king to his rebels, and is perhaps the origin of the traditional English belief in the meanness of the grasping Scot who will do anything for money.

With the Civil War over and the king a prisoner in Parliament's hands, the Presbyterians and the Independents came into open conflict. Presbyterianism, which for a hundred years had been a revolutionary creed, now became a counter-revolutionary one. Anglican noblemen and High Churchmen, who had hitherto hated Presbyterianism, became Presbyterians, believing that the Presbyterians and the Scottish Covenanter army could alone save them from the menace of Independency and from the religious toleration which they identified with political anarchy. As in other revolutions, the moderates who had led the movement in the early stages had become alarmed at the forces which they had unleashed. As early as December 1644, Essex had feared that 'our posterity will say that to deliver them from the yoke of the king we have subjected them to that of the common people'.

The Presbyterians controlled both the House of Lords and the House of Commons; Cromwell and the Independents controlled the victorious Roundhead army. Parliament demanded that the army should be disbanded now that the war was over; but owing to their financial difficulties they were reluctant to pay the soldiers the wages due to them, which gave Cromwell an excuse to refuse to disband the army. In the summer of 1647, hearing that the Presbyterian Parliamentary leaders were organising a military force and planning to carry out a *coup* against the Independents, Cromwell ordered the army to march on London, and sent an officer to seize the king who was being held prisoner by Parliament in Northamptonshire. Charles now became a prisoner in Cromwell's hands. Cromwell offered to restore him to the throne if he would undertake to grant religious toleration; but Charles, though he tried to play off the army and Parliament against each other by negotiating with both behind the other's back, refused either to become a Presbyterian or to grant religious toleration.

Cromwell himself came into conflict with more extremist forces. Many of his soldiers demanded not only religious freedom but also political democracy. They formed committees of 'Agitators' in every regiment, with every regiment sending a representative to the army's Council of Agitators. The Agitators put pressure on Cromwell to take vigorous action against the king and the Presbyterian Parliament. They read the writings of Lilburne, who, after his release from prison by the Long Parliament in 1640, had fought with distinction during the Civil War, but had afterwards been imprisoned by the Presbyterian Parliament. He and his followers became known as 'Levellers'. Whereas the Presbyterians demanded that the army, like the king, should submit to the authority of Parliament, Lilburne thought that the army, having fought for the people's freedom against the king, should now fight for it against Parliament.

Cromwell and most of his officers, whom the levellers called 'the Grandees', opposed the Agitators' demands for political democracy. In October and November 1647 he and other Grandees met the leading Agitators in the village church on the riverside at Putney. For thirteen days they held discussions about the future form of government in England, the Agitators arguing that all Englishmen, except servants and other wage-earners, should have the vote at Parliamentary elections, and the Grandees insisting that the existing property qualification must be maintained. The Levellers' demand that all males except wage-earners should have the vote would have excluded the personal servants of the aristocracy and gentry and some of the artisans in the towns, but would have transferred control of Parliament from the gentlemen to the small independent yeomen farmers in the countryside, and from the merchants to the craftsmen in the towns. The reports of the debates have been preserved, but almost certainly only in an abbreviated form; and it is difficult to disentangle the precise ideas, if any, which lay behind the biblical language of the speakers. But the Levellers' position was clearly expressed by one of their spokesmen, Colonel Rainsborough, at Putney: 'I think that the poorest he that is in England hath a life to live as the greatest he.' Cromwell, on the other hand, believed that it was essential to maintain the distinction between the nobleman, the gentleman and the yeoman.

In May 1648 the Second Civil War broke out, as the result of secret negotiations between the king, the Presbyterian leaders in Parliament, and the Scots. The Scots and the Presbyterians agreed to restore Charles as king; and Charles, though he refused to become a Presbyterian himself, agreed to establish Presbyterianism for a trial period of three years as the official state religion in England as well as in Scotland, with no religious toleration for the Independent sects. A Scottish army composed of both Cavaliers and Covenanters invaded the north of England; a group of Cavaliers started a revolt in Kent and Essex; some Presbyterians, who had been officers in the Roundhead army in the First Civil War, seized Pembroke; and a mutiny by Presbyterians and Cavaliers broke out in the fleet. Cromwell and the army, though greatly outnumbered by all their enemies, did not falter. They held the king responsible for starting the Second Civil War. Before setting out to fight the enemy they held a meeting of the Army Council at Windsor, and passed a resolution that 'it was our duty, if ever the Lord brought us back again in peace, to call Charles Stuart, that man of blood, to an account for the blood he had shed'.

The mutiny in the fleet was suppressed. The Cavaliers in Kent and Essex were driven into Colchester, where they held out for several months but were eventually forced to surrender. Cromwell captured Pembroke after a six-weeks' siege, and then marched against the Scots in the north. Although he had only 8,600 men against 20,000 Scots, he defeated them by a brilliant tactical manoeuvre at Preston, and the remnants of their army retreated into Scotland. In the First Civil War, both sides had treated their captives as prisoners-of-war, for the Cavaliers had been deterred by the threat of reprisals from executing their Roundhead prisoners as traitors; but the army now regarded the leaders of the Cavalier and Presbyterian rebels as criminals, and they were shot or beheaded.

The army and the Independents, having defeated their enemies, were ready to carry out their pledge to bring Charles

Stuart to justice. They marched on London and occupied the City and Westminster, and on 6 December 1648 carried out a purge of the members of the House of Commons. When the MPs assembled at 8 a.m. for the daily sitting of the House, they found soldiers at the door under the command of Colonel Pride. He held in his hand a list of the MPs' names, which had been drawn up on the previous evening by the army commanders and the leaders of the Independent minority in the House of Commons. Pride allowed only 80 of the 500 MPs – the Independents and a handful of neutral members – to enter the House. The rest were turned back, and 41 of the leading Presbyterians among them were arrested and held prisoners for two days before being released.

The remaining 'Rump' of the Long Parliament passed a resolution on 1 January 1649 establishing a republic, abolishing the House of Lords, constituting itself as the supreme governing body, and appointing a Council of State to govern the country. It voted to set up a High Court of Justice to try Charles Stuart for his crimes against his people, especially for starting the Second Civil War. The court consisted of 152 Commissioners, but nearly half of them refused to attend, and only 78 sat when the trial opened on 20 January in Westminster Hall. Charles, who was brought before the court, behaved with great dignity, refused to plead, and denied the jurisdiction of the court to try him. Many of the judges were most reluctant to pass sentence on the king and to sign the death warrant, but Cromwell, who was one of them, used all his energies to overcome their reluctance. Charles was beheaded on the balcony of his palace at Whitehall at 2 p.m. on 30 January. The headsman wore a mask to conceal his identity; he was probably the public executioner.

It was the first time in history that a king had been executed by his subjects, though deposed sovereigns like Edward II and Richard II had been assassinated by their captors, and Mary, Queen of Scots, had been executed after a trial by Elizabeth I's judges. There can be no doubt that most of the spectators in Whitehall, who watched the execution under the eye of Cromwell's soldiers lining the street, were shocked at the act of regicide, as were the majority of the people of England, for they had all been brought up to believe in the duty of passive obedience to the prince, in the divine right of kings, and the inviolability of 'Sacred Majesty'. The publication of a book which was supposed to have been written by Charles I, but was in fact a forgery by a Church of England clergyman, aroused great sympathy for the 'martyr' king. The government of the Commonwealth, which showed remarkable tolerance towards the Cavaliers, made no serious efforts to suppress the book.

The king's execution was regarded by his judges as a matter of principle, without regard for political expediency. The cry of the soldiers in Westminster Hall, when the sentence of death was passed on Charles, was 'Justice! Justice!'. One of the leading regicides, when facing the vengeance of the Cavaliers at his own trial in 1660, proudly claimed that they had put the king to death openly, in the full light of day. The aim of the regicides was to proclaim, whatever the political consequences and whatever the cost to themselves, that a king who offends against God and the liberties of his people may be brought to trial and punished by his subjects.

The news of Charles's death was received abroad with the greatest indignation. In France the Abbé Bossuet, who denounced it in a sermon, coined the expression 'Perfidious England'. No foreign government, except some of the Protestant cantons of Switzerland, recognised the English republic, or took energetic measures to prevent the assassination of its representatives abroad by Cavalier refugees. The Scottish Covenanters, in their hatred of the English Independents, supported the cause of Charles's eldest son, the prince of Wales, who had escaped to Holland, and proclaimed him as King Charles II. In Ireland, the English Cavaliers made a truce with the Irish Catholic chieftains whom they had been fighting in order to wage war against the English Commonwealth. Prince Rupert fitted out ships in Portuguese ports and attacked English shipping on the high seas.

The government in London, which was dominated by Cromwell, dealt first with the Levellers and Agitators in the army, who mutinied in the summer of 1649. Cromwell chased the mutineers to Burford in Oxfordshire, where he executed the leaders. He then sailed for Ireland, and spent a year overcoming the resistance of the Cavaliers and Catholics. He was in most circumstances a merciful man, but the English Protestants regarded the Irish Catholics as barbarians beyond the laws of humanity, partly because of racial prejudice and partly because of the atrocities, real and alleged, which had been committed against the English settlers in Ireland during the Irish Catholic revolt of 1641. Even in the First Civil War, when both sides had respected the status of their English prisoners-of-war, Parliament had passed an Act requiring their army to put to death any Irish papist whom they captured fighting for the Cavaliers. At the capture of Drogheda and Wexford during his Irish campaign, Cromwell not only massacred the defending garrison when he captured the town by storm, which was justified by the seventeenth-century laws of war, but also killed all the Catholic priests whom he encountered. His name has been hated in Ireland for over three hundred years.

Having crushed the resistance in Ireland, Cromwell invaded Scotland. Here he was fighting not papists but Presbyterians whom he regarded as erring Protestants and as former allies who had strayed from the fold; but though he urged them: 'I beseech you in the bowels of Christ, think it possible you may be mistaken', the Scottish Covenanters were as certain as Cromwell that the Protestant God was on their side. For once Cromwell allowed himself to be outmanoeuvred by the Covenanter army, who cooped him up in the fields to the south of Dunbar and threatened to starve him into surrender. But the Covenanter commander, under pressure from the Presbyterian ministers who accompanied his army, came down from the hills to do battle with Cromwell's smaller force. As he saw the enemy advance, Cromwell said: 'God is delivering them into our hands', and by a brilliant tactical manoeuvre he won a great victory.

The young King Charles II was very different in character from his father. He was intelligent, witty, lascivious, tolerant, pragmatic, flexible and cunning, and had learned from painful experience the need to manoeuvre and compromise. He had hoped that his devoted follower, the marquis of Montrose, would restore him to power in Scotland with the help of the Scottish Cavaliers; but Montrose, who led an expedition from Norway to the Orkneys, was defeated and captured in the far north, and hanged as a traitor in Edinburgh by order of Argyll and the Covenanters. Charles II then joined forces with the men who had executed Montrose. He sailed from Holland to Speymouth, took the Covenant, became a Presbyterian, and was crowned king of Scotland at Scone by Argyll. He pretended to be a loyal Presbyterian, but Presbyterian discipline irritated his pleasure-loving nature as much as Presbyterian political philosophy conflicted with his concept of royal authority. He came to the conclusion that 'Presbytery was not a religion for gentlemen'.

For nine months Cromwell waited at Edinburgh for a suitable opportunity to deal with Charles II and the Covenanters, who were at Stirling. Then in the summer of 1651 he laid a trap for them. He advanced across the Forth and besieged Perth, deliberately leaving the road to England open. Charles and the Scots marched on London, taking the western road through Lancashire and being joined by the northern Cavaliers. Cromwell, after spending two days capturing Perth, set off in pursuit, hurrying down the eastern road through Northumberland and Yorkshire at the rate of twenty miles a day through the hot August weather. He was joined by the Commonwealth forces in England and trapped Charles at Worcester, where on 3 September he destroyed the Cavalier and Covenanter army and won the final battle of the war.

Charles II succeeded in escaping to France after a series of adventures and narrow escapes, thanks to the devotion of loyal Cavaliers. Three days after the Battle of Worcester, he was nearly caught at Boscobel in Shropshire, where he hid in the branches of an oak tree while Cromwell's soldiers, who were looking for him, stood talking beneath the tree. Disguised in woman's clothes, he travelled south, and after unsuccessfully trying to embark at Bristol and at Charmouth in Dorset, he passed into Sussex and on 15 October sailed from Shoreham to France.

The English Commonwealth had not yet found a permanent form of government. The 'Rump' of the Long Parliament which remained after Pride's Purge consisted of less than 80 of the MPs who had been elected in 1640; but they refused to take any steps to appoint a new legislative body. Cromwell lost patience with them, and in April 1653 led a body of soldiers into the House and dispersed them by force. He assumed the sovereign power, and in December took the title of Lord Protector. He was not personally vainglorious, and had throughout his military and political career always been content to take second place behind some figure-head when he thought this was for the good of the cause; but as Lord Protector he believed that he would be more likely to win the respect of the gentlemen and merchants if he lived in a semi-royal state. He moved into the royal palaces at

Whitehall and Hampton Court, and was addressed as 'Your Highness', though the life at his court was much simpler than in the days of the monarchy.

He was unable to find a legislative system which satisfied him, and tried various unsuccessful experiments. In July 1653 he summoned a Parliament consisting of 120 of his nominees; they were Independent supporters, and came from a lower social class than MPs usually did. This assembly was known, from the name of one of its members, as the Barebones Parliament. Its measures for protecting tenants and for simplifying legal procedure annoyed the landowners and lawyers, and to conciliate them Cromwell dissolved the Barebones Parliament and replaced it with a new Parliament of a traditional type, consisting of representatives elected by the merchants and country gentlemen; but for the first time in English history it contained representatives from Scotland. He grew impatient with the endless debates, and dissolved it.

In the spring of 1655 he was confronted with an unsuccessful Cavalier insurrection in Wiltshire and Dorset, and after suppressing it he imposed a military dictatorship. England was divided into eleven regions, each governed by one of Cromwell's major-generals, who had absolute powers in their districts and were subject only to Cromwell and his Council in London. This was deeply resented by the gentry, whose traditional powers as JPs were interfered with by the regional dictators, and 'the rule of the major-generals' was remembered with horror by their descendants for several centuries. It lasted less than two years, for Cromwell, still wishing to win the goodwill of the country gentlemen, ended the system of military government in the spring of 1657.

At this time, he seriously considered taking the title of king and establishing a hereditary monarchy. This would undoubtedly have pleased the merchants and gentlemen, and might perhaps have established the new regime; but the plan was strongly opposed by his leading generals, who realised that it would weaken his dependence on the army, and he reluctantly abandoned it. In 1658 he summoned a new Parliament of elected representatives of the merchants and gentlemen, and also appointed an Upper House of his own nominees, instead of the single-chamber system which had existed since 1649. But he again became irritated by the Parliamentary bickerings, and dissolved Parliament.

Cromwell adhered to his principle of religious toleration for all sects except Catholics, though he was unable to prevent his Parliaments and the local JPs from harassing and persecuting the new sect of Quakers which George Fox founded in the middle of the Civil War. He managed with some difficulty to persuade his supporters to agree to permit the Jews to return to England for the first time since their expulsion by Edward I, for he was conscious of the financial advantages which England would derive from their presence. His government was not popular in the country. The suppression of theatres and May Day festivities, for which he is often criticised today, was not begun by him, but by the Presbyterians of the Long Parliament during the Civil War; but he maintained the ban, though his love of music led him to permit the first opera ever to be performed in England. He annoyed the country gentlemen by forbidding race-meetings after the insurrection of 1655, for he was afraid that they could be used as an excuse for Cavaliers to assemble for a new revolt.

During his five years as Lord Protector he never left London, except to go to Hampton Court. This was because of the danger of assassination. Both the Cavaliers and the Levellers made repeated plots to kill him, but he survived four assassination attempts. He changed his guard every day as a precaution against assassins, and slept in a different room in his palace every night.

He pursued a vigorous foreign policy, and forced the kings and governments who had ostracised the regicide republic to respect and fear it, and to seek his friendship and alliance. This was largely due to the brilliant successes of his admiral, Robert Blake, an ardent Puritan and Republican who had never been to sea until he was fifty, but had distinguished himself during the Civil War by his heroic defence of Lyme Regis and afterwards of Taunton. Thanks largely to Blake, Cromwell won the war against Holland that he had inherited from the government of the Rump Parliament, though he was distressed at having to fight against another Protestant state. He was much more ready to go to war with Spain – a war in which Protestant and national interests coincided, and which was in the glorious traditions of Elizabeth I's days. Blake was also successful in a series of naval engagements against Prince Rupert, and in frightening the Portuguese and French governments into refusing Rupert shelter in their ports. He displayed English naval power in the Mediterranean when he bombarded Algiers and forced the Dey to release his Christian captives.

Queen Christina of Sweden established friendly relations with Cromwell. The French government made a military alliance with him against Spain, under which England acquired the port of Dunkirk, her first bridgehead in Europe since the loss of Calais a hundred years before.

Cromwell died at the age of fifty-nine on 3 September 1658, the anniversary of his victories at Dunbar in 1650, and at Worcester in 1651. His funeral in Westminster Abbey was an impressive state ceremony; but within less than two years his regime had fallen. His son Richard, who had never shown any ability or interest in politics, was chosen as Lord Protector; but in April 1659 he was overthrown by a group of Cromwell's old generals. In May the Republicans overthrew the generals and restored the survivors of the Rump Parliament which Cromwell had dissolved in 1653; and in October Major-General Lambert overthrew the Rump. The Rump then appealed to Major-General Monck, the commander-in-chief in Scotland, to overthrow Lambert and restore their authority.

Monck was a professional soldier, a bluff, brutal man with no strong religious principles, though he called himself a Presbyterian. At the start of the First Civil War he had fought for Charles I, but after being taken prisoner he had joined the Roundheads in the Second Civil War. He won Cromwell's respect by his services as a commander both on land and at sea, though Cromwell was warned on one occasion that Monck was plotting with the exiled Charles II. It shows how greatly Cromwell had changed his attitude in the course of the years that he should appoint a man like Monck to high command; for no one could have been further removed from the zealous yeomen Independents whom Cromwell had chosen as his officers in Ely in 1643 because they were 'godly' men who knew what they were fighting for. Cromwell was right in believing that Monck would always be loyal to him personally; but he had no loyalty whatever to the 'Good Old Cause'.

Monck was probably planning to restore Charles II as king

before he ostensibly became the champion of the Rump against Lambert in the autumn of 1659. Lambert, who had marched with his army to Newcastle, was lulled into inactivity by Monck's pretence that he wished to negotiate a peaceful settlement. He waited until his army had been wasted away by desertions; for, unlike Monck, who was backed by the wealthy Scottish Presbyterian merchants, he could not find the money to pay his soldiers. On 1 January 1660 Monck began his march from Coldstream, crossing the frozen Tweed, and advancing without encountering any resistance, through snow all the way, until he reached London on 3 February. The members of the Rump greeted him as their saviour, but within a fortnight he had overthrown their authority and summoned the other MPs of the Long Parliament who had been expelled in Pride's Purge. The MPs voted to invite Charles II to return, and dissolved themselves. The king sailed from Holland and landed at Dover on 25 May. Four days later, on his thirtieth birthday, he entered London amid the cheers of the people.

CHAPTER 11

THE
RESTORATION
AND THE
'GLORIOUS
REVOLUTION'
(1660–1714)

The Restoration of 1660 has been remembered by later generations as a happy event unmarred by revenge on the part of the king and his supporters. This is true only from the point of view of the moderate Parliamentarians who had led the Roundheads in the early days of the struggle against Charles I. The surviving members of the High Court of Justice who had sentenced Charles to death were put on trial for high treason as regicides and executed with all the old barbarities of hanging, drawing and quartering at Charing Cross. Several other Republican leaders, who had had no part in the king's trial, were also executed. The bodies, not only of Cromwell, but of Pym and Blake, were disinterred from Westminster Abbey, and Cromwell's head was stuck on London Bridge. Most of the prominent Independent politicians, including several members of the Rump who had invited Monck to march from Coldstream, were imprisoned for life or for shorter terms. But the Roundheads who had done nothing more than fight in the First Civil War were pardoned, and those who had afterwards resisted Cromwell or supported the Restoration were treated with favour by Charles II. Monck was created duke of Albemarle and honoured as the chief pillar of the throne.

A series of disasters struck the country early in the reign. Dunkirk was lost when Charles II sold it back to France four years after Cromwell had acquired it. In 1665 the Great Plague caused nearly 70,000 deaths in London out of a total population of 460,000, of whom two-thirds fled from the city to escape the pestilence. The Great Fire of London, which raged for four days in September 1666, devastated a large part of the city. A war with Holland went badly, and in 1667 the Dutch sailed up the Medway and burned the dockyard at Chatham. The Great Fire at least had its compensations, for it enabled Sir Christopher Wren's great new building projects to be carried out.

At court, the king made love to a succession of mistresses, to whom he awarded titles and large grants of land and money, and by whom he had a considerable number of illegitimate children. His courtiers followed his example with women, and ate, drank and gambled heavily. In the city, the same loose morals prevailed among all classes; the theatre flourished, with the women's parts being played for the first time by actresses, not by boys, in comedies about lovers and mistresses involved in comic situations and hilarious misunderstandings. The wealthier classes lived in more spacious, more comfortable and more luxurious houses than their fathers and grandfathers, and wore more elaborate and ostentatious clothes, with increasingly large periwigs. Coffee-houses were opened, where the pleasures of coffee, chocolate, tobacco, newspapers and gossip could be enjoyed.

At the universities of Oxford and Cambridge, the authorities stamped out both popery and Nonconformity; enforced High Anglican worship and ritual; preached the doctrine of the divine right of kings and passive obedience; denounced the regicides who had spilt the 'sacred blood' of King Charles the Martyr; and burned the books of Knox and Milton which justified resistance to royal authority. In Durham and Nottinghamshire, miners worked deeper beneath the surface than in earlier times, often for eighteen hours a day, with women and small children working at their side, to send coal to London in increasing quantities, and causing the capital to be covered in winter with a thick fog of smoke from which the rich tried to escape by moving out of town to Kensington or Highgate. In the country, the squire and the parson ruled the village; led a vigorous outdoor life, riding and hunting; ate huge meals, drank a great deal of ale, and cursed Puritans, Roundheads, dissenters and poachers. The artisans in the towns and the agricultural labourers in the country had a lower standard of living than their parents, but could at least enjoy the village fairs which had been banned under the Commonwealth.

The more extreme Royalists were unsuccessful in their attempts to repeal all the legislation passed in the first two years of the Long Parliament. The clock was put back to 1641, but no further. The king accepted the necessity of obtaining Parliamentary sanction for all new legislation and for raising taxes; and the criminal jurisdiction of the Council and the Court of Star Chamber, with the use of torture, was not revived. But the advances since 1641 – the Republic and religious toleration – were destroyed.

The king himself, with his tolerant character and his scientific interests, was inclined to favour religious toleration of all sects who were prepared to worship peacefully and refrain from seditious activity. He had been deeply impressed by the devotion which the Catholic gentry had shown to his father's cause during the Civil War; he had been helped by several Catholics in his escape after Worcester; his mother and his sister Henrietta Maria, who had married King Louis XIV of France's brother, the duke of Orleans, were Catholics; one of his illegitimate sons was a Jesuit. He was also conscious that the Presbyterians had played a vital part in his restoration and were, for the moment at least, his enthusiastic supporters. He therefore proposed that both Catholics and Presbyterians should be granted toleration.

The Catholics were willing to accept this proposal as a preliminary step; but no one else would agree to it. The Cavaliers in the House of Commons and the bishops in the House of Lords were determined to reimpose the domination of the Church of England as it had existed under Elizabeth I and Charles I and to persecute both Catholics and Presbyterians. The Presbyterians considered that religious toleration was sinful, and that only Presbyterianism should be permitted. It was only because Cromwell and the Independents had granted religious toleration to the Protestant sects that the Presbyterians had supported the Restoration; and it was for them a matter of fundamental principle never to agree to their own toleration if other religions were also to be tolerated. Their spokesmen had declared on several occasions that they would prefer to have a government which persecuted them and the Catholics rather than one which gave toleration to both.

In 1662 the 'Cavalier Parliament' passed the Act of Uniformity which imposed a Book of Common Prayer which was virtually identical with Elizabeth I's Prayer Book, and made it illegal for anyone to attend any other religious service. Their policy was implemented by the Lord Chancellor, Edward Hyde, earl of Clarendon. After unsuccessfully trying to persuade Charles I to compromise in 1641, Hyde had supported him in the Civil War and had been Charles II's closest adviser during his years of exile. The Act of Uniformity was followed by a series of statutes which became known as the 'Clarendon Code'. They forbade Protestant 'Nonconformists' – the term originated at this time – to hold any office in local government, and ejected Nonconformist vicars from their benefices; a proposal by the House of Lords to pay them a pension was rejected by the House of Commons. The Five Mile Act made it a criminal offence for any ejected Nonconformist vicar to come within five miles of any city or borough, or of any parish at which he had been vicar.

Although Charles II would have liked to grant religious toleration to the Presbyterians, he was determined to break the power of the Scottish Covenanters and the Church which had started all the trouble for his father in 1638; and the irritations which he had experienced at their hands in 1650 had removed any feelings of gratitude which he might otherwise have had for their support at that time and in 1660. When the marquis of Argyll, who had crowned him king at Scone in 1651, came to court after the Restoration, he was immediately arrested and tried and executed for high treason. Despite the hesitations of the king and of some of his advisers, the government forced the Church of Scotland to be reorganised with bishops instead of being controlled by the congregations and the General Assembly. This led to resistance from the Presbyterians, and several of their leaders were arrested.

In 1666 the Covenanters rose in revolt; but after the experiences of the past twenty years the Scottish nobility were no longer prepared to support them, and the government suppressed the revolt with great severity. There were repeated revolts in

Scotland during the remainder of Charles II's reign, but all were savagely crushed. Charles was told by his advisers that the restrictions on his powers in England did not apply in Scotland, where he could rule as an absolute monarch. Torture, which was still legal there, was regularly used in the examination of the rebels. The Covenanters held illegal prayer-meetings in the hills of the south-west; the government troops hunted them down and massacred them. The young extremist preachers among the Covenanters, following in the tradition of Knox and his successors, exercised the powers of the Old Testament prophets to depose wicked kings, and declared that Charles II, by breaking the oath to the Covenant which he had sworn in 1650 and by his betrayal of God's truth, had forfeited his throne and should be put to death. The government troops, acting under powers granted to them by the Scottish Parliament, stopped people at random in the rebellious districts, ordered them to say 'God save the King', and immediately shot dead all who refused. The horrors of 'the Killing Time' and of the dungeons of Dunnottar Castle in Kincardineshire, where the Covenanter rebels were confined, has remained to this day a bitter memory for the people of Scotland.

In England, where Parliament impeached Clarendon but continued to support the same policy, Charles was irked by their insistence on religious persecution, by their quarrelling, and by their power to limit his authority. He envied the position of Louis XIV who, after surviving a civil war during his childhood, had established an absolute autocracy in France and was the most powerful sovereign in Europe. Charles told the French ambassador that he was sure that only a Catholic king could be a true autocratic king. By 1669 he was discussing with his most intimate advisers the possibility of his becoming a Catholic and making England a Catholic state, with toleration being granted to all law-abiding Protestant sects. But he kept his intentions a strict secret and took no premature step.

After several months of very secret negotiations through unofficial envoys, Charles's sister Henrietta Maria came to England in May 1670 and stayed for a month with Charles in Dover Castle. They negotiated the secret Treaty of Dover, whereby Charles agreed to make war against the Dutch as Louis XIV's ally and as soon as possible to declare himself a Catholic. Louis agreed to pay him £225,000 a year so that he need not rely on Parliament to authorise taxation, and to send 6,000 French troops to suppress any opposition which might arise in England when Charles announced his conversion. Only the clauses of the treaty which provided for the military alliance against Holland were made public. The alliance was not popular in England; but though the English were suspicious of the French and of Louis XIV, they had no objection to another war of revenge against their old enemies and commercial rivals, the Dutch.

The war broke out in 1672. The French armies overran Holland; but the Dutch made a determined resistance under their twenty-two-year-old stadholder, Prince William of Orange. In the same year, Charles tested the reaction of his subjects to his plans, and made a bid to gain the sympathy of the Nonconformists, by issuing, under his royal prerogative, a Declaration of Indulgence, remitting the penalties which had been imposed on Nonconformists who practised their religion, and granting them toleration for the future. The Anglican Parliament challenged the legality of the king's 'dispensing power', and denied that he might lawfully dispense any section of his subjects from the need to comply with the law. He was forced by Parliamentary pressure to withdraw the Declaration of Indulgence and allow the persecution of Nonconformists to continue.

In 1673 Parliament passed the Test Act, which required every army officer, every civil servant, every JP, and anyone in any position of authority in national or local government or in the universities, to take an oath declaring that he did not believe in transubstantiation. This was an oath which no Catholic could take. Charles's brother James, the duke of York, openly declared himself a Catholic, and as he refused to take the oath against transubstantiation, he was forced to resign his office of Lord High Admiral, though he had distinguished himself in several sea-battles against the Dutch. James was an obstinate and opinionated man whose chief disadvantage, as a politician, was a scrupulous honesty which prevented him from resorting to any subterfuge or manoeuvre.

The fear of popery, of Louis XIV, and of Charles II's intentions caused a number of Opposition politicians to form a new political party. They soon became known as 'the Whigs', whereas the king's supporters were called 'the Tories'. Both names originated as terms of abuse invented by their opponents. The word 'Whig' probably derives from 'whiggamore', a cattle-drover, and was used contemptuously by the king's men to describe first the Scottish Covenanters and then the Protestant Opposition in England. A 'tory' was an Irish robber lurking in the bogs, and the Whigs called their opponents 'Tories' to suggest that they were pro-Irish Catholic bandits.

The Whigs were led by Anthony Ashley Cooper. He was a country gentleman from Wiltshire who had fought in the Civil War first for the king and afterwards for Parliament. Under the Commonwealth he had at first supported Cromwell, but had then turned against him, and had actively worked for the Restoration. Charles II created him earl of Shaftesbury and appointed him Lord Chancellor; he was the last man who was not a lawyer to hold the office. He was as cynical and lascivious as all the other courtiers; but despite his frequent shifts of political allegiance he was undoubtedly a sincere opponent of popery and of royal absolutism. When he realised that Charles was planning to become a Catholic autocrat he resigned from the government and organised the Whigs as a very effective political force. He gained the enthusiastic support of the merchants of the City of London and of the apprentices and the people.

The opposition from Shaftesbury made Charles more dependent on subsidies from Louis XIV, and Louis continued to pay them regularly. Charles occasionally tried to appease the English Protestants, and to exercise a little gentle blackmail on Louis, by a show of friendship with the Dutch, and in 1677 arranged the marriage of Mary, the eldest daughter of James, duke of York, to William of Orange; but the secret understanding with France was not weakened.

The impending conflict came to a head in 1678 when an unscrupulous adventurer, Titus Oates, informed the Privy Council that he had been a trainee at the Jesuit college at St Omer (which the French had just captured from Spain), but had repented, and felt obliged to disclose that the Jesuits, and the Catholics generally, were planning to assassinate King Charles and establish papal domination in England. As Charles and the Council were sceptical about the truth of his statement, he visited a Middlesex JP, Sir Edmund Berry Godfrey, and swore a deposition about the popish plot. A few weeks later, Godfrey was found murdered in a ditch on Primrose Hill; he had been strangled, then stabbed after death with his own sword. None of his money or valuables had been taken. The public was convinced that he had been murdered by the Jesuits, though some believed that Oates had arranged the murder in order to convince the people that there really was a popish plot.

It caused an outburst of anti-Catholic hysteria in London. Three Catholics were tried and convicted of the murder on the evidence of a man who in later years admitted that he had committed perjury; and several other Catholics were executed for high treason on Oates's evidence. Shaftesbury and the Whigs took the opportunity to demand that Parliament pass an Act excluding the Catholic duke of York from the throne and enacting that Charles should be succeeded as king by James, duke of Monmouth, his illegitimate son by an aristocratic Welsh girl, Lucy Walter, who had been his mistress when he was a refugee in Holland at the age of nineteen in 1649. The Whigs claimed to have found evidence that Charles had secretly married Lucy Walter before Monmouth was born; but Charles denied this, and firmly refused to agree to the exclusion of his brother James from the throne. In order to get James away from London and from the political limelight, he sent him to govern Scotland, where James intensified the persecution of the Covenanters; and when the Whigs in Parliament pressed on with the Exclusion Bill, Charles dissolved Parliament, relying on the money which he received from Louix XIV to enable him to dispense with taxation.

It was during the struggle with the king over the Exclusion Bill that the Whig Parliament passed the Habeas Corpus Act, which has been called one of the four pillars of the British Constitution – the other three being Magna Carta, the Petition of Right of 1628, and the Bill of Rights of 1689. The Act, which was only passed because the votes were wrongly counted in the House of Lords division lobbies, merely gave statutory recognition to, and slightly strengthened, the old procedure of the common law courts by which, if anyone is held in illegal imprisonment, his friends can immediately secure his release by obtaining a writ of habeas corpus from the common law judges. This procedure, while extremely effective for the purpose for which it is intended, cannot help anyone held in *lawful* imprisonment, which includes persons detained without trial or justification under the provisions of an Act of Parliament; and it has hardly ever been of use to those suffering arbitrary arrest at the hands of the government. Neither the Whigs in 1682, the Radicals in 1817, the Irish Nationalists in 1881, the British Fascists in 1940, nor the detainees in Northern Ireland in 1971, have been able to invoke it.

Charles II allowed the fury aroused by the Popish Plot to run its course, and then struck when the time was ripe. In reply to the Whig clamour for a new Parliament, he issued writs for another general election, at which the Whigs again obtained a majority; but he summoned the new Parliament to meet in March 1681 not at Westminster, but at Oxford, where it would be free from the influence of the London apprentices and demonstrators. He tricked Shaftesbury into believing that he was about to agree to the Exclusion Bill, while he arranged for a new subsidy from Louis XIV and stationed troops at strategic points in the south of England. He then summoned the members of the House of Commons to come to the House of Lords, which sat in Christ Church College, to hear a message from the throne. They came happily, expecting to hear him announce his capitulation over the Exclusion Bill; instead, he dissolved Parliament, and soon afterwards arrested Shaftesbury and other leaders of the Opposition.

It was impossible to get a London jury to convict Shaftesbury of sedition. He was released on bail, went into hiding in London, and escaped to Holland before he could be re-arrested. He died a few weeks after reaching Amsterdam. Some of the Whig leaders then planned an insurrection in the spring of 1683 which was to begin with the assassination of the king and the duke of York at Rye House in Hertfordshire on their return journey to London from the races at Newmarket. A fire in the stables at Newmarket caused the race-meeting to be cut short, and Charles and James returned to London some days before the plotters expected. The plot was discovered, and arrests, trials and executions followed. Among the victims were Lord William Russell, who had been a party to the assassination plot, and the author and politician, Algernon Sidney. The only evidence against Sidney was the draft of an essay on the advantages of a republic over a monarchy which had been found in his study, but which he had never published. The Lord Chief Justice, Sir George Jeffreys, ruled that this was sufficient to convict him of high treason, and he was beheaded.

Charles then proceeded to revoke the charters of the City of London and other boroughs in which Whig influence was strong. He abolished their right to elect their mayors and aldermen, and appointed the mayor and borough officials by royal decree. He also abolished their right to send MPs to the House of Commons. For the last four years of his reign, Charles II ruled as an absolute monarch without summoning another Parliament, and worked closely with the duke of York. A flood of Tory books and pamphlets, as well as the poems of John Dryden and the plays of Thomas Otway, advocated the doctrines of the divine right of kings and the duty of passive obedience, and vilified and ridiculed Shaftesbury and the Whig leaders. All Whig and Opposition writings were banned under a rigid censorship. The methods of fifty years before – the Star Chamber, torture, and ear-croppings – had become obsolete; Charles II and his judges operated by coercing juries, by sentences of imprisonment and floggings, and above all by sentencing the defendants to enormous fines which it was quite impossible for them to pay, and then ordering them to be detained in prison until the fine was paid. This meant that they would never be released, especially as they had to pay the expenses of their maintenance in prison, in the usual way, in addition to the fine.

Charles II died at Whitehall at the age of fifty-four in February 1685. A Catholic priest, Father Huddleston, who had helped him to escape after Worcester, was smuggled into the palace and received the dying king into the Roman Catholic Church. The duke of York succeeded to the throne as King James II of England and VII of Scotland. Within a few months, the earl of Argyll sailed from Holland to western Scotland and launched an insurrection; but he was defeated, captured and executed. In June, the duke of Monmouth landed at Lyme Regis and was proclaimed king at Taunton. He was joined by many of the Protestant dissenters in the south-west, including a number of old Roundhead soldiers; but James sent an army against him under the command of an incompetent French-born courtier, Louis Duras, earl of Feversham, with Lord Churchill, the future duke of Marlborough as second-in-command. The rebels were defeated in the swamps of Sedgmoor in Somerset. In the 296 years which have elapsed since Sedgmoor, no battle has been fought on English soil.

Monmouth was found hiding in a cornfield, and was taken to London. King James granted him an interview, but only to inform him, as he lay grovelling on the ground pleading for mercy, that he must die under the Act of Attainder which Parliament had passed when they heard of his landing. James's conduct aroused criticism, for it was the invariable practice of a king, when petitioned to show mercy, only to grant the petitioner an audience if he had decided to pardon him.

James sent the Lord Chief Justice, Lord Jeffreys, to try the rebels who had followed Monmouth. This brilliant lawyer, who had been appointed Chief Justice of the King's Bench at the age of thirty-five and had shown his mettle by his handling of the trials of the Rye House plotters, was determined to obtain convictions, even from juries who sympathised with the defendants – if necessary, by reminding the jurors that they could be punished for giving a 'perverse' verdict. He was also determined to use his position on the bench to make Royalist and Tory propaganda, and to denounce the villainy of regicides and Presbyterians. He reviled the prisoners, and sentenced many of them to death, and others to be flogged or sent as slaves to Barbados. He was bitterly hated by his victims and their supporters; but he would not be remembered today as the infamous 'Judge Jeffreys' if his enemies had not triumphed three years later.

The Anglican Tories accepted, with misgivings, a Catholic king as the sovereign of a Protestant realm and Supreme Governor of the Church of England. They supported him against Argyll and Monmouth because of their belief in the duty of passive obedience and their hatred of rebellion, and because they found the Non-conformist yeomen and artisans who formed the bulk of Monmouth's army too reminiscent of Cromwell's Independents. But the merchants and gentlemen mistrusted the Catholics, the French, and absolute monarchy. In October 1685 Louis XIV revoked the Edict of Nantes, which for eighty-seven years had ensured religious toleration for the Protestants in certain parts of France, and began a savage persecution. Many Protestants escaped abroad, risking severe punishment if caught escaping, and several thousands came to England as refugees. Louis's action aroused great indignation in England, and the English Protestants contributed to the relief of the refugees. King James permitted the subscriptions, and himself gave £500; but this did not appease the popular anger against his co-religionists.

Two years later, he issued a Declaration of Indulgence, in which he suspended the operation of the penal laws against Catholics and Protestant Nonconformists. He released the Nonconformist leaders from prison, and invited them to Whitehall, making determined efforts to win their support against their persecutors of the Church of England. But most of them did not trust him, and were more willing to listen to the appeals from the Anglican Whigs for an alliance against popery and absolute monarchy. James appointed Catholic officers to high command in the army, and a Jesuit priest to his Privy Council, granting all of them a dispensation, under his royal prerogative, from the obligation to take the oath against transubstantiation prescribed by the Test Act. He also appointed Catholic noblemen as his leading counsellors in Scotland. They intensified the campaign against the rebellious Covenanters, for the Declaration of Indulgence, though applying to the Scottish Presbyterians, did not extend to the prayer-meetings in the hills.

In May 1688 James re-issued the Declaration of Indulgence, and ordered the Church of England clergy to read it out to their congregations from the pulpits. Seven of the bishops, led by the archbishop of Canterbury and the bishop of London, asked for an audience with James, and presented him with a petition requesting him to withdraw his order for the reading of the Declaration of Indulgence in the churches. He told them that their petition was seditious; and the fact that it had been printed and distributed in London before it was presented to him seems to justify his suspicion that it was part of a co-ordinated Whig agitation, though nearly all the seven bishops were Tories and zealous monarchists. Soon afterwards he ordered that the seven bishops be arrested and sent to the Tower, and prosecuted for sedition, though he apparently intended to pardon them after their conviction.

Only four of the hundred London vicars obeyed the order to read the Declaration of Indulgence in their churches; and in the country it was read in less than five per cent of the churches.

The arrest and prosecution of the seven bishops alarmed both the Tories and the Whigs. They were even more worried when, on

10 June, James's queen, Mary of Modena, gave birth to a son. James had had two daughters by his first marriage to Clarendon's daughter, Anne Hyde, before he became a Catholic; the eldest, Mary, had married William of Orange, and the youngest, Anne, Prince George of Denmark. Both the princesses and their husbands were Protestants. Mary of Modena's baby son, who would displace his half-sisters in the line of succession to the throne, would certainly be brought up a Catholic by his Catholic father and mother. The Protestants afterwards believed the story that the baby was a changeling who had been smuggled into the palace at Whitehall by the Jesuits in a warming pan; but this was certainly untrue. The birth of the Catholic heir convinced the Whigs that they must at once get rid of James.

The seven bishops were tried at Westminster Hall. As they were brought there from the Tower by barge, the river was lined with thousands of people cheering them, and crying 'God bless your lordships!' On 30 June they were found Not Guilty by the Middlesex jury. James was reviewing his troops on Hounslow Heath. As he approached the camp, he heard the soldiers cheering. He was told that they were cheering, not his arrival, but the news which had just been received that the bishops had been acquitted.

On the same day, seven prominent personages, including the bishop of London and Charles II's former Tory minister, Danby, signed a secret letter to William of Orange, inviting him to invade England in order to protect the freedom of the people. His mother was the daughter of Charles I, and his wife was James II's daughter. He and she could therefore claim to be the heirs to the throne if James II and his baby son were set aside as Catholics.

William of Orange was greatly tempted by this implied offer of the crown of England, chiefly because of the additional strength which it would give to Holland and the Protestant cause in the struggle against Louis XIV's domination of Western Europe; but he was a cautious man by temperament, and feared that if he invaded England, Louis would at once attack Holland. French agents discovered about the approach that the English Whigs had made to William; and Louis warned James. Although he was engaged in a war against Austria and the German states, he stationed an army corps on the Dutch frontier to deter William. On 2 September the French ambassador at the Hague publicly informed the Dutch Parliament that France would declare war if William invaded England.

But James now made a tremendous blunder, either from a wish to conciliate his people, or, more probably, out of pure national pride. He formally repudiated the alliance with France, and stated that he would rely only on his own resources and his subjects' loyalty to repel the threatened invasion. Louis was so angry that he decided to wash his hands of James for the time being. He withdrew his army from the Dutch frontier, and sent it to invade the Rhineland. This was an error of judgment on his part, for the consequences of William's seizure of England were to be disastrous for him, as well as for James.

On 19 October William sailed from the Texel with 600 ships carrying 15,000 soldiers, but was driven back by contrary winds. Neither James nor Louis took advantage of this warning and respite; and on 1 November the 'Protestant wind' changed and blew William down the Channel to Torbay in Devon. He landed on 5 November, and advanced a few miles to Axminster, where he waited, inactive, for four weeks, not venturing to advance until the English rose in his support, and ready to sail back to Holland if they did not. But in the north, Danby rose against James, and seized York for William.

James placed his army under Churchill's command, and marched with it to Salisbury. Here Churchill, who had sensed the mood of the other Tory noblemen, deserted to William, and he and his officers rode through the night to Axminster. James thereupon withdrew his army to Andover, and William began a slow advance towards London. James's daughter and son-in-law, Princess Anne and Prince George of Denmark, were the next to desert him.

James lost his nerve, and decided to escape to France. He slipped out of Whitehall by a secret passage and crossed the Thames by barge from Millbank to Vauxhall. He took with him the Great Seal of England to prevent it from falling into William's hands, and apparently tried to throw it into the river, for it was afterwards found on the bank. He drove in a hackney carriage from Vauxhall to Sheerness, and embarked in a fishing boat in the Isle of Sheppey; but the local population, who thought that he was an escaping Jesuit, manhandled him and brought him back to Faversham. He was rescued by some of his loyal gentlemen, and returned to Whitehall. He was still there when William arrived on 18 December and took up his residence half a mile away in St James's Palace.

William was only too eager that James should escape abroad, as he wished to avoid the embarrassment of holding his father-in-law a prisoner and having to decide what to do with him. He sent a body of men to escort him to the coast, and ordered them to give him every opportunity to escape. On 23 December James sailed for France, where he was welcomed by Louis XIV, who placed the Palace of Saint-Germain-en-Laye at his disposal, and continued to recognise him as king of England.

Jeffreys tried to escape disguised as a seaman. As he waited for a ship in an inn at Wapping, he was recognised by a man whom he had once sentenced to be flogged. The man told the neighbours and the officers of the watch. The officers arrived in time to prevent Jeffreys from being lynched by the people, and took him as a prisoner to the Tower, where he died five months later of the stone in the bladder from which he had long suffered.

- Nearly the whole nation had united behind William, and this caused him some political embarrassments. Old Roundheads, Republicans, regicides and Levellers emerged from years of exile or retirement to offer their services to the hero who had accomplished a second revolution against the hated Stuart monarchy and had undone the Restoration of 1660; but he was also supported by zealous High Church Tories who still worshipped the memory of King Charles the Martyr, and had turned against James II only because he was a Catholic and had proclaimed religious toleration. William managed to retain the goodwill of all of them, chiefly by threatening to go home to Holland if they failed to sink their differences and reach a working compromise.

In January 1689 a special Convention Parliament met and discussed how to solve the problem of the succession and government. The Whigs adopted a revolutionary attitude, proclaiming that James had forfeited his throne because he was a papist and had broken his contract with his people; the Tories tried to maintain that there had been no break with constitutional legality. They argued that James II's action in throwing the Great Seal into the Thames and escaping to France must be interpreted as a declaration of abdication on his part; and as the so-called prince of Wales was not James's son but a baby who had been smuggled into the palace in a warming pan, the vacant throne passed to the next in line, his daughter Mary. But as William insisted that he as well as Mary should be given the crown, they were proclaimed as joint sovereigns, King William III and Queen Mary II; and when Mary died in 1694, William continued to reign as sole king.

The Whig position, that James had forfeited the crown for breach of contract, was officially adopted; but in later times the established aristocracy, the gentry and the constitutional lawyers all preferred to forget this aspect, and to stress the legal continuity of the regime established in 1689. Even in the twentieth century historians and constitutionalists have tended to obscure the fact that the reigning dynasty, the Parliamentary system, and the rule of law of modern Britain are all based on an act of revolutionary illegality.

The Convention of 1689 also passed the Bill of Rights, which was re-enacted later in the year by the first Parliament of the new reign. It enacted that the king could not levy taxes or maintain an army without the consent of Parliament, and that no proceedings could be taken against any MP for any action or speech in Parliament. It proclaimed that the king's dispensing power, by which he had claimed to be able to dispense some of his subjects from the penal laws and the Test Act, was illegal 'as it hath been assumed and exercised of late'. Excessive fines and other 'cruel and unjust punishments' were prohibited. A proposal that judges should be irremovable by the king, unless he had been requested to remove them by resolutions passed in both Houses of Parliament, was not adopted in 1689, but was enacted twelve years later in the Act of Settlement.

Some of the Tories were worried about the legality of the deposition of James II, and a majority of the bishops, including five of the seven Bishops whom James had prosecuted in 1688, refused to take the oath of allegiance to William and Mary; but there was no armed resistance to the new king and queen in England. In Scotland, John Graham of Claverhouse, Viscount Dundee, who had been one of the most active officers of Charles II and James II in the suppression of the Covenanters, raised a force of Highland clansmen to fight for James. He defeated William's troops at Killiecrankie in Perthshire, but was killed at the moment of victory, and his army disintegrated. There was no further organised opposition in Scotland.

In August 1691 the government offered a pardon to all James's supporters who took the oath of allegiance to William and Mary before 1 January 1692. All the Highland clans did so except the Macdonalds of Glencoe, whose chief decided, as a gesture of protest, to wait until the last day before taking the oath. On 31 December he arrived at Fort William to take the oath, but had come to the wrong address, and was held up by the snow in his attempt to reach Inverary, where the oath was administered. He therefore did not take the oath until 6 January. Sir John Dalrymple, Master of Stair, the Secretary of State for Scotland, welcomed the excuse to extirpate the troublesome Macdonald clan, and obtained King William's authority to do so. He sent the earl of Argyll's Campbell clansmen, who had always hated the Macdonalds, to Glencoe. After enjoying the Macdonald's hospitality for a fortnight, the Campbells murdered their hosts on the night of 12 February 1692, though some of the Macdonalds escaped to die in the snow on the neighbouring hills. It was a sign of the times that the massacre caused so much indignation in England and Scotland that Dalrymple was forced to resign and withdraw from public life for some years. The extermination of a Highland clan would have aroused little comment fifty years earlier.

In the spring of 1689 James II landed in Ireland with French troops. The Irish Catholics rose in his support, and he occupied Dublin and nearly all the country. He summoned an Irish Parliament which granted religious toleration to both Catholics and Protestants and restored to the native Irish the lands which had been confiscated and appropriated by the English settlers in Cromwell's time. Only the town of Londonderry held out for William. The people of the town were the descendants of the Scottish Presbyterians who had settled in Ulster eighty years before.

James besieged Londonderry. An aged Presbyterian minister, George Walker, inspired the citizens to resist. When the governor wished to surrender, he was placed under arrest, and the people, with the apprentices in the forefront, prepared to fight to the end. After a four-months' siege, the navy which William had belatedly sent to relieve the town managed to break through the boom that the besiegers had constructed, and to bring supplies to the starving inhabitants. This forced James to raise the siege.

In the following year, William himself arrived in Ireland with his army, and on 1 July 1690 defeated James and his French and Irish forces in a battle on the River Boyne, near Drogheda, in which James's generalship was even more faulty than William's. James promptly returned to France, and though the war continued for another fifteen months, it ended with a French evacuation and an Irish capitulation. The defeated Irish Catholics were treated much worse than those in England. Although the surrender terms provided for religious toleration, the English settlers and Parliament insisted on overruling them. All forms of Catholic worship were proscribed; Catholics were forbidden to hold any public offices, or to be schoolmasters, to send their children to be educated abroad, or to own horses valued over £5. A reward of £5 was paid by the government to any English settler who killed an Irish 'Tory'. There was wholesale expropriation of the land that still remained in the ownership of Irish landowners; and the flourishing Irish wool industry was deliberately destroyed by discriminatory tariffs and taxation.

The war with France continued for eight years. Louis made no further attempt to invade English territory, but waged the war against William and his Dutch and English troops in the Netherlands. The French usually had the best of the fighting; but though William was not a great general, he was dogged in defence and held his own. The size of the armies employed and the increased fire-power of the artillery and small-arms gave a foretaste of the sufferings which modern war would bring; at the Battle of Landen (Neerwinden) in 1693, where the French won a decisive victory, the two sides together lost 20,000 men – the highest casualties that had ever been suffered in a battle. The war ended in a draw. By the Treaty of Ryswick of 1697 both parties agreed to restore all the towns and territory which they had captured since the outbreak of hostilities; but Louis XIV agreed to recognise William as king of England. This was a moral defeat for Louis, who had won all his previous wars.

In England, William tried to avoid antagonising the Tories, but he relied chiefly on Whig support. While the Church of England continued to be the official religion, toleration was granted to all Protestant sects; only the Catholics and the Unitarians were exempted from it, for all office-holders were required to swear that they believed in the Trinity, but did not believe in transubstantiation. In Scotland, the Presbyterian Church was re-established without bishops, and the surviving Covenanters were allowed to live in peace; but the Scottish Church never again tried to control the state or to act as a revolutionary force. A small number of Tory zealots and a few scheming politicians in England entered into secret contact with James II at Saint-Germain; but only a handful of 'Jacobites' were executed for high treason by William's government.

As William and Mary had no children, Parliament had to provide for the succession at William's death, and in 1701 passed the Act of Settlement. It provided that if William died childless, he was to be succeeded by James II's daughter Anne, who was living at William's court. If she died without heirs – she had had ten miscarriages, and none of her five children had survived – the crown was to pass to the Electress Sophia of Hanover and 'the heirs of her body, being Protestant'. The Electress Sophia was the twelfth of the thirteen children of Elizabeth, queen of Bohemia, the daughter of James I; but once again the hereditary principle was violated, as the children of Sophia's elder brothers and sisters were bypassed. The Act of Settlement provided that if any British sovereign should either become or marry a Catholic, he should thereupon forfeit the crown in favour of the next heir in line from the Electress Sophia; and it enacted that any person who questions the right of Parliament to alter the succession to the crown shall be guilty of high treason. The Act is still in force (as amended by His Majesty's Declaration of Abdication Act of 1936) and is the sole title of Queen Elizabeth II to the crown of England.

In September 1701 James II died at Saint-Germain. On his deathbed he was visited by Louis XIV, who promised him that he would recognise his thirteen-year-old son, James, as king of England. In the eyes of his Jacobite supporters, the boy became King James III of England and VIII of Scotland, and reigned for sixty-five years until his death in 1766; for the government and people of England, he was 'the Old Pretender'.

Louis's recognition of the Old Pretender was a signal for the renewal of the war with England. Austria had felt threatened by the decision of the king of Spain to appoint Louis's grandson as his heir, and the War of the Spanish Succession began, with England,

Austria, Holland, Denmark and the North German states fighting as allies against France, Spain and Bavaria.

In February 1702 William III's horse stumbled over a molehill when he was riding in the park at Hampton Court. The king, who was already suffering from pleurisy, was thrown, and died a fortnight later from his illness and his injuries. The Jacobites celebrated by drinking the health of 'the little gentleman in black velvet' (the mole who had built the molehill).

Anne succeeded William as queen, and Churchill, now duke of Marlborough, replaced the dead king as commander-in-chief. Marlborough commanded the English armies in the field; and his wife Sarah, who was a close personal friend of the queen, virtually controlled affairs at home. He operated against the French troops in the Netherlands while his ally, the Austrian commander Prince Eugène of Savoy, fought them in northern Italy.

In the summer of 1704 Louis XIV sent an army under Marshal Tallard to Bavaria. Marlborough made an unexpected march from the Netherlands up the Rhine, and after linking up with Prince Eugène, won an overwhelming victory over the French at Blenheim, taking Tallard prisoner. It was the first occasion, since Louis had come to the throne as a child sixty-one years before, that the French armies had been decisively beaten on a battle-field. Two years later, Marlborough defeated the French at Ramillies in the Netherlands, and in 1708, together with Eugène, won another great victory at Oudenarde. Louis then tried to open peace negotiations; but the Allies rejected his overtures, and Marlborough and Eugène invaded north-eastern France.

In September 1709 they fought a very bloody battle at Malplaquet. The casualties amounted to 32,000 on both sides, which broke the record established at Landen of being the highest ever known in a battle. Eugène and Marlborough were justified in claiming the victory; but they lost nearly twice as many men as the French – a quarter of their whole force – and this prevented them from advancing any further. At Malplaquet, as at Blenheim and Oudenarde, the two Allied generals worked together in a perfect collaboration, though neither of them had any authority over the other.

Shortly before Malplaquet, the duchess of Marlborough quarrelled with Queen Anne and was replaced as the queen's

211

favourite by her Tory rival, Mrs Abigail Masham. This brought the Tories to power in England for the first time since 1688. They carried on with the war, but obstructed Marlborough's campaigns, and worked behind the backs of their Austrian ally for a separate peace with France. Another brilliant campaign by Marlborough in the Netherlands in 1711, when he outmanoeuvred the French at the 'Non plus ultra' lines, led to no result; and by the Treaty of Utrecht, which ended the war in 1713, Louis XIV obtained better terms than he could have hoped for four years earlier. But his prestige had suffered greatly. Under the peace treaty, England gained Gibraltar, and Louis XIV withdrew his recognition of the Old Pretender and recognised Anne as queen of England.

England's gains in the War of the Spanish Succession were moral rather than material. All Europe knew that her armies had beaten and humbled the most powerful despot in Europe; and future generations of Englishmen, like the subjects of Queen Anne, have regarded Marlborough's victories as the foundation of English supremacy. For the French, the *grand siècle* had ended; for the English, the eighteenth century, the century of prosperity and imperial conquest, had begun.

CHAPTER 12

THE
EIGHTEENTH
CENTURY
(1714–83)

The great struggles and civil wars of the sixteenth and seventeenth centuries had been fought chiefly on religious issues, but had resulted in profound political and social changes. England in 1702 was a very different place from England in 1529. The monasteries, the ecclesiastical heresy tribunals, and the burnings at the stake had gone; the Star Chamber, interrogation under torture, the ear-croppings, the proclamations and injunctions imposing new religious beliefs, the constant meddling of the Council, the sheriffs, and the JPs in the daily lives of the people, had come and gone. The struggle against Louis XIV, which had begun as a fight against Catholic despotism, had ended as an almost exclusively national war. Drake's seamen had fought above all for the Protestant religion; Marlborough's soldiers fought for England.

The eighteenth century, more than any other, is today an object of romantic and nostalgic fascination to the English middle classes. It was certainly a golden age for the nobility. Hitherto, security had not been one of the privileges of the aristocracy. In every generation during the previous four hundred years at least one nobleman had been executed as a traitor, and others had been imprisoned for sedition. By 1714 this risk had almost disappeared, though there was still the possibility of a return of the Stuart kings and of Jacobite upheavals, and it was not until 1747 that the last nobleman, Lord Lovat, died on the scaffold.

Some, though not all, of the aristocracy in the eighteenth century were very rich. Their income came largely from the rents paid for their land, which was still mainly agricultural, but also included the growing towns, and coal mines. They also held shares in new profitable ventures, such as banking, insurance, and overseas development companies dealing with speculative enterprises in America and India. Some of the wealthiest noblemen, like the duke of Newcastle, had an income of over £100,000 a year. They paid less than 3p in the £ in combined taxes and rates; and their agricultural labourers earned about £15 a year.

They lived in very large houses surrounded by many acres of gardens, parks and fields. These houses were often on the same sites as the small turreted fortresses and manor houses where their ancestors had lived; but they had been enlarged into baroque mansions under Charles II, Queen Anne, or the early Hanoverian kings. Foreign visitors were astounded that anyone but a king could live in such impressive palaces.

They controlled Parliament. They held a clear majority in the House of Lords, for the creation of many new peerages after 1660 had enabled them to outnumber the bishops, and since the reign of Henry VIII no abbots sat there. They also controlled the House of Commons. One-fifth of the members of the House of Commons were the sons or brothers of peers, and most of the rural constituencies were 'pocket boroughs' where the influence of some nobleman, as the landlord or patron of the local tenants and tradesmen, ensured that the voters, who had to declare how they were voting to the returning officer at the polling stations in the presence of the nobleman's representatives, could be relied on to vote for his nominees. The young William Ewart Gladstone, standing in 1832 as the duke of Newcastle's candidate for Parliament in the duke's pocket borough at Newark, stated in his address to the electors:

> Why do you return me to Parliament? Not because I am the Duke of Newcastle's man, simply; but because, coinciding with the Duke in political sentiment, you likewise admit that

one possessing so large a property here, and faithfully discharging the duties which the possession of that property entails, ought in the natural course of things to exercise a certain influence. You return me to Parliament, not merely because I am the Duke of Newcastle's man; but because both the man whom the Duke has sent, and the Duke himself, are your men.

The gentry, too, felt a new sense of security. In earlier times, though they had been less at risk than the nobility, they were always liable to be ruined through their connection with a nobleman who had been executed or arrested, and, unlike the privileged nobleman, to be examined under torture and put to death, not by the axe, but by being hanged, drawn and quartered. By the eighteenth century their status, in relation to the nobility, had improved. Previously the class barriers between them had been clearly marked. The Sumptuary Laws prohibited gentlemen from wearing the colours, and their wives the ornaments, of the lords and ladies of the nobility; and at official banquets they were not served with the delicacies reserved for noblemen. Noble ladies had sometimes married their stewards or other gentlemen of their households, but it had always caused comment. By the eighteenth century, the gentlemen considered themselves to be almost, if not quite, the social equals of the noblemen. They often went to the same schools and university colleges, though there the noblemen still had a few special privileges. The nobleman was entitled to be awarded a university degree without passing an examination, which a commoner had to take; and at Eton and Harrow a peer's son was addressed as 'Mr', instead of only by his surname – a practice which continued till the twentieth century.

The gentry and the merchants, like the nobility, acclaimed the 'Glorious Revolution' of 1688, which they praised as a bloodless revolution, conveniently forgetting the events in Scotland and Ireland. They regarded Oliver Cromwell as a wicked usurper and regicide, but William III as the liberator. The Glorious Revolution had brought, not a republic, 'the rule of the Major-Generals', and levelling doctrines, but the 'Protestant Succession', the sovereignty of Parliament, and the 'rule of law'. This became the post-revolutionary ideal. The men of the Middle Ages had idealised the vow – the vows of celibacy of priests, monks and nuns; the oath of allegiance of the knight to his lord; and the vow of the Crusader to go to the Holy Land. The men of the sixteenth and seventeenth centuries had idealised the duty of obedience to their prince and the divine right of kings, or the Word of God as revealed in scripture. The men of the eighteenth century and their successors idealised the rule of law.

In a literal sense, there was nothing new about the rule of law. The rule of law had applied in the days when ecclesiastical courts condemned heretics, and the sheriffs burned them under the legal provisions of the Act for the Burning of Heretics. It had applied when noblemen were beheaded without trial under the provisions of an Act of Attainder. But when the men of the eighteenth century spoke of the rule of law, they meant the rule of laws made by a Parliament of gentlemen and merchants controlled by the nobility and free from royal compulsion, and interpreted and enforced by the common law courts with judges who had the same political, economic and social outlook as the nobles and gentlemen, and with juries who, because of the necessary property qualification for jurymen, also shared this outlook.

The judges were hardly ever noblemen, but came from the ranks of the gentry, or more often were the sons of merchants, vicars, solicitors, or other middle-class professional men. They had all been barristers of one of the four Inns of Court. Unlike in other countries, in England a judge was always promoted from the ranks of the barristers, and had therefore always begun his career as an advocate for defendants and private persons as well as for the crown, before he was promoted to the judicial bench. Since the Act of Settlement of 1701, he could no longer be removed by the king, except by resolution of both Houses of Parliament. He was not afraid to give judgments against the Crown, and could be relied upon to protect the liberty and the property of the nobility, the gentry, and the merchants – and even, if the occasion ever arose, of the artisans and husbandmen – against the king's officers. He could also be relied upon to deal severely with poachers, highwaymen and pickpockets.

The judges and the political commentators prided themselves that in England the king was under the law and that all men were equal before the law. Nobles and gentlemen had their privileges, but preferential treatment in the courts was not one of them. To

216

foreigners living under autocratic monarchs, the English legal system seemed a model of fairness and justice. Voltaire, who in France had had no remedy when he was assaulted by a nobleman's servants and imprisoned in the Bastille without trial because he had insulted the nobleman, was deeply impressed, when he came to England, to find himself in a country where such things could not occur. Englishmen, comparing their courts of law, not with those of foreign despots, but with the English theoretical ideal, were sometimes less enthusiastic. Fielding, who was a JP in Westminster as well as a novelist, portrayed in his *Joseph Andrews* the lawyer who assures Lady Booby that 'the laws of the land are not so vulgar to permit a mean fellow to contend with one of your ladyship's fortune. We have one sure card, which is to carry him before Justice Frolic, who upon hearing your ladyship's name will commit him without any further question'. As late as 1803 the Attorney-General, Perceval, who was the son of a peer, appearing for the prosecution at Cobbett's trial for sedition, reminded the jury that Cobbett's father had been a man from the lowest social class and used this as a reason why they should be inclined to mistrust the sincerity of Cobbett's motives.

If the rights of private property and the well-established rules of the common law proved inconvenient, they could be swept aside by that other great principle of the Glorious Revolution, the sovereignty of Parliament. The Whigs, in the period after 1688, passed Landlord and Tenant Acts which did not, like the legislation of the twentieth century, grant legal privileges to tenants, but altered the common law in favour of landlords by allowing them to seize goods which were formerly exempt from distress for rent, and to charge double rent if the tenant stayed on after receiving notice to quit. Far-reaching powers of arrest, search, and confiscation of property were given to the Customs and Excise officers in their operations against the smugglers who became an increasing problem for the government in the course of the eighteenth century. These powers are still in force today, and are more extreme and arbitrary than any held by other government officials. They originated, not under Tudor or Stuart despotism, or in the modern socialist state, but in the days of freedom and the rule of law under the Whig administration of Sir Robert Walpole in the early eighteenth century.

Other statutes created more than two hundred new offences punishable by death, most of them connected with robbery, theft or poaching. In many respects, crime was more prevalent in the eighteenth century than it had been for several hundred years. There was a great deal of crime and vice in the slums and inns of London; and drunkenness had increased after the Revolution when imported Dutch gin competed with English ale in popular favour. The roads were infested with highwaymen. In the seventeenth century, new materials had been used for road-building, and travel was now easier than ever before. Before the Civil War, the state of the roads made it almost impossible for horsemen to travel through the mud at a rate of more than thirty or forty miles a day except on two or three roads in the country; by Charles II's reign, riders, and even coaches, often covered a hundred miles a day. But if the roads were better, they were more dangerous. Highwaymen robbed travellers even as close to London as Hampstead Heath. The inadequate local constabulary could not have coped with the criminals, even if all the constables, government officials and JPs had been incorruptible.

Those who were arrested had a good chance of acquittal, for in criminal trials the common law of England strained the law in favour of the defendant, acting on the principle that it was better that ninety-nine guilty men should go free rather than that one innocent man should be punished. If the defendant was convicted, the punishment was very severe, because the judges believed that, as the chances of being caught and convicted were small, the punishments must be the heavier in order to be an effective deterrent. There was also very little chance of a convicted man being pardoned, having his sentence reduced, or being released from imprisonment before he had served his full sentence; for though the king's power of pardon had been preserved after the Revolution of 1688, it was viewed with suspicion as being associated with the illegal dispensing power, and as an arbitrary royal interference with the rule of law. There was no country in the world where a man had a fairer trial than in England, and few in which he was more severely punished if convicted.

When Queen Anne died in 1714, the crown passed without disorder, under the provisions of the Act of Settlement, to the elector of Hanover, Georg Ludwig, the son of the Electress

Sophia, who became King George I. Sophia had died shortly before Queen Anne, and failed by fifty-three days to become queen of England. In the following year the Old Pretender landed in Scotland and started an insurrection, but it was defeated by the government without much difficulty.

The control of the English government over Scotland had been tightened in Anne's reign by the Act of Union of 1707, which abolished the Scottish Parliament. Since 1603, England and Scotland had been two kingdoms, each with a Parliament and government, and ruled by the same king; henceforth they would form one United Kingdom, both sending MPs to the same Parliament at Westminster. From this time onwards, it became increasingly common to refer to the united kingdoms of England and Scotland as 'Great Britain', and to their people as 'the British', though many Englishmen continued to speak of England and the English when they meant the United Kingdom, which for the French and other foreigners was always 'l'*Angleterre*', '*England*' or '*Inghilterra*'.

After the brief Tory interlude during the last five years of Anne's reign, power returned again to the Whigs, who held it uninterruptedly for the next forty-eight years. George I chose Sir Robert Walpole as his chief minister. The traditional story that Walpole was appointed to be the first Prime Minister, and created the Cabinet, because George I could not speak English, is untrue; for George spoke some English and sometimes presided, like earlier kings, at the meetings of his Council. But he spent much time in Hanover, and left Walpole a freer hand than any earlier minister had been allowed. Walpole started the practice of discussing many matters, not at full meetings of the Council, but at a sub-committee, which was known as 'the Cabinet Council'. Soon the Cabinet had replaced the Privy Council as the chief executive and policy-making body in the state. The Privy Council henceforth met only for formal business, though the origin of the Cabinet as a sub-committee of the Council is shown by the fact that still today every Cabinet minister must first be appointed a Privy Councillor.

Walpole was a jovial and very portly gentleman from Norfolk. He was wholly lacking in idealism, and used bribery to buy votes in the House of Commons; but he was sincerely devoted to the Protestant Succession and the achievements of the Glorious

Revolution. He was the typical Whig country gentleman installed in Number 10, Downing Street, which he was the first Prime Minister to use as a London residence. When he received his morning's post-bag, he always opened the letters from his gamekeeper in Norfolk before the state papers. He ate and drank heavily, rode and hunted whenever he could, and, despite his enormous bulk, pursued women undeterred by the rebuffs which he received.

He remained as Prime Minister until George I's death, and continued in office when George II succeeded his father, serving as Prime Minister for nearly twenty-one consecutive years. He was not popular, for the people resented the taxation which he imposed, particularly the excise duties on tobacco, which led to much law-evasion, smuggling and discontent and were the indirect cause of the Porteous riots in Edinburgh in 1736. The men of the 1730s did not appreciate the charm of the eighteenth century; they yearned for 'Good King Charles's golden days', and for the old times 'when mighty roast beef was the Englishman's food' and 'our soldiers were brave and our courtiers were good'.

Walpole's economic and financial policy helped ensure the prosperity of the merchants and the growth of English trade. He wished above all to keep England out of war. He succeeded in accomplishing this during the War of the Polish Succession of 1733–4, when, as he proudly told George II's queen, Caroline: 'Madam, there are 50,000 men slain this year in Europe and not one Englishman.' But this did not altogether please a nation which remembered Marlborough's triumphs and wished again to show its ascendancy. In 1739 Walpole was forced by public opinion to declare war on Spain over disputes about slave-trading rights and smuggling, after an English sea-captain had aroused great indignation by alleging, rightly or wrongly, that his ear had been cut off by a Spanish naval officer eight years before. When Walpole heard the church bells ringing in London to celebrate the declaration of war, he commented that though they were now ringing their bells, they would soon be wringing their hands. The war went badly, and he fell from power in 1742.

The War of Jenkins' Ear developed into the War of the Austrian Succession when Frederick the Great, king of Prussia, invaded Silesia and went to war with the Empress Maria Theresia of

Austria. France supported Prussia, and England supported Austria. In the middle of the war the French, as a diversion, sent the Old Pretender's son, Prince Charles Edward, to start a Jacobite revolt in Scotland. The Young Pretender landed in north-west Scotland with seven men in August 1745, and was immediately joined by most of the Highland clans. Before the end of the year he had captured Edinburgh, defeated an English army at Prestonpans, just south of Edinburgh, and had invaded England, passed through Lancashire, and reached Derby. Here he was persuaded by his commanders, much against his will, to abandon his plan to march on London, and to retreat to Scotland.

It is a matter of speculation as to what would have happened if he had advanced; it is certain that retreat led to disaster. After marching aimlessly around Scotland for five months, he met the government forces which had been sent against him under George II's son, the young duke of Cumberland, on Culloden Moor near Inverness. His Highlanders were routed, hunted down and massacred with great cruelty, at the orders of 'Butcher' Cumberland; but Charles himself escaped after many adventures in the Western Highlands and islands, and was eventually carried in a French ship to France. It was the last Jacobite rising. The Highlands were occupied by English and loyal Lowland Scottish troops; the clan system was destroyed; and in due course the English government successfully harnessed the fierce fighting spirit of the Highlanders by recruiting them into special regiments in the English army.

The War of the Austrian Succession ended in 1748, but, after eight years' peace, was resumed as the Seven Years War in 1756. This time the alliances were reversed, with England allied to Prussia, and France to Austria. A great war leader appeared in England – William Pitt, the grandson of a merchant who had made a fortune in India by discovering a diamond of great value. Pitt had become an MP and had made his name by bitterly attacking Walpole's peace policy, and the incompetence of the Whig governments that succeeded Walpole. He had held only minor political offices until in 1756, at the age of forty-eight, he was appointed a Secretary of State (in effect, Foreign Secretary). He was soon turned out of office by the Whigs, who hated him; but they were forced by public opinion to reappoint him as Secretary of State in the duke of Newcastle's government in 1757.

He was a brilliant, arrogant, neurotic man, who suffered at times from fits of insanity, but was an imaginative statesman and an efficient administrator as well as a superb orator in the flamboyant style in fashion in the House of Commons in his time. He was fully convinced 'that I can save this nation and that nobody else can'.

He had great confidence in the military genius of Frederick the Great, and decided to finance the king of Prussia to wage war in Europe while England fought the French at sea, in Canada and in India. By the end of the seventeenth century, British merchants of the East India Company had firmly established themselves in Bombay, Madras and Bengal in the territories of the 'Great Mogul', the Emperor Aurangzeb, the Muslim ruler of the subcontinent from Kashmir to Cape Comorin. Aurangzeb's empire disintegrated after his death in 1707 in one of those rapid eclipses which can befall a great imperial power; and within forty years a handful of French and British settlers were contending for the mastery of India. A young man in the service of the East India Company in Madras, Robert Clive, turned out to be a brilliant general, and waged war with great success against the French colonists in India and against the Indian princes whom they enlisted as their allies. In 1757 Clive won his victory at Plassey which ensured that England, not France, should acquire the empire of the Great Mogul.

Two years later, another brilliant young general, James Wolfe, whom Pitt had appointed to command the English forces in Canada at the age of thirty-three, won the Battle of Quebec after he and his men had taken the extraordinary risk of climbing the Heights of Abraham under cover of darkness before defeating the French on the plateau at the summit; but both Wolfe and the French general, Montcalm, were killed in the battle. The English navy also won a great victory in 1759 over the French ships in Quiberon Bay off the west coast of Brittany to complete what David Garrick, in the patriotic song 'Hearts of Oak', called 'this wonderful year'.

George II died in 1760, and was succeeded by his twenty-two-year-old grandson, George III. The young king was determined to rule as well as to reign; within a year he had forced Pitt to resign, and in 1762 he ousted the duke of Newcastle and the Whigs, and appointed his friend Lord Bute as Prime Minister. As in the War of the Spanish Succession, the Whigs were replaced in the hour of victory by an administration who were eager to make peace; but though Pitt, in a great speech in the House of Commons, denounced the terms of the Treaty of Paris, which ended the war in 1763, as being too lenient to France, England gained India and Canada from the Seven Years War.

Within twenty years she had lost the most important of her colonial territories in America. These stretched along the Atlantic coast from Maine to Georgia, but went no further west than the River Ohio, though the undeveloped lands between the Ohio and the Mississippi were ceded by France to Britain by the peace treaty of 1763. The colonies had all developed independently of each other, linked only by their allegiance to the king of England. Virginia was founded by the Lincolnshire adventurer, Captain John Smith, in 1607; Massachusetts was founded thirteen years later by Puritan settlers who sailed in the *Mayflower* from Southampton to a land where they could worship free from the tyranny of the Church of England; Rhode Island was founded by Independents expelled from Massachusetts, who found territory where they could worship free from the tyranny of the Presbyterians of Boston; Pennsylvania was founded by William Penn and his Quakers in 1681. New York and New Jersey were captured from the Dutch, and Delaware from the Swedes, during Charles II's reign. Maryland and North and South Carolina were developed by agents of English noblemen under Charles I and Charles II; and Georgia by Protestant immigrants from the continent of Europe in the middle of the eighteenth century.

As soon as the Seven Years War had been won and all danger from the French removed, the colonists in America began to demand some degree of self-government and to protest against being taxed by the king and the Parliament in London. Following in the English seventeenth-century tradition, they demanded 'No taxation without representation'.

George III was determined to reassert the royal authority in both Britain and America, without breaking the law. As a convinced Protestant, he accepted the principles of the Revolution of 1688 on which his title to the throne depended, and made no attempt to use the methods of Charles II and James II. Instead, he created a party in Parliament. He had the advantage, unlike the Whigs, that as king he was in a position to give them titles and the perquisites of office. His party, which became known as 'the King's Friends', gained a majority in the House of Commons and the House of Lords, and he appointed Lord North as his Prime Minister. Having successfully broken the power of the Whigs in England, he was equally determined to overcome the resistance of the colonists in America.

The Americans, with the support of the Whig Opposition in England, resisted the attempt to tax them under the Stamp Act of 1765, and, by a mass refusal to obey the law, forced the British government to repeal the Act. But new taxation was imposed from Westminster without the colonists' consent; and King George, by a mixture of threats and concessions, succeeded in both angering and encouraging the colonists. There were clashes between the soldiers and the people in America, which led to incidents such as the 'Boston Massacre' of 1770, when the soldiers fired on the crowd, and the Boston Tea Party almost four years later, when demonstrators threw into the sea boxes of tea which were being imported from England. In 1775 the American War of Independence began with a battle between British troops and the colonists at Lexington; and on 4 July 1776 the Americans issued their Declaration of Independence at Philadelphia.

The attempt to crush the colonists by force was condemned by the Whigs at Westminster. Pitt, who had been created earl of Chatham, denounced it in a series of brilliant speeches in the House of Lords. The American resistance aroused great sympathy among opponents of absolutism in France and elsewhere in Europe, and the young Marquis de La Fayette came from France to join the American army. The Americans chose as their commander-in-chief George Washington, a gentleman and landowner of Virginia, who had served as an officer in the British army against the French in America. He was not a brilliant general, but was a patient and dogged commander who was never discouraged by difficulties or setbacks, and in the first three years of the war held his army together in several dangerous retreats and in harsh conditions.

At first the war went badly for the Americans, but in 1777 they defeated the British General Burgoyne in the Saratoga campaign. Next year, France intervened. The American representative in Paris was Benjamin Franklin, a seventy-two-year-old philosopher and scientist who, among his other achievements, had invented the lightning conductor. He worked to persuade King Louis XVI of France to intervene on the American side and take the opportunity of avenging the French defeat in the Seven Years War. Such a step was certain to antagonise the Americans' Whig supporters in England, but Franklin and his colleagues were realists, and thought that French troops would be more useful than English sympathy.

In 1778 France went to war with England. Chatham, who was dying, came to the House of Lords to declare that, despite his former sympathies for the Americans, he now believed that England must wage war with all determination against France and the rebellious colonists. He collapsed in the middle of his speech, and died five weeks later. In 1779 Spain, and in 1780 Holland, also entered the war on the American side.

In 1781 the British commander in Virginia, Lord Cornwallis, was trapped at Yorktown and surrendered with his army to Washington. The war ended two years later with the peace of Versailles. England recognised the independence of the American colonies, which constituted themselves as the United States of America. France regained only Senegal and a few islands and outposts by the peace treaty. Nor did the defeat in America prevent the English people from continuing for another two hundred years to believe that they had never lost a war.

CHAPTER 13

SOCIAL UPHEAVAL
AND
COUNTER-REVOLUTIONARY WAR
(1783–1815)

Although the Whigs blamed George III and his Tory government for the loss of the American colonies, they were unable to put an end to royal and Tory rule. In 1783 the king appointed as his Prime Minister Chatham's younger son, William Pitt, who was only twenty-four years of age. In the House of Commons the Whigs carried a vote of censure on Pitt's government, but Pitt refused to resign. He remained as Prime Minister for three months while he was repeatedly defeated in the House, until the king dissolved Parliament. He had calculated correctly, for at the general election of 1784 Pitt won a majority in the House of Commons, and remained in office as Prime Minister for the next seventeen years.

He soon found himself in the midst of a growing controversy about the slave trade. The first Europeans to traffic in Negro slaves were the Portuguese under Prince Henry the Navigator in the middle of the fifteenth century. Prince Henry's sea-captains bought Negroes from the African chiefs in Guinea and brought them back to Portugal as slaves; this was justified on the grounds that, as slaves in Portugal, they could be taught to be Christians. It was a well-meaning Christian missionary, Las Casas, who introduced Negro slavery to the West Indies and started the slave trade between Africa and America. When Columbus discovered the New World, the Spaniards proceeded to enslave the native population and work them to death, and within twenty-five years the West Indians were in danger of being exterminated. Las Casas had their welfare at heart. He was told that African Negroes were more robust and would be able to stand the strain of heavy work better than his beloved Indians. He persuaded the Emperor Charles V to authorise the importation of Negro slaves from Guinea to the West Indies.

By 1565 Elizabeth I's sea-captains were challenging the Spanish monopoly of the slave trade and were taking blacks from Africa to America. It was the beginning of a period of 250 years during which English merchants and seamen played the leading part in bringing some five million Negroes by force from Africa to the West Indies, the United States and South America. The ships were loaded at Bristol and Liverpool with rum for West Africa, where the cargo was sold and the ships re-loaded with slaves who had been kidnapped from their native villages by African warriors and sold to the English traders. They were carried to the West Indies, where the ships were loaded with sugar for the voyage home to England. The mortality among the slaves on the sea-voyage and in the West Indian ports was very high, averaging 17 per cent, for they were packed in much too tightly in order to enable a large number to be carried and thus increase the merchants' profits; and disease spread in the terrible conditions in the ships' holds.

In the West Indies the slaves were auctioned to the highest bidder. The household slaves were often well-treated, but those set to work in the sugar and cotton plantations were grossly overworked by overseers, and usually died young. They were disciplined by flogging and other cruel punishments, including mutilation, castration and burning alive. Both Louis XIV and the Catholic kings of Spain issued codes to protect the slaves against the worst ill-treatment, but the codes were often evaded in practice by the slave-owners in the French and Spanish colonies. Conditions were worse in the British and Dutch colonies, where the elected colonial legislatures were much less inclined than the autocratic kings in Europe to restrain the brutalities of the planters.

During the second half of the eighteenth century, a small minority of Christian gentlemen in England, who were shocked on religious and moral grounds by the existence of slavery and the slave trade, began an agitation for their abolition. They scored their first success in 1772 when they succeeded in an action on a writ of *habeas corpus* to free a slave who had been brought to London by his master from the West Indies. The Lord Chief Justice, Lord Mansfield, after trying unsuccessfully to avoid having to give a ruling in the case, gave judgment (overruling an earlier legal opinion of 1729) that there could be no slavery in England, and that any slave became free as soon as he set foot on English soil. The Abolitionists followed up this success with a campaign exposing the horrors of conditions in the slave-ships, and in 1789 the House of Commons voted to set up a commission to consider the abolition of the slave trade.

Pitt was sympathetic to abolition, but he was under strong pressure from the supporters of the trade. The merchants of Bristol and Liverpool and the West Indian planters believed that they would be ruined if the slave trade were abolished, and they organised a strenuous opposition, in Parliament and in the press, denouncing the Abolitionists as ignorant do-gooders and, after the outbreak of the war against the French Revolution in 1792, as agents of revolutionary France. They argued that British economic prosperity and international competitiveness depended on the slave trade, and were supported by many sections of the Establishment, especially by the king, the admirals, and the bishops. A bill to abolish the trade was twice defeated in the House of Commons; on two other occasions it passed, but was defeated in the House of Lords.

The slave trade was eventually abolished by Britain in 1807. The British government thereafter took the lead in urging other governments to follow suit, and used the British navy to suppress slave-trading by foreign traders. The Abolitionists meanwhile switched their efforts to the abolition of slavery itself. This proposal too was vigorously opposed; but after a number of unsuccessful slave revolts in the West Indies had been suppressed with great cruelty, and these cruelties had been denounced by the Abolitionists in England, Parliament passed an

Act in 1833 abolishing slavery throughout the British Empire after 1 August 1834, and substituting a milder form of forced labour, known as apprenticeship. The Abolitionists then claimed that the embittered slave-owners were treating their apprentices even worse than when they had been slaves, and apprenticeship was finally abolished, and the Negroes given their freedom, in 1838.

The supporters of slavery often argued that the conditions of the slaves in the West Indies were better than those of the free labourers in the mills and factories of Lancashire. During the last quarter of the eighteenth century, the great transformation in English life known as the Industrial Revolution had got well under way. The invention of steam power had made it possible and profitable to produce goods in factories, employing a substantial number of workmen working together, rather than in cottage industries and in artisan's craftshops where a master craftsman worked alone with his family or with one or two employees. Enterprising manufacturers opened factories in the towns of Lancashire, Yorkshire and the Midlands, and attracted the necessary labour by offering higher wages than those paid to agricultural labourers in the villages. The population moved rapidly from the country to the towns. This coincided with improvements in public health and medicine, and the elimination of some of the worst plagues, which led to a sharp reduction in the death rate and an increase in population. The population of England, which had been between 3 and 4 million in the sixteenth century and 5 million in 1700, rose from 9 million in 1780 to 25 million in 1850. In 1780, 20 per cent of the population lived in towns; by 1850, the proportion was 60 per cent.

There has been a great deal of controversy, both at the time and among later historians, as to whether the condition of the common people improved or worsened during the Industrial Revolution. Some maintain that it led to great suffering in the 'dark satanic mills' of which Blake wrote in his poem 'Jerusalem' in 1804, and in the urban slums in which the mill workers lived. Others claim that these conditions, though bad compared with those of later times, were better than the state of the country people in the eighteenth century; that the discontent was due to the fact that the improvements led to expectations of even greater improvements which were not immediately fulfilled; and that wages, and working and living conditions, have improved, slowly but continuously, ever since the Industrial Revolution began. It is difficult to decide this question, owing to the subjective features involved in comparing the lives of an agricultural labourer toiling in the fields and of the factory worker working at a loom in a factory. Thomas Babington Macaulay, a good Whig, had no doubt that the Industrial Revolution had brought progress and had improved the condition of the people, and that those who said that things had been better in the good old days were merely indulging in the silly habit of idealising the past, like other generations before them. He believed in 1848 that this process would continue; that by the twentieth century wages and conditions would have improved so much that the agricultural labourer in Dorset would be dissatisfied with a wage of fifteen shillings a week, and that a carpenter in Greenwich might be earning £3 a day; but that when this had come about, the fortunate people of the twentieth century would nevertheless yearn for the good old days of Queen Victoria.

There is no doubt that people in the countryside, who under the free system of the eighteenth century were able to leave their jobs and take any other work they could obtain, eagerly accepted the offer from the northern entrepreneurs of relatively high wages in return for very long hours of work and strict factory discipline; but as more and more of them came to the towns to apply for these jobs, the wages fell, while the long hours and the discipline remained. They were required to work up to sixteen or eighteen hours a day, six days a week, in hot, unhealthy, and often dangerous conditions, for it did not pay the employer to provide air and light in the mill or to fence the dangerous machinery. Many employers banned talking, singing or whistling during working hours, believing that these distractions interfered with production, and also, perhaps, disapproving of such frivolities from a lower-middle-class Nonconformist standpoint. Disobedience to the ban on talking or singing, as well as shoddy work and late arrival in the mornings, was punished by what were called 'fines', but in law were deductions from wages made under the terms of the contract of employment into which the workman had voluntarily entered. The workmen could earn more money for their families if their wives and children also worked in the mill or factory, and small children could be profitably employed there carrying out work under the looms and in other spaces which were too small for a grown adult.

Workmen who worked very hard, and lived a frugal life while they saved part of their wages, could sometimes make enough money to become employers and open their own mill. They were often the worst employers. They became respected local figures, and were sometimes even accepted in London society, though they were refused admission to Almack's, the most select of the London clubs, and the duke of Wellington resented the fact that they aspired to dance with the daughters of the aristocracy.

The Whig doctrine of freedom did not allow for any legal restriction to be placed on the right of the employer and employee to enter into any contract which they thought would be to their advantage; but when it was known that children of five or six were working eighteen hours a day in mills and sometimes falling into the machines and losing their arms or legs, public opinion began to demand that some restrictions should be imposed. The first Factory Act was passed in 1802; it limited the hours of work of child apprentices to twelve hours a day and provided for their religious instruction, but applied only to some establishments. The next act, which was passed in 1819, applied only to cotton mills and factories: it prohibited the employment of children under nine, and limited the working hours of young persons between the ages of nine and sixteen to thirteen and a half hours a day, including a one and a half hours' break for meals. The Act was largely evaded. It was not until after 1830 that any adequate steps were taken to enforce safety regulations or to limit hours of work in factories.

The development of the mills made the old cottage weaving industry unprofitable. This caused so much resentment that in 1811 there was an outbreak of violence in the industrial districts of the Midlands and the north of England, in which workmen destroyed the looms and other mechanical inventions in the factories, which they held responsible for unemployment. The rioters were known as Luddites, a word which had come into use some forty years before because a crazy youth named Ned Ludd happened on one occasion to break a machine in a fit of insanity. The government responded by passing Acts of Parliament which made loom-breaking an offence punishable by death, and several of the rioters were hanged.

A further incentive to country dwellers to go to work in the towns came from the lowering of wages and the standard of living of the agricultural labourers in the last years of the eighteenth century. After 1760 a large number of commons were enclosed and converted into the private property of some nobleman or other large landowner. This could, of course, be done legally under the provisions of a private Act of Parliament. In the north of Scotland the duke of Sutherland and other landowners ejected the local crofters and destroyed their cottages, in order to convert the region into a grazing area for sheep. The local population resisted, and in 1814, after the government had sent in troops, the duke's agents drove out the inhabitants, in some cases by burning their roofs over their heads. One old woman was dragged out of her cottage and died as she watched it burn.

The poor in both town and country suffered from the high price of bread, under the provisions of the Corn Laws of 1815, which had been passed by the Tory government, in defiance of the protests of the Whigs and the principle of free trade, to help both the farmers and the landowners to whom they paid rent. It enacted that no foreign wheat could be imported until the price of wheat had risen to eighty shillings a bushel – a high price when the agricultural labourer was earning between eight and ten shillings a week. It was only in 1846, after a strong and long agitation by the Whigs and Liberals, that Sir Robert Peel's Conservative government agreed to abolish the Corn Laws.

The distress in the countryside exacerbated the war between poachers and gamekeepers, though the most persistent poachers were not hungry labourers searching for food but members of well-organised professional poaching gangs who were supplying the middle classes in London and other towns with the game of which they would otherwise have been deprived under the Game Laws. These laws, which had been enacted in the reign of Charles II, restricted the right to hunt and shoot to members of the nobility and landowners owning more than a hundred acres. By the end of the eighteenth century the Game Laws were being denounced as a shameful example of aristocratic privilege, though they were stoutly defended by the nobility and their spokesmen on the grounds that they were necessary to encourage the nobility to hunt, which was essential if they were to be efficient cavalry officers in wartime.

The landowners placed man-traps and concealed spring-guns in their woods to catch the poachers, and Parliament passed Acts increasing the penalties for poaching; poachers could be imprisoned, whipped and transported for seven years to Van Diemen's Land (Tasmania), which was occupied by Britain soon after Australia was incorporated into the British Empire in 1788. Both Australia and Van Diemen's Land were used as penal settlements to which criminals in Britain were deported, and detained under savage discipline, until the system of transportation was ended in 1853. The severe penalties gave poachers an incentive to resort to violence to resist arrest, and many of them used their firearms against gamekeepers. An Act was thereupon passed in 1803 which made it an offence punishable by death for a poacher to fire at a gamekeeper. Men were executed under this Act for inflicting even minor wounds on gamekeepers.

England was beginning to move into the new society produced by the Industrial Revolution when the French Revolution broke out in 1789. The aristocratic and middle-class intellectuals who led the revolutionary movement in its early stages had been inspired by the example of free England, and intended to draft a constitution on the English model. The meeting of the States-General at Versailles, and the voting of the Declaration of the Rights of Man, in the summer of 1789 were therefore welcomed in political and intellectual circles in England; and the English rejoiced when the people of Paris, on 14 July, stormed the Bastille and released the seven prisoners who were the only captives still confined there. But though the Whig leader, Charles James Fox, declared that the storming of the Bastille was the greatest and the best event in the history of the world, his political colleague, the Irish Whig Edmund Burke, who had supported the American Revolution, immediately sounded the alarm, and warned that the revolutionary movement in France would constitute a threat to the British and European social order. He was answered by Thomas Paine, the son of a craftsman in Norfolk who, after being a Customs' officer, had gone to America to support the colonists' struggle and was the first person to suggest to them that they should declare their independence and establish a republic. Paine's book *The Rights of Man* was a vigorous defence of the French Revolution; and in London, Birmingham and Glasgow, radical groups formed the Corresponding Society, the Friends of the People, and other organisations to further the principles of a democratic revolution on the French model.

In the late summer of 1792 the extremist Jacobins seized power in France, imprisoned the king and queen and the royal family, murdered the aristocrats in the prisons, and declared a republic. This outraged everyone in England except the radicals of the Corresponding Society and the extreme section of the Whigs. In November the French revolutionary government published a manifesto in which they offered French support to any people who rose in revolt against their tyrants. Pitt considered that the manifesto was a threat to the British government; he prepared to join Austria and Prussia, who had already invaded France, in making war on the Revolution. Paine was prosecuted for sedition for publishing *The Rights of Man* and fled to France. In January 1793 the French government executed Louis XVI and invaded Belgium, and Britain declared war.

In Britain, the war was seen, not only as a national war against the hereditary enemy, France, but as a counter-revolutionary crusade. Taking advantage of the fact that the English language, with its Latin and Germanic origins, often has two words with identical meanings, they distinguished between Freedom and Liberty, between British 'freedom under the law' and the 'licentious liberty' of France. The pamphleteers and journalists violently denounced the crimes of the Jacobin regicides; the London theatres closed in mourning when the news arrived in October 1793 of the execution of Queen Marie Antoinette; and the activities of the Committee of Public Safety and the Revolutionary Tribunal, and the guillotining of the aristocrats in Paris in the presence of the applauding *tricoteuses* – the women who knitted as the guillotine fell – aroused the deepest indignation. A rising young MP, George Canning, started a journal, *The Anti-Jacobin*, in which he denounced the French revolutionaries and their British supporters with biting sarcasm; he castigated the British sympathiser with the French Revolution, in words which were to be often quoted in the next two hundred years, as

A steady patriot of the world alone,
A friend of every country – but his own.

The government acted to prevent the spread of revolution from across the Channel. Public meetings and political lectures were banned. The radical leaders, Thomas Hardy and Horne Tooke, were prosecuted for high treason for their speeches at a public meeting, but to Pitt's anger were acquitted by a London jury. Some less prominent radicals were convicted and executed. In Scotland, the radical advocate, Thomas Muir, was tried before the old Scottish judge, Lord Braxfield, who nearly fifty years before had been counsel for the crown in the forfeiture cases after the rising of 1745. Braxfield sentenced Muir to fourteen years' transportation. His conduct at the trials of the radicals at which he presided earned him a reputation with his opponents of being the Judge Jeffreys of Scotland.

The majority of the people undoubtedly supported the war against France, though it is difficult to know how far the patriotic mobs who attacked the houses of the anti-war radicals were representative of the population. The government had too much respect for the rule of law to approve of this violence and the attempted lynchings, and used all efforts to suppress them. The patriotic song, 'God save great George our King', which had first been sung in 1745 to the tune of an old hymn, became a great favourite with Tory and pro-war supporters, who often assaulted persons who refused to rise to their feet while it was being sung. It became the national anthem. In the theatres the audience often interrupted the performance to sing 'God save the King' until it became the accepted rule to sing it only at the beginning or the end of the performance – a practice which continued until the second half of the twentieth century.

Britain fought the war, like her earlier wars of the eighteenth century, with a small professional army, though the French revolutionary army was raised by compulsory military service of the whole population. The British army was composed entirely of volunteers. The officers bought their commissions, and were drawn almost exclusively from the nobility and the country gentlemen. The other ranks came from the lowest strata of society, from volunteers who had enlisted because of poverty, a desire for adventure, or to escape criminal proceedings, or bastardy summonses by pregnant girls. The navy was similarly composed of gentlemen officers and volunteer paupers; but in the navy enlistment was augmented by the operation of the press-gang, which was legally entitled to seize any seafaring man in any port and force him to join the king's navy. During the war against France, the navy carried these methods of forcible enlistment so far as to stop United States ships on the high seas and seize any member of their crew whom they suspected of being deserters from the British navy or merely British subjects who had emigrated to the United States, even if they had acquired US citizenship. This practice involved Britain in a war with the United States from 1812 to 1815, in the course of which the British burned the White House in Washington, but were defeated by General Andrew Jackson at New Orleans before news had arrived that the British and American delegates at Ghent had signed a peace treaty which was a victory for neither side.

Among the officers in both the army and the navy there was the highest morale, discipline and gallantry, inspired by loyalty to the king, by *esprit de corps*, and by the traditions of their class and background. The rank-and-file were controlled by the strictest discipline, including severe floggings. Sometimes offenders received as many as five hundred or even a thousand lashes with the cat-o'-nine-tails. Whipping had played a part in English life from the earliest times, having been freely used by the medieval Church, and at all times by parents and schoolmasters on children. But the savage flogging in the army and navy was not introduced until after the Revolution of 1688, though various forms of painful punishments had been applied in the forces in earlier times. The officers believed, in Wellington's words, that their soldiers were 'the scum of the earth', and that only by the threat and use of the lash could they be kept under control and made into splendid soldiers. General Duff declared in the House of Commons: 'That it was as easy to chain the North wind as to manage British soldiers without the aid of corporal punishment.'

The British army was unsuccessful against the French in the Netherlands, where the exploits of the king's son, the duke of York, as commander-in-chief led to nothing except the composition of a song which has become a well-known nursery rhyme, though the incident to which it referred was fictitious:

> Oh the noble Duke of York,
> He had ten thousand men,
> He marched them up to the top of the hill
> And he marched them down again.

236

At sea, the British navy was almost always successful, and, much more clearly than in earlier wars, established Britain as the greatest naval power in the world. It produced an outstanding admiral, Horatio Nelson, the son of a vicar of Norfolk. He combined a brilliant, daring and imaginative tactical ability with strong Tory principles and a fanatical anti-Jacobin zeal. He increased his popular reputation as a heroic figure by losing both an eye and an arm in action during the war. He became in his own time, and has remained ever since, the greatest national hero of the British people, and more than any other individual fulfilled the boast that 'Britannia rules the waves'.

In 1794 the Reign of Terror ended in France when Robespierre and his extremist Jacobins were overthrown by the more moderate 'men of Thermidor'. The government, the Tories and the press in Britain refused to recognise that any change had occurred in France, and saw Robespierre's downfall as just another example of the Jacobins killing each other as well as respectable aristocrats. The French revolutionaries found a great general, the young Napoleon Bonaparte, who in 1796 won a series of shattering victories over the Austrians in Northern Italy. After his successes, the French made tentative peace proposals. Pitt was prepared to enter into peace negotiations; but Burke, in the last weeks before his death, published a pamphlet, *Letter on a Regicide Peace*, in which he denounced the idea of ever negotiating with the Jacobins who had killed their king and queen. His pamphlet made a great impression in Britain, and this, combined with the opposition of George III, made it impossible for Pitt to negotiate with the French.

At this time there were two serious mutinies in the navy, at Spithead and at the Nore; but both were suppressed with the usual hangings and floggings. In Ireland, the national discontent broke out in a widespread insurrection in 1798. Unlike the struggles of the seventeenth century, this was not a fight between Catholics and Protestants, but a radical revolutionary movement in which radicals and democrats from both Catholic and Presbyterian families fought to overthrow the British monarchy and establish a republic on the French model. They relied for success on the help of French soldiers, and sang: 'The French are on the sea, the French are in the bay, they'll be here without delay'. But only a token force of French troops arrived, for Napoleon sent the main force of his army and navy, not to Ireland, but to Egypt in order to secure the route to India.

The Egyptian expedition was a disaster for France. Nelson destroyed the French fleet at the Battle of the Nile by a brilliant manoeuvre, sailing between the fleet at anchor and the shore and bombarding it from this unexpected quarter. Napoleon was thus cut off from his base, and could do nothing but win a number of useless victories against Britain's Turkish ally in Egypt and Syria. In October 1799 he abandoned his army and, slipping through Nelson's fleet, returned to France to make himself dictator by his *coup d'état* of 18 Brumaire.* The French army in Syria held out for another two years before capitulating to the British.

The Irish rebellion was suppressed with great severity. The revolutionary leader, Wolfe Tone, was sentenced to death by a court martial, in breach of the established principles of the English rule of law. His counsel, the famous Irish advocate John Philpot Curran, applied on the eve of his execution to the common law courts in Dublin for a writ of *habeas corpus* to save him; but Tone committed suicide in his cell before the court could give a decision.

The Irish rebellion caused the British government to tighten its control over Ireland by abolishing the Irish Parliament and having Irish MPs, like the Scottish MPs, sitting in the House of Commons at Westminster. It also forced Pitt to abandon the scheme which he had in mind for abolishing the legal restrictions on the Irish Catholics. On this point he encountered the determined opposition of George III, who thought that for him to consent to Catholic Emancipation would be a breach of his coronation oath to uphold 'the Protestant religion by law established'.

In 1803, another unsuccessful insurrection broke out in Dublin under the leadership of the young intellectual, Robert Emmet. He was in love with Curran's daughter, Sarah, and his execution for high treason inspired the Irish poet, Thomas Moore, to write his poem to Sarah Curran: 'She is far from the land where her young hero sleeps'. The revolts and executions in Ireland created a widespread popular cult, which still exists in Ireland as it does in

---

* The name given to the date 9 November in the new calendar adopted by the French revolutionaries.

France, of heroic martyrs who sacrifice their lives on the barricades or on the scaffold in order to achieve their political ideals. This feeling is fundamentally opposed to the English ideal of the rule of law.

The British government, unable to wage war on land against the French on a large scale, financed the war effort of the Austrians; but the Austrian armies were again defeated by Napoleon at Marengo. The enthusiasm for the war began to wane in England, and the new government, which had succeeded Pitt's administration, opened peace negotiations. Peace was signed at Amiens in 1802. But it was of short duration. Both sides accused the other of failing to comply with the peace terms, and in 1803 Napoleon, in an outburst of rage, insulted and violently denounced the British ambassador, Lord Whitworth, for the British failure to evacuate Malta, as had been agreed under the Treaty of Amiens. War was declared, and Pitt returned as Prime Minister. While he again formed and financed a coalition with Austria and Russia against France, Napoleon, who made himself Emperor of the French in 1804, planned to strike at the heart of his greatest enemy by invading England.

He massed a large army at Boulogne, and throughout the summer of 1805 the English expected the invasion at any time. Fortifications known as Martello Towers were built along the south coast, and volunteers enrolled to fight the French when they landed. The patriotic enthusiasm was intense; even some of the radicals enlisted, for though they had formerly sympathised with the French Revolution, they had lost faith in Napoleon after he took the title of emperor. The fleet on which Napoleon depended to transport his troops across the Channel was blockaded in the Channel, Atlantic and Mediterranean ports. Nelson bottled up the French ships in Toulon for eighteen months; but in January 1805 they slipped out of the harbour. After months of evasion and chase across the North Atlantic, Nelson encountered the French fleet off Cape Trafalgar in northwest Spain. It had been joined by the Spanish ships, for Spain, though an absolute monarchy, had made an alliance with revolutionary France in the hope of recovering Gibraltar and Jamaica from Britain. On 21 October 1805 Nelson won a great naval victory at Trafalgar, but he himself was killed in the battle.

The Battle of Trafalgar did not in fact save England from

invasion, because a month before it was fought Napoleon had abandoned his invasion plan and had marched his army at Boulogne into Bavaria to fight the Austrians and Russians; but Trafalgar destroyed the French fleet as an effective fighting force, and ensured that he would never again plan a direct attack on England. When the news of the victory reached Britain sixteen days after the battle, it was hailed as the greatest triumph, and the dead Nelson as the greatest hero, that the country had ever known, though it was not until 1843 that a very high monument was erected to him a few yards from Charing Cross at the centre of a newly constructed square which was named Trafalgar Square.

Six weeks after Trafalgar, Napoleon won a great victory over the Austrian and Russian armies at Austerlitz in Moravia, and forced the Austrian emperor and the tsar to make peace. In London, Pitt was dying of drink, though he was still only forty-six. When he heard the news of Austerlitz, he was utterly depressed, and, looking at the map of Europe on the wall in his house, said: 'Roll up that map; it will not be wanted these ten years.' He died a month later. His friends reported that his last words were: 'Oh, my country! How I leave my country!'; but the story spread that in fact they were: 'I think I could eat one of Bellamy's veal pies.'

In October 1806 Napoleon destroyed the power of Prussia at the Battle of Jena, and after occupying Berlin issued the Berlin Decree in November, which placed an embargo on all trade with England and compelled all the conquered states of Europe to enforce the embargo. The British retaliated by enforcing a blockade against France; and thanks to the power of the British navy, and the quality of British manufactures, France and occupied Europe suffered more than Britain from the effect of the blockade and counter-blockade.

In 1808 Napoleon invaded Spain. The British government sent a young general, Sir Arthur Wellesley, with an army to Portugal to hold it against the French, and another under Sir John Moore to help the Spanish resistance in northern Spain. Moore was defeated and killed after a heroic retreat which made him a popular hero in England. Wellesley held the lines of Torres Vedras and saved Lisbon. Next year he was created Viscount Wellington. Before leaving London to take up the command in

Portugal, he had told a guest at a dinner party that he had carefully studied Napoleon's tactics, and had no doubt that he could defeat him in battle.

He soon took the offensive against the French in Spain, and after five years of warfare drove them across the Pyrenees and invaded France. Meanwhile Napoleon had invaded Russia, had lost his whole army in a disastrous retreat, and had been defeated by the armies of the German states at the Battle of Leipzig. In 1814 the Prussian, Austrian and Russian armies, as well as Wellington, invaded France, and Napoleon was forced to abdicate, and to accept the kingdom of Elba which the victorious Allies offered him. In March 1815 he returned to France, the whole nation flocked to his support, and he became emperor again for the Hundred Days; but the Allied powers refused his offer of peace, and prepared an army in the Netherlands under Wellington's command to invade France and overthrow him. He tried to forestall them by invading Belgium and destroying the Allied armies before they were ready; but on 18 June he was defeated at Waterloo, where Wellington's men held out and broke the strength of the French army, until Blücher and the Prussians arrived to complete the destruction of the enemy.

Wellington led the Allied armies to Paris, and Napoleon, after unsuccessfully trying to escape to the United States, surrendered to the British warship *Bellerophon* off the west coast of France. The Allied governments sent him as a prisoner in British custody to the British island of St Helena in the South Atlantic, where he died six years later.

241

CHAPTER 14

VICTORIAN
GLORY
(1815–1902)

Trafalgar, Waterloo and the Industrial Revolution had made
Britain the greatest nation in Europe, with the highest prestige
abroad and unbounded self-confidence at home. At first, under
her Tory government, she used her great power to restore and
bolster up the old autocratic regimes in Europe. In Spain, where
there had been a popular rising of the people against the foreign
tyranny of Napoleon, the Liberals, forgetting their traditional
friendship for revolutionary France, had played an active part
in the national uprising, and in the course of it had proclaimed
the democratic Constitution of 1812 which gave the vote at
Parliamentary elections to large sections of the people; but after
the defeat of Napoleon, the Constitution of 1812 was abrogated,
thanks largely to Wellington's influence, and the king of Spain
became once more an absolute sovereign. In France, the Bourbon
monarchy was restored; in Italy, the Habsburg and Bourbon
dynasties, and the ecclesiastical despotism of the papal government; and in Prussia and Holland, the old Conservative and
Protestant autocrats.

The British Foreign Secretary, Lord Castlereagh, gave his full

242

support to the plans of the Holy Alliance of Russia, Austria and Prussia to crush revolutionary movements and Liberalism throughout Europe, if necessary by armed intervention. In 1821 the Austrian chancellor, Metternich, sent Austrian troops to crush the revolutionary outbreaks in Italy and next year the Holy Alliance authorised the Bourbon government of France to intervene in Spain and to suppress the Spanish Liberal government and restore King Ferdinand. In 1823 the French troops marched in, and Ferdinand, in breach of a promise of amnesty, hanged and imprisoned the defeated Liberals.

The British government did not protest against the intervention in Italy and Spain, but they were alarmed at the domination of Europe by the Holy Alliance, and completely reversed their foreign policy. In August 1822 Castlereagh committed suicide in a fit of insanity. He was succeeded at the Foreign Office by Canning; but though the change of policy has been attributed to Canning's appointment, it had in fact been decided on by Castlereagh shortly before his death. Canning threatened to use the British navy to prevent Spain from suppressing the national revolts which had broken out in her South American colonies. Referring to the French intervention in Spain, he declared that if France must rule Spain, it should be Spain without the Indies, and claimed that he had 'called the New World into existence to redress the balance of the Old'. All the Spanish territory on the mainland of the American continent, from Cape Horn to California, became independent states, and the Portuguese colony of Brazil also gained its independence.

There was a similar change at this time in the government's internal policy. Soon after Pitt's death the earl of Liverpool became Prime Minister, and held office uninterruptedly for fifteen years. George III, who had first had bouts of madness in 1788, became permanently mad in 1811, and his royal powers were exercised by his eldest son, George, the prince of Wales, as prince regent. The prince, who was on very bad terms with his father, had originally been close to the Whigs; but after he became regent he abandoned them for the Tories, and he continued his pro-Tory policy when he became King George IV in 1820. The Whig Opposition thereupon backed the cause of his wife, Queen Caroline, when the King tried unsuccessfully to divorce her for her adultery with an Italian servant, though

George's own love affairs were notorious. The Whigs succeeded in arousing so much opposition to the divorce bill that the government withdrew it.

Towards the end of the eighteenth century, the radical section of the Whigs had challenged the whole basis of the power of the landed aristocracy by demanding a reform in the constituencies of the House of Commons so as to allow the growing towns in the Midlands and North of England to be represented in the House and abolishing the 'rotten boroughs'. The oft-cited case of Old Sarum in Wiltshire, which was represented in the House of Commons by the nominee of a peer although there was not a single inhabitant in the constituency, was only the worst example of a system under which about 100 constituencies, each with fewer than 500 voters, had the right to elect an MP, whereas cities like Birmingham and Manchester, with populations of 75,000, were not entitled to send any member to the House of Commons. The demand for Parliamentary reform was stifled at the outbreak of the war with France in 1793, when any attempt to interfere with the perfection of the English Constitution was seen as a conspiracy by unpatriotic Jacobins to injure the king and the nation.

After the end of the war in 1815, the agitation was renewed. A demonstration held at Spa Fields in London to demand reform was broken up by police and in February 1817 the prince regent's carriage was attacked by the mob. Parliament then passed legislation which curtailed the freedom of the press, allowed the government to detain its political opponents without trial, and enacted that if fifty or more persons attended a meeting which had been called without the consent of the lord lieutenant of the county, they should be guilty of an offence punishable by death. In August 1819 a crowd of 80,000 people assembled in St Peter's Fields in Manchester to hear the radical orator, Henry Hunt, address a meeting in favour of Parliamentary reform. The local JPs ordered the yeomanry to disperse the crowd with their sabres, and about a dozen people attending the meeting, some of them women, were killed, and over 400 were injured. The Opposition called it the 'Massacre of Peterloo' in mocking imitation of Waterloo; but the prince regent sent the JPs a message of thanks and congratulation, and Wellington strongly supported their action. Hunt was sentenced to two and a half years' imprisonment for his speech at the meeting, and the government passed the 'Six Acts', which placed further restrictions on political agitation.

In 1820 a group of radicals, from their headquarters in Cato Street off the Edgware Road in London, tried to murder the Cabinet while they were dining at a house in Grosvenor Square; but the plot was betrayed by one of the many informers and *agents provocateurs* employed by the government. The conspirators were executed, as were a number of Scottish radicals who tried to start a ludicrously abortive insurrection in Glasgow in the same year.

The radical intellectuals blamed Castlereagh for the repression, as well as for his reactionary foreign policy and for his severities when he was Secretary for Ireland at the time of the rising of 1798. Shelley wrote after Peterloo:

> I met Murder on the way;
> He had a mask like Castlereagh;
> Very stern he looked, yet grim;
> Seven bloodhounds followed him.

Byron called him a 'cold-blooded, smooth-faced, placid miscreant', and after his suicide wrote that he would lament his death when Ireland had ceased to lament his birth.

Under Canning's influence the Tory government became less repressive. A peaceful campaign developed in Ireland for the removal of the remaining disabilities imposed by law on the Catholics, above all for their right to sit in the House of Commons. The radicals and Liberals, and most of the Whigs, supported the demand for 'Catholic Emancipation', and Canning favoured it. Soon after Canning's premature death, Wellington's Tory government gave way over Catholic Emancipation, and all the Catholics' demands were granted in 1829. Thirty years later, practising Jews were allowed to sit in the House of Commons; and in 1888 Charles Bradlaugh, after a long struggle, won the same right for atheists.

The winning of Catholic Emancipation encouraged the agitation for Parliamentary reform. In the general election of October 1830, the Whigs won a clear majority in the House of Commons, and returned to power, having been in Opposition for all except three of the previous sixty years. The Prime Minister was Lord Grey, who as a young man in 1794 had nearly been arrested for his support of the French Revolution and his opposition to the war. In July 1830 the Bourbon King Charles X of France had been overthrown by a revolution which put his Liberal cousin Louis Philippe on the throne; and in August a revolution in Brussels had driven out the government of the autocratic King of the Netherlands and created the new Belgian nation. The Whig return to power in England was seen by European Conservatives as a further advance in the new revolutionary wave which was engulfing Europe.

Lord Grey's government introduced the Reform Bill in the House of Commons. It provided for the abolition of the rotten boroughs and the grant of representation in Parliament to the industrial towns of the Midlands and the north. It was strenuously opposed by the Tories, who knew that it meant the end of the control of the House of Commons by the nobility. After the second reading had been carried by one vote in the House of Commons, the bill was defeated in committee; but Lord Grey won the general election of May 1831 with an increased majority. The Reform Bill then passed the House of Commons, but was thrown out by the House of Lords. There was no way in which the government could outvote the Tory majority in the Lords except by the creation of more Whig peers, and Lord Grey asked the new king, William IV, to do this. William had always been a Tory, and hesitated to use his royal prerogative to compel the Tories to accept a measure which he did not like; but while he hesitated, the people rioted in London and Birmingham, and the country seemed to the aristocracy and the middle classes to be on the verge of revolution. Wellington and the Tories freed the king from the necessity of creating new peers. The Tory peers in the House of Lords abstained, thus allowing the Reform Bill to become law. It passed by the votes of the minority of Whig peers on 4 June 1832.

But the fears of the British and foreign Conservatives that Lord Grey's government was a harbinger of revolution were soon set at rest. A few weeks before it came into office, riots broke out in the agricultural districts of Sussex, Hampshire and Wiltshire. They were spontaneous outbreaks by the agricultural labourers, and usually took the form of a band of men, armed with sticks, calling on the local gentlemen and demanding money to relieve their poverty. With the encouragement of Lord Melbourne, who was Lord Grey's Home Secretary, the local JPs and militia suppressed the rising, and the common law judges punished the participants with great severity; although no one had been killed or seriously injured by the rioters, several of the labourers were executed, and more of them were transported for many years to Van Diemen's Land.

In 1834 Grey was succeeded as Prime Minister by the more conservative Melbourne, who immediately came into conflict with the radical members of his party, and with the working-class political organisations, over the New Poor Law. This set up a national administration for the poor law in place of the old system which had been administered by the local JPs, and carried through a complete reorganisation of the principles on which the poor law was administered. Its object was to discourage paupers from applying for public assistance, and to encourage them to take employment at low wages, by making the conditions under which poor relief was given as unpleasant as possible. All 'outdoor' relief in the paupers' homes was abolished, and relief could henceforth be obtained only in poor law institutions, which became known as 'the workhouse' and as the 'Poor Law Bastilles'. The three Poor Law administrators – the 'Pashas of Somerset House' – and their subordinate officers drafted regulations which, by enforcing segregation of the sexes, the separation of families, long working hours, boring work, shortage of sleep, unpalatable food, no smoking, no visitors, and no excursions, would make the workhouse more disagreeable than the worst-paid job outside, and the workhouse overseer, in the words of one of the Poor Law Commissioners, 'the hardest taskmaster and the worst paymaster that the idle and the dissolute can apply to'.

The campaign against the New Poor Law, and the denunciation of the horrors of the workhouses, was vigorously carried on by the Socialists and by humanitarians of all parties, most notably by Charles Dickens in his novel *Oliver Twist*, which was published in 1837; but Melbourne's government, with the support of most of the Tories, stood firm, and only minor modifications were introduced into the harsh regime of the workhouses.

By the 1830s, a new phenomenon, the trade unions, was having an important influence on economic and political life.

There are records of combinations between workmen, and strikes, as early as the reign of Henry VIII; but it was not until the beginning of the Industrial Revolution that they had an important effect. The trade unions immediately ran into difficulties with the common law judges, who extended the law of conspiracy in order to deal with the threat from trade unions to the interests of the employers and the nation's commerce. The judges held that although a solitary individual can lawfully injure another person, even from motives of malice, provided that his action is neither a crime nor a civil wrong, if two or more persons combine to commit an action which harms another, they are guilty of the crime and tort of conspiracy, even though their action would be lawful if committed by a single person. This meant that an employer could lawfully do what was illegal if done by his united workmen.

The common law was strengthened by the Combination Act of 1799, which was passed during the war against revolutionary France and the anti-Jacobin hysteria in Britain. The Act made it an offence for two or more workmen to combine in order to obtain higher wages or a reduction of working hours, and violated the accepted principle of English law by forbidding appeals to the Court of King's Bench and requiring defendants to incriminate themselves. It also made it an offence for anyone to contribute to the legal expenses of defendants who were prosecuted under the Act.

In the less repressive atmosphere which followed the death of Castlereagh, the Radical MP Francis Place succeeded by some very skilful Parliamentary manoeuvring, in securing the enactment of a bill which legalised trade unions in 1825. But their activities were still frustrated in many ways by the judges. When in 1834 six agricultural labourers at Tolpuddle in Dorset joined together to form an agricultural workers' trade union, and took an oath of loyalty to the union, they were prosecuted under an Act against unlawful oaths, which had been passed during the repression of 1817, and sentenced to seven years transportation. The trade unions and their radical supporters organised a campaign of protest which culminated in a demonstration in London when 30,000 people marched from Copenhagen Fields to Whitehall with a petition to Lord Melbourne for a pardon for the 'Tolpuddle martyrs'. Melbourne refused to receive the petition, and Lord Brougham and Lord Londonderry, in the House of Lords, said that the demonstration was a defiance of the rule of law. For three years the government refused the demand for a pardon, believing that the principle of the rule of law would be seriously weakened if they gave way to popular pressure. Only when the protests had subsided were the men set free and brought back from Australia and Van Diemen's Land before completing their sentences.

In 1831 the miners in the Durham coalfields went on strike in support of a demand that no child under the age of eleven should work underground for more than nine hours a day. In 1842 a great wave of strikes spread through the cotton mills of Lancashire; and in 1844 there was another great miners' strike in Durham. Nearly all these strikes were ultimately unsuccessful. The employers broke the strike by bringing workmen from Ireland and offering them higher wages than the Irish rates, which were always substantially lower than those paid in England.

The most powerful mineowner in Durham was the marquess of Londonderry, who was Castlereagh's half-brother, and had served as a general under Wellington in Spain. He regarded the strikers as an enemy to himself and to society, who must be fought with all the means which he could command. As most of the miners were his tenants, he ejected them from their houses; and he threatened to take similar action against any shopkeeper in the district who helped relieve the distress of the strikers' families by supplying them with food and necessaries on credit. By these means, he succeeded in forcing the strikers to return to work on his own terms. From the first, the employers were conscious that trade unions could completely undermine their power over their workmen. They refused, in nearly every case, to recognise the existence of trade unions or to negotiate with their representatives, and many of the strikes of the 1830s and 1840s were an attempt to force the employers to negotiate.

The trade unions also participated in political campaigns, especially in the agitation for a ten-hour working day for women and children. The leading part in this struggle was played by a Tory MP, Lord Ashley, who afterwards inherited his father's title of earl of Shaftesbury. Ashley was chiefly responsible for the enactment of three great reforming statutes: the Factory Act of 1833 first placed effective restraints on the length of the working day; the Act of 1842, despite the strong opposition of Lord Londonderry, prohibited women and children from working in mines; and the Ten Hours Act, after being defeated on several occasions, eventually passed in 1847.

The unions and organisations of working men put forward demands in the People's Charter, whose supporters became known as the Chartists. They demanded universal manhood suffrage, the abolition of the property qualification for MPs, voting by secret ballot at Parliamentary elections, the payment of MPs, and that a general election should be held every year. This last demand is the only one which has not now been granted; but all the demands were rejected by the government and the House of Commons in 1839.

The Chartists made their last attempt in the 'year of revolutions', 1848. In January a revolution broke out in Palermo which overthrew the government of the king of Naples. In February a revolution in Paris forced King Louis Philippe to abdicate, and a republic was established. In March the governments were overthrown by revolution in both Vienna and Berlin. Encouraged by the revolutionary ferment in Europe, the Chartists planned for a demonstration of 200,000 people to assemble at Kennington Green on 10 April and march to Westminster to present to Parliament a petition in favour of the Charter. The government banned the demonstration, and called on the nobility, the gentry, and the middle classes and their servants to volunteer to serve as special constables, under the command of the old duke of Wellington, to protect the capital from the Chartists. 170,000 men enrolled as special constables and barred the Chartists' way to Parliament Square; and the Chartist leaders called off the proposed march. Soon afterwards the Chartist movement split and petered out.

Its eclipse was to some extent due to the strong Low Church religious influence which increasingly pervaded the popular reforming movement during the Victorian era, and caused the General Secretary of the Labour Party, Morgan Phillips, in the middle of the twentieth century, to say that the British Labour movement had been influenced much more by Methodism than by Marxism. John Wesley, the son of a Lincolnshire rector, founded the Methodist movement in the middle of the eighteenth century as a form of 'enthusiastic' religion within the Church of

England which appealed to the poor in town and country instead of to the Establishment in the 'squire and parson' society of the time. He and his supporters were ridiculed and victimised, but were not subjected to the intensive persecution which dissenters had suffered at earlier periods; and the nobility and gentry came increasingly to welcome the spread among the lower classes of a deep religious faith which emphasised the duty of servants to obey their masters and to accept without complaint the position in society in which it had pleased God to place them.

Other religious movements appeared in the middle of the nineteenth century. The Salvation Army was founded by William Booth, who, like other contemporary religious philanthropists, had witnessed during his adolescent years the bitter clashes between the working classes and the authorities in the industrial areas in the 1840s. He had been sympathetic to the Chartists and the Socialists, but was put off by their advocacy of revolutionary violence and their atheism. His movement, which concentrated on exposing the evils of drunkenness and alcohol, encountered fierce opposition both from the Englishman who loved his beer and his gin, and from the brewers whose profits were threatened by Booth's Salvation Army. His followers risked, and occasionally lost, their lives while facing the brutal violence of their enemies in the slums of London, the ports and the industrial towns; but their steadfastness and passive submission to ill-treatment ultimately won the respect both of the Establishment and of the people.

The defeat of the Chartists in 1848 was a great boost to the already high morale of the British Establishment. All over Europe the absolute monarchies, with their centralised *gendarmerie* and large armies, had been overthrown by revolution; but in England, the forces of revolution had been defeated by the middle classes enrolled as special constables, and the rule of law had triumphed. British power and prosperity had never been higher, and Englishmen's self-confidence was unbounded as they contemplated their empire in five continents, their unrivalled diplomatic influence, their ascendancy in international trade, and their political institutions, with their constitutional monarchy, their Parliamentary system, their class structure, and their 'freedom under the law'. They were convinced that their political, economic and social system was the best in the world, and as near to perfection as any merely human institution could ever be. They wrote proudly of their 'youthful Queen, the Queen of half the world', for William IV's niece, Princess Victoria, had succeeded to the throne at the age of eighteen in 1837. They believed literally in the words of their patriotic song, *Rule Britannia*, which James Thomson had written for his masque 'Alfred' to Arne's music in 1740:

> The nations not so blest as thee
> Must, in their turns, to tyrants fall;
> While thou shalt flourish, great and free,
> The dread and envy of them all.

They were proud of their great capital, London, which, with a population of over two million, was the largest city on earth. The author of a history text-book for schools, who cited a passage in which Julius Caesar referred derogatively to the dwellings of the ancient Britons, could not refrain from adding a footnote: 'But what today is Caesar's Rome compared to ever-growing London, the greatest capital in all the world?' They wrote about events taking place 'at Manchester', 'at Paris', 'at Vienna', 'at New York', but 'in London', which was the only town big enough, and great enough, for people to be 'in' it, not 'at' it.

It was believed that the national glory and prosperity were the result of the observance of the precepts of the Protestant religion, and the punishment by law, and even more by public censure and ostracism, of those who violated its moral code; by respect for law and order; and by thrift and hard work. It was known that some members of the aristocracy were idle and extravagant, but they were despised if they continued to indulge in these vices after they left the university. Already in the lecherous and spendthrift era of the Regency, William Wilberforce and the members of his Society for the Suppression of Vice, though mocked by their critics as the 'Clapham Saints', had had considerable success in dissuading the aristocracy from whoring, drinking and gambling; for many Regency rakes had obeyed Wilberforce's exhortation that if they found it impossible to desist from these vicious practices, they should at least commit them in secret and not in the presence of their servants.

Landowners of land on the fringe of London and the large cities granted leases for ninety-nine years to tenants at nominal rents on condition that the tenants erected and maintained houses and other buildings on the land, thus ensuring a great rise in value when the land reverted to the landlord's great-grandson in ninety-nine years' time; for in England, unlike in any other country in the world, a landowner could be sure that neither government legislation nor economic decline would interfere with the rights of his descendants or cause the value of the land to fall. It never occurred to them that an Act of Parliament in 1954 would deprive their great-grandchildren of the benefits which they had planned for them.

England was not a country in which an exclusive aristocracy surrounded itself with legal privileges and prevented enterprising members of inferior classes from rising in society. English peers not only played cricket with the villagers, and sent their wives to labourers' cottages with comforts at Christmas, but also invited to their houses bankers and manufacturers, including Jewish bankers and north-country manufacturers. They sometimes married the daughters of the bankers and manufacturers, and occasionally married an illegitimate shop-girl who had become a beautiful and successful actress, or a very pretty American girl. The self-made man, who had risen from poverty and the humblest origins to become wealthy and successful was the hero of Victorian society. The explorer Sir Henry Morton Stanley, who achieved international fame by finding Dr Livingstone in Africa, was a workhouse boy and rose to be received and knighted by Queen Victoria as well as becoming rich. He was greatly admired for his success.

Lord Palmerston, who was Foreign Secretary for sixteen years between 1830 and 1851 and Prime Minister for nine years between 1855 and 1865, described England, in one of his greatest speeches, as

> a nation in which every class of society accepts with cheerfulness the lot which Providence has assigned to it; while at the same time every individual of each class is constantly striving to raise himself in the social scale – not by injustice and wrong, not by violence and illegality – but by persevering good conduct and by the steady and energetic exertion of the moral and intellectual faculties with which his Creator has endowed him.

A popular song exhorted the working man to

> Work, boys, work, and be contented,
> As long as you've enough to buy a meal;

The man, you may rely,
Will be wealthy by and by,
If he'll only put his shoulder to the wheel.

It was this self-confidence in their virtues which made the English believe that they had the moral right, as well as the naval power, to interfere in every part of the world to protect the rights of British subjects and the honour of the British flag, and to help moderate Liberals in their internal struggles against right-wing autocrats and radical extremists – a policy which hostile foreigners called 'bullying small nations'. This policy became particularly associated in the public mind with Palmerston; but it was the British nation, not Palmerston, who was the real author of the policy. The French statesman and historian, Tocqueville, described Victorian England as a warlike, but not a military, nation. Britain fought her wars with her small volunteer army of paupers serving under aristocratic officers, by hiring foreign mercenaries, and by subsidising Continental allies with their large land armies. The middle-class Englishman, the business and professional man, was not expected to join the army; it would indeed have been almost impossible for him to do so, for he would not have found it easy to buy a commission, and it would have caused great embarrassment to his officers if he had enlisted as a private. He could cheer on the soldiers from the safety of his English home and office, thousands of miles from the battle zone; for his duty was to ensure British prosperity by making money, just as the duty of his employees was to enable him to do this by working hard; while the duty of the aristocracy, who very largely monopolised the Foreign Office, was, in Palmerston's words, to use British diplomatic and military power 'to open and to secure the roads for the merchant'.

The popular image of England, often portrayed in cartoons in *Punch* and elsewhere, was of John Bull, the imaginary national prototype, spoiling for a fight with a big bullying European autocrat or with some Asiatic barbarian tycoon – a fearless, pugnacious and aggressive John Bull, convinced of the justice of any cause for which he fought. If a British subject was imprisoned or ill-treated in a foreign country, and did not receive an apology and compensation, Palmerston would send the British navy to blockade the ports of the offending state; and the same course would be adopted if the foreign state did not repay its debts to British investors. Palmerston desisted from such action only when dealing with a nation which was too strong to threaten, or too far away from the coast to allow the British navy to come within striking distance of it. Britain was not the only great power which adopted these methods in the nineteenth century, but she was best able to carry it out successfully because of her incomparable navy.

It was their conviction of their moral superiority over all other nations which inspired the British government and people in their dealings with the native populations in Asia and Africa. When confronted with a cruel enemy during the Indian Mutiny in 1857, the British commanders, several of whom were Scottish Calvinists, felt justified in resorting to the most ruthless methods, including the infliction of physical and mental suffering and calculated affronts to the native religion, not only out of a belief that severity would deter, but because they felt themselves to be the instruments of an avenging Old Testament God. When they burned the emperor of China's Summer Palace in Peking, after smashing all the priceless antiques, in order to punish him for having permitted the torture of British subjects within the precincts of the palace, neither the historic nor the artistic value of the objects which they destroyed was a factor to be taken into consideration as compared with their duty to carry out the civilising mission of John Bull.

But by the middle of the nineteenth century an opposing point of view was being expressed by a vociferous minority in Britain. This was the attitude which was referred to, both admiringly and derisively, as 'the Nonconformist conscience', though it was not limited to those who were Nonconformists in religion. It was expressed most powerfully by the Lancashire manufacturer, John Bright, and by William Ewart Gladstone, who in fact was not a Nonconformist but a High Anglican. Gladstone became the leader of the Liberal Party, and was four times Prime Minister between 1868 and 1894; and although his attitude was unpopular among large sections of the British people, and aroused intense opposition and dislike from Queen Victoria, it had in the long run a profound effect on British political thought and action.

Gladstone declared that 'the rights of the savage, as we call him' were as high as those of Englishmen, and denounced 'the policy of denying to others the rights that we claim ourselves'. He opposed the 'Opium War' in 1840, when Palmerston went to war with China to compel the Chinese government to repeal the laws which prohibited the import of opium from British India. To Macaulay and to most MPs, the evils of opium-smoking were not as great as those which would result from interfering with the freedom of British merchants to trade with willing Chinese purchasers. Gladstone likewise opposed other cases of aggressive diplomacy in which Palmerston indulged. His attitude, that international morality should prevail over British national interests, was violently denounced as unpatriotic; but the representatives of the Nonconformist conscience, like their aggressive opponents, were deeply convinced of British moral superiority. They believed that the British people could rise above the selfish and primitive nationalist feelings which animated all other nations; for no foreign government was impeded, in the pursuit of its national interests, by an influential Nonconformist conscience at home.

Though the Nonconformist conscience of the Liberals and pacifists condemned Palmerston's aggressive foreign policy, the European radicals welcomed it, for it was often directed against royal despots, like the kings of Naples and Greece, and at the Austrian and Russian emperors who upheld them. In 1849 Palmerston intervened to prevent Turkey from yielding to the Russian and Austrian demands that she should extradite to Russia and Austria the Polish and Hungarian revolutionaries who had rebelled against the tsar and the emperor of Austria; and this made him a hero of the European radicals. The British people worshipped the radical Italian revolutionary, Garibaldi, who in 1860 overthrew the tyrannical regime of the king of Naples when he sailed to Sicily with his 'Thousand' volunteers and defeated 20,000 Neapolitan troops. Many British volunteers joined Garibaldi's forces, and he was cheered by half a million people in the streets when he visited London in 1864. The Austrian ambassador in Paris, finding himself trapped in the middle of a group of revolutionary radicals and Socialists during the street-fighting which followed the *coup d'état* in 1851 by the future Emperor Napoleon III, put on a fake English accent, because he thought that revolutionaries would be friendly to him if they believed that he was an Englishman. French Conservatives, contrasting the British indignation at the execution of a few revolutionaries in Naples with the mass hangings and shootings carried out by British soldiers in India, thought that the English deplored cruelty only when the victims were 'Reds'.

Palmerston's combination of threats and diplomatic finesse was nearly always successful in avoiding a major war; but thanks to a chain of events for which he was only partly responsible, Britain became involved in the Crimean War against Russia in 1854, in alliance with France and Turkey. For the first time in history, a newspaper correspondent accompanied the British army during a war, and the *Times* correspondent in the Crimea, William Howard Russell, exposed the incompetence of the army high command in Turkey and in the Crimea which had permitted such disasters as the charge of the Light Brigade at Balaclava, the sufferings of the soldiers besieging Sevastopol, and the neglect of the wounded in the base hospitals at Scutari. In Britain, the public indignation was directed against the duke of Newcastle, the Secretary of State for War, who was held responsible for the disasters; and for the first time there was a widespread lack of confidence in the ability of the aristocracy to lead the nation in wartime. The middle-class politician, Layard, ran a campaign against the aristocracy, speaking at public meetings and raising the slogan 'The right man in the right place'; but Palmerston himself, who had become Prime Minister in the darkest hour of the war, remained almost universally popular, and strenuously maintained that English freedom would be endangered if the army were commanded by a professional military hierarchy instead of by the nobility.

Palmerston's flamboyant personality, and his image as the personification of the aggressive John Bull, made him so popular that his opponents despaired of ever gaining office during his lifetime; and he was still Prime Minister when he died in 1865, a few months after increasing his majority at the general election – a feat which was not repeated by any Prime Minister until 1959. His chief anxiety during his last years was neither the apparent strength of France under the Second Empire of Napoleon III, nor the rise of Prussian power in Europe after Bismarck's appointment as Prime Minister in Berlin, but the potential menace to British world supremacy from the United States.

The American Civil War broke out in 1861, when the Southern states seceded from the United States because they feared that

Abraham Lincoln's government was intending to abolish Negro slavery in the South. Political attitudes towards the Civil War varied in Britain, where the blockade imposed by the United States navy prevented the cotton of the Southern states from reaching England, and caused acute economic distress among the millworkers in Lancashire. The radicals strongly supported the cause of the North, seeing the Civil War as a crusade against slavery; but Palmerston's government hoped that the war would lead to secession by the South and the break-up of the United States as a nation, though his government refrained from entering the war on the side of the South, or even from giving the South diplomatic recognition. When the North won the Civil War, and the United States emerged as a united nation with a powerful army and navy, Palmerston feared the worst as far as the future was concerned.

The death of Palmerston cleared the stage for the struggle between Gladstone and Disraeli which dominated British politics for the next fifteen years. Benjamin Disraeli was a fascinating and contradictory character. He was the son of a Jewish writer who was baptised with his family into the Church of England when Benjamin was aged thirteen. Like his father, Disraeli became a writer, and a very successful author of amusing and perceptive novels with a background of contemporary British politics. He was elected to the House of Commons in 1837 as a Tory MP. He combined a sympathy with the sufferings of the working class which was unusual in the 1830s with a profound admiration for the English monarchy and aristocracy. The obsequious flattery which he lavished on Queen Victoria was not solely due to a cynical desire to ingratiate himself with her and further his political ambitions; it was also an expression of his romantic concept of royalty. He enjoyed the friendship shown to him by English peers, and even more the attentions lavished upon him by their wives.

He was an opponent of Palmerston, and condemned his foreign policy; but after he and the Conservative Party – as the Tories were now called – had been routed by Palmerston in the general election of 1857, when they opposed Palmerston's aggressive policy in China, he decided that at any general election John Bull would always beat the Nonconformist conscience; and after Palmerston's death he stepped into his shoes.

He likewise adopted his opponents' policy when, after opposing the Liberal government's proposals to give the vote to some of the working class in the towns, he himself introduced a more radical measure which in 1867 granted what was virtually universal manhood suffrage in the urban areas, though it was only in 1885 that Gladstone's Liberal government extended it to the country districts. In this matter, both Disraeli and Gladstone acted against their party interests, for the urban working class regularly voted Liberal, and the country labourers Conservative.

After spending nearly all his political career in Opposition, and being Prime Minister for only ten months in 1868, Disraeli became Prime Minister for the second time in 1874 at the age of sixty-nine, and during his six years of office established himself as one of the great statesmen of British history. His first achievement in foreign affairs was to acquire for the British government, by a quick diplomatic and financial *coup*, a majority shareholding in the Suez Canal Company, and thereby control over the Suez Canal, which had been built a few years previously by French capital despite the opposition of Palmerston's government.

Disraeli, who was created earl of Beaconsfield in 1876, next encountered the international crisis caused by the Russo-Turkish War of 1876-7. He continued Palmerston's policy of bolstering up the Turkish empire in order to prevent Russia from capturing Constantinople and thus controlling the Middle East and the Mediterranean. But this involved supporting the oppressive rule of the Sultan and his Muslim officials and soldiers over the Christian populations of the Balkans, who looked to Russia for support. Disraeli, like Palmerston, succeeded in persuading most of the clergymen of the Church of England that, in the Reverend Charles Kingsley's words, the Muslims were 'fighting on God's side' against Russia and the Christians; but Gladstone and the Nonconformist conscience were outraged when Disraeli dismissed the stories of the Turkish atrocities against the Christians in Bulgaria as 'coffee-house babble' and gave Turkey full diplomatic support. Gladstone demanded that the Turks should be expelled 'bag and baggage' from the Balkans, and believed that Disraeli had debased British political life; Disraeli proudly boasted that his policy was 'as selfish as patriotism', and castigated Gladstone as 'a sophistical rhetorician, inebriated with the exuberance of his own verbosity' and his supporters as 'the friends of every country save their own'.

Russia won the war against Turkey, and forced the Turks, by the Treaty of San Stefano, to agree to the creation of a new independent Christian state of Bulgaria; but Disraeli, at the Congress of Berlin in 1878, forced Russia to yield most of the advantages which she had gained from the war and the Treaty of San Stefano, and to return most of the new Bulgaria to Turkey. He returned to London from Berlin to an enthusiastic welcome from the crowds at Charing Cross Station and the warmest congratulations from the queen. He declared that he had won 'Peace with honour'.

Disraeli lived long enough to inaugurate the new policy of imperialist expansion in Africa; but it was only after his death in 1881 that Robert Cecil, marquess of Salisbury, who succeeded him as leader of the Conservative Party, presided over the greatest period of colonial acquisition in British history. In the last quarter of the nineteenth century nearly all the African continent was annexed by the European powers, and Britain secured by far the largest part of it. In 1882 Gladstone's government rather reluctantly sent troops to Egypt to suppress a popular Arab nationalist rising against the Khedive's government; and though General Gordon was killed in an unsuccessful attempt to conquer the Sudan, the British public resolved to avenge Gordon's death and acquire the territory as soon as possible. This was accomplished in 1898.

The Nonconformist conscience did not condemn the war against the Arab nationalists in the Sudan, who had alienated sympathy by their cruelties, their anti-Christian fervour, and especially by their ruthless slave-trading activities among the Negro population of Central and West Africa. The British Liberals objected only when the victorious British troops in the Sudan blew up the tomb of Gordon's conqueror, the Mahdi, who had been buried there fourteen years earlier, and, after burning his corpse, threw the ashes into the River Nile. The Liberals were much more indignant about the Boer War. Only a small minority of British Liberals and Socialists in 1899 realised the intensity of the fierce racialism of the South African Boers and their determination to keep down the black population in their territories; and the Jameson Raid in 1895, the financial schemes of Cecil

Rhodes and his backers, and the aggressive policy of the Conservative government convinced them that Britain was waging an unjust war against the Boers for the benefit of unscrupulous financiers. The majority of the people of Britain, like the aged Queen Victoria, passionately supported the war, and violently condemned as 'pro-Boer' the Liberals who opposed it. The anti-war radical Liberal MP, David Lloyd George, was nearly lynched when he tried to address a public meeting in the ultra-Conservative city of Birmingham, and only saved his life because the police smuggled him out of the hall disguised in a policeman's uniform.

The British forces suffered a series of defeats in the opening months of the war, but by the autumn of 1900 had defeated the regular Boer armies in the field. The resistance was carried on by Boer guerrillas. In order to break the resistance and to deprive the guerrillas of the food and shelter which they received from their civilian co-patriots, the British troops burned the farms of the Boers and herded the men, women and children into detention centres which were officially known as 'concentration camps'. Typhoid spread in the camps, and 30,000 of the Boer detainees died. This caused great bitterness among the Boers, and outraged the Nonconformist conscience in England. The Liberal leader of the Opposition in Britain, Sir Henry Campbell-Bannerman, made himself very unpopular by saying at a public banquet: 'A phrase often used is that war is war. . . . When is a war not a war? When it is carried on by methods of barbarism in South Africa.'

The Boers capitulated in 1902, and the Transvaal Republic and the Orange Free State were annexed to the British Empire. In the previous year Queen Victoria had died after a reign of nearly sixty-four years – the longest of any English sovereign – and her son had succeeded as King Edward VII at the age of fifty-nine. The new King, with his bonhomie, his love of gambling, his enormous appetite, and his love affairs, had been publicly censured by some religious leaders, but was very popular with large sections of his subjects. Never has a nation greeted the dawn of a new reign and a new century with more optimism than the people of Britain in 1901. In the music halls they enthusiastically sang the patriotic songs, old and new, and none more appropriate than Leslie Stuart's hit, 'Soldiers of the Queen', which explained that it was because of the valour of the soldiers of the Queen that 'we tell them all that England's master', and that 'we've always won'.

How long would the power of the British empire continue? Disraeli, a few years before his death, said at the Lord Mayor's Banquet at the Guildhall in November 1878 that some people believed that even the greatest empires did not endure for ever, and that the British empire would one day pass away, like the empires of Genoa, Venice and Holland. Disraeli did not think so. He believed that a nation like England 'is more calculated to create empires than to give them up', and that 'if the English people prove themselves worthy of their ancestors . . . their power will never diminish.'

CHAPTER 15

THE GROWTH OF
DEMOCRACY
AND THE
GREAT WAR
(1902–22)

A great change took place during the second half of the nine-teenth century in the attitude of the British aristocracy and middle class towards the working class. Until the 1840s, they were quite indifferent to the sufferings of the poor. They believed that poverty was as inevitable as disease, and that the aristocracy and middle class, with their high standards of courtesy and education, had no need to concern themselves with the lives of the uncouth members of the lower orders. This attitude is revealed in the reports in Hansard of question time in the House of Commons, with ministers refusing to take any action or even to show concern when the tiny handful of radical MPs brought to their notice cases of pregnant mothers left to die of cold and hunger in the workhouse and of children brutally treated in prison. It is also shown in the popular middle-class literature of the time, in the stories of virtuous gentlemen and well-bred ladies and children confronted by rude, aggressive, drunken working men. All this had changed by the 1860s. Ministers in the House of Commons at least expressed their distress at reports of oppression and injustice; and in the novels, virtuous working-class girls were seduced by aristocratic blackguards. Captain Gronow, writing his memoirs in 1862, stated that when he was a young man everyone tried to claim that they were related to a peer, but that now they seemed eager to keep such a relationship as dark as possible. The aristocracy still had many admirers and hangers-on, but after the Crimean War they were on the defensive.

In December 1905 the Conservative government resigned, and Campbell-Bannerman formed a Liberal government, which in January 1906 won the general election with a large majority. In 1908 he resigned on the grounds of ill-health – he died a fortnight later – and was succeeded as Prime Minister by the more cautious barrister, Asquith. But if Asquith was a moderating influence compared with Campbell-Bannerman, this was more than offset by the promotion of two members of Campbell-Bannerman's government, Lloyd George and Winston Churchill, Lloyd George being appointed Chancellor of the Exchequer and Churchill entering the Cabinet as President of the Board of Trade and afterwards becoming Home Secretary. Lloyd George, a solicitor from Criccieth in north Wales, had been a radical from his earliest years. Churchill, who was the son of the Tory politician Lord Randolph Churchill and the grandson of the duke of Marlborough, had been a cavalry officer in the Sudan and a war correspondent in the Boer War, where he had been taken prisoner and had escaped. He had then entered the House of Commons as a Conservative MP, but had crossed the floor of the House and become a Liberal.

The Liberal government embarked on a far-reaching programme of social reform which led to the biggest political conflict since the days of the Reform Bill of 1832. Lloyd George introduced a system of national insurance and old age pensions; the recently conquered Boers were granted home rule in South Africa in 1909 which in due course led bloodlessly and legally to their establishing South Africa as an independent sovereign state; and exceptional privileges were granted to trade unions.

The position of the trade unions had changed during the previous fifty years. When the Chartist movement collapsed after 1848, the unions abandoned their independent political activity, and in politics confined themselves to supporting Liberal candidates at Parliamentary elections; but in 1900 they united with the Independent Labour Party which had been formed in 1893 after the first Labour MP, Keir Hardie, had been elected to the House of Commons in the general election of 1892. Together they formed the Labour Party – a new political party which was closely linked, both organisationally and financially, with the trade unions, and which aimed to return Labour and trade union MPs to the House of Commons.

The conduct of strikes had on the whole become less violent; and an increasing number of employers had decided that it was to their advantage to recognise trade unions and negotiate collective agreements with the union leaders. This led to a new relationship between the employers and the trade union leaders. The union leader of the 1890s was a very different figure from his persecuted, defiant and almost revolutionary predecessor of the 1830s. By 1893 the rank-and-file union member in the factory viewed with some suspicion his union official who went to the office dressed in a good overcoat and a top hat, and carrying a rolled umbrella, and who lunched and dined with the factory owner.*

The unions had achieved more by political lobbying than by industrial action. Having lost most of the great strikes by which they tried to improve the position of the working men, they secured the enactment of a number of statutes in the last quarter of the nineteenth century which limited working hours and enforced stricter safety standards in mines and factories; while Gladstone's government in 1871, and Disraeli's in 1875, abolished nearly all the statutory restrictions on trade unions and strikes. The unions were nevertheless repeatedly frustrated by the decisions of the judges. Some of these decisions were so surprising as to convince the unions that the courts were strongly biased against them. A long series of judicial rulings have led the trade unions today to regard the judges, not as impartial arbitrators, but as their most determined enemies.

No sooner had Campbell-Bannerman's government come to power than the Trade Disputes Act of 1906 was passed, in the face of strong opposition from the Conservatives. It exempted trade unions and all members of trade unions from liability to pay

* See the letter written in 1893 by a rank-and-file trade union member, quoted in the Webbs' *History of Trade Unionism*.

damages for any action that they committed in the course of a strike or trade dispute. The Act transformed the trade unions from victimised into privileged bodies. In 1909 the judges struck another harsh blow at trade unions when they ruled that it was illegal for the unions to use their funds to pay the salaries of Labour MPs and to work for the return of Labour candidates at Parliamentary elections. Again the Liberal government stepped in and in 1913 passed an Act of Parliament to reverse the effect of the court's decision by permitting the trade unions to use their funds for these political purposes.

The Conservative majority in the House of Lords reluctantly passed the Trade Disputes Act of 1906 and Lloyd George's national insurance and pensions legislation; but in 1909 they precipitated a political crisis by defeating his budget, though it was a long-established constitutional convention that the House of Lords did not interfere with money bills. The landowners and wealthy classes had become conscious of the extent to which taxation could be used, not merely as a means of raising revenue, but as an instrument to destroy their status in society. Income tax, which had originally been imposed as a wartime measure by Pitt in 1799 at two shillings in the pound (10 per cent), was introduced as a permanent tax by Peel's government in 1842; after falling to 2 pence in the pound (less than 1 per cent) under Disraeli's government in 1875, it had risen to 1 shilling in the pound (5 per cent) by 1908. Death duties had first been introduced by Gladstone when he was Chancellor of the Exchequer in 1853, and were strengthened by the Liberal Chancellor of the Exchequer, Sir William Harcourt, in 1894; they rose as high as 15 per cent on the largest estates. As early as 1856 Palmerston had feared the effect of death duties on the social order, and wrote: 'I consider hereditary succession to unbroken masses of landed property to be absolutely necessary for the maintenance of the British Constitution.'

Lloyd George's budget in 1909 imposed new taxes on landed property, increased income tax to 1 shilling and twopence, and introduced a new tax, supertax, afterwards called surtax, at sixpence in the pound, raising the combined income tax and supertax on higher incomes to 1 shilling and eightpence in the pound (8 per cent). The House of Lords refused to pass the budget.

The extreme wing of the Liberal Party launched a strong attack on the aristocracy and the landlords. Lloyd George, in a vigorous speech at Limehouse, denounced landowners and dukes. Liberal pamphlets attacked the nobility, exposed their vices, and listed those who owed their titles to the fact that one of their female ancestors had gone to bed with Charles II. They demanded legislation to abolish the House of Lords, or at least to curb its powers so that it would no longer be able to prevent the House of Commons from enacting legislation.

The government fought a general election in January 1910 on the issue of the power of the Lords to reject the budget; and though they lost over a hundred seats, they and their allies, the Labour party and the Irish party, had a majority over the Conservative Opposition of 124. The House of Lords now gave way and passed the budget; but this no longer satisfied the Liberals, who introduced a bill to abolish the power of the House of Lords to reject a money bill, and in the case of other legislation provided that the power of the Lords should be limited to delaying the passing of a bill for a little over two years.

No bill restricting the powers of the House of Lords could become law unless the peers in the House of Lords passed it. This the Conservative majority in the Lords absolutely refused to do, though they offered to support a reform of the House of Lords which would modify the hereditary principle. Edward VII found himself in the same position as William IV in 1832: he was asked by his Prime Minister to use his royal prerogative to create new peers so as to enable a measure of which he personally disapproved to become law. At the height of the crisis, he died in May 1910. The new king, his son George V, tried to persuade the parties to reach a compromise, and when this failed, insisted that there should be another general election before he exercised his royal prerogative to create new peers. The political situation grew more tense. In the country, Conservative hostesses wrote to their Liberal neighbours and informed them that in view of their political attitude they would no longer be welcome in their houses.

The Liberals won the general election of December 1910, gaining twenty-three seats and losing twenty-four to the Conservatives; in the new House there were 272 Liberal, 272 Conservative, 84 Irish Nationalist and 42 Labour MPs. The king then agreed, if necessary, to create the new peers. When Asquith announced this in the House of Commons, he was shouted down by the Conservative MPs, and was unable to make himself heard for twenty-five minutes; but the House of Lords, faced with talk from Liberal extremists of making every hundredth elector in Whitechapel a peer, gave way, as they had done in 1832. The Conservative Parliamentary Party decided, against the opposition of the 'Diehard' Tory peers, to abstain in the division over the Parliament Bill, and it passed in the House of Lords in August 1911 by a majority of 17.

The Irish Nationalist MPs had their own motives for supporting the Parliament Bill, for the House of Lords was the insurmountable obstacle to the realisation of Irish Home Rule. The grant of Catholic Emancipation in 1829 had not brought peace to Ireland; the struggle continued for national independence and for the rights of the tenants against the English landlords in Ireland, many of whom were absentee nobles living in London and on their English country estates. In 1846 the failure of the potato crop had caused a famine in Ireland, and during the next three years 1½ million people died of hunger. The government refused to ban the export of wheat during the famine, or to give poor relief to the people in their homes; both these measures would have violated Whig economic theory. They sent troops to guard the vehicles taking the wheat to the docks, and enforced the workhouse regulations in all their rigour, though many women preferred to die of starvation rather than have their hair shaved, a condition imposed by the workhouse authorities.

The bitterness caused by the 'great hunger' was increased by the suppression of an insurrectionary movement in 1848 and by the sentences of transportation for life to Van Diemen's Land imposed on the revolutionary leaders. The mass emigration to America, which, with the deaths during the famine, reduced the population of Ireland from 8 million in 1845 to 4 million in 1890, was more of a tragedy in personal terms than was shown in the statistical tables; and incidents such as the ploughing up of the paupers' graves, in which the victims of the famine were buried, were remembered from generation to generation.

In 1865 a revolutionary nationalist society, the Fenian Brotherhood, began a terrorist campaign of assassination and bomb-throwing which the British public considered to be far more reprehensible than identical acts of terrorism committed by revolutionaries in Russia or Italy. The execution of captured terrorists aroused more resentment in Ireland, especially the hanging of three Fenians – the 'Manchester martyrs' – who were involved in the accidental shooting of a policeman while helping two fellow-Fenians to escape from prison. Other Fenians, like the revolutionary socialist Michael Davitt, were sentenced to long terms of imprisonment in the new penitentiaries, with their system of solitary confinement, in conditions which were much harsher than those 'prison universities' in which political prisoners were confined in tsarist Russia and the other continental autocracies. The British authorities, unlike almost every other government in the world, refused to recognise the category of 'political prisoner', arguing that, under the British rule of law, no one was punished for his political opinions, but only after being convicted of a criminal offence.

The agricultural tenants in Ireland felt great resentment at the practice of the land agents of their absentee English landlords of increasing the rent of any tenant who had added to the value of the land by the improvements which he had made at his own expense. Their resentment was increased by the fact that in Ulster the tenants were protected against this practice by the custom known as 'tenant-right' by which an ejected tenant was entitled to compensation for any improvement which he had made; but the British Parliament refused to extend tenant-right to other parts of Ireland.

When at last tenant-right was granted, the tenants were still dissatisfied; and there were also complaints of tenants being evicted for voting against their landlords' candidates at Parliamentary and local elections. In 1879 Davitt and his revolutionary colleagues founded the Land League, which organised rent strikes, and by propaganda and intimidation induced nearly all the agricultural population to refuse to accept a tenancy of a farm from which a tenant had been ejected for non-payment of rent. Oppressive land agents were ostracised by the local population; the most notorious of them, the earl of Erne's land agent in County Mayo, Captain Boycott, gave his name to a new word in the English language. Occasionally a land agent, or a tenant who moved into a farm from which his predecessor had been ejected, was found murdered on a lonely country road.

Gladstone's government suppressed the Land League and arrested its leaders; and the repression was intensified under Lord Salisbury's Conservative government. The government found it difficult to get juries to convict in political cases, for the Nationalist barrister and MP, Tim Healy, who often appeared for the defence at the trials, adopted the simple expedient of objecting to every juror who wore a tie. The Conservative Secretary for Ireland, A. J. Balfour – 'Bloody Balfour' to the Irish Nationalists – abolished trial by jury for many political offences; and demonstrators were killed when troops opened fire.

Meanwhile the Irish Nationalists had launched a political campaign to achieve Home Rule, with self-government by a Parliament in Dublin under the sovereignty of the queen of England. They found a skilful leader in a Scottish Protestant, Charles Stewart Parnell, who tried to force the British government to grant Home Rule by disrupting Parliamentary business at Westminster. This led to the practice of ending discussion by the 'guillotine' procedure of a majority vote of the House. Parnell made an alliance with Gladstone and the Liberals, which was disrupted when Parnell became involved in a divorce scandal. After a long struggle, Gladstone's last government succeeded in persuading the House of Commons to pass the Home Rule Bill in 1893; but it was thrown out by the Conservative majority in the House of Lords.

It was only after the Parliament Act of 1911 had limited the power of the House of Lords that the Liberal government was able to reward its Irish nationalist allies for their support over the Parliament Bill by proceeding with a new Home Rule Bill. The House of Lords could now only delay the bill for just over two years. The Conservative leaders therefore decided to resort to extra-Parliamentary methods to defeat Home Rule. Two eminent Conservative barristers and political leaders, Sir Edward Carson and F. E. Smith, played the leading part in the campaign. Carson, who was a native of Southern Ireland, was a former solicitor-general; Smith was a future attorney-general, and, as Lord Birkenhead, was to become Lord Chancellor. They stirred up the Protestant population of Ulster to oppose a project which would result in placing them under the government of Catholics in Dublin instead of the Protestant British government in Westminster.

They organised the signing of the Covenant, in imitation of the Covenant signed by the Ulstermen's Scottish Presbyterian ancestors in the revolutionary religious struggle in Scotland in 1557 and 1638. At great meetings in Ulster, speaking from a platform-table draped with the Union Jack, Carson and F. E. Smith called for resistance in language which went very close to inciting armed violence and civil war. Any Home Ruler who used similar language would certainly have been prosecuted for sedition; but the Liberal government dared not bring the Conservative leaders to trial. The government could not rely on the sympathy of the judges, of an English jury, or of their armed forces.

The leaders of the Conservative party in England gave their full support to Carson and F. E. Smith, and launched the slogan: 'Ulster will fight and Ulster will be right!' In 1914 it was discovered that Carson and his supporters were stockpiling arms which were being shipped to them in Ulster from Germany. The Liberal Secretary of State for War thereupon asked the British generals whether they would be prepared to serve against the Conservative rebels in Ulster, or whether they would prefer to resign. They unanimously answered this extraordinary question by informing him that they would all resign. The government thereupon abandoned their plans to suppress Carson and his Ulster Volunteers.

The Liberal government was also in conflict with the suffragettes. As early as 1870 a bill to give women the vote had passed its second reading in the House of Commons; but, like similar bills in later years, it failed to become law. In 1903 Mrs Emmeline Pankhurst and her daughters organised a small group of zealous women of all social classes to campaign for women's suffrage. Asquith's government declared their sympathy with the suffragettes' demands; but as they refused to give Parliamentary time for the discussion of bills for women's suffrage, the women resorted to 'direct action'. A mass demonstration of women was held in Parliament Square, though this was illegal under the provisions of an Act of 1817 which banned meetings within one mile of the Houses of Parliament while the Houses were in session. The police dispersed the demonstration with a good deal of violence.

The allegations of police brutality, and the many arrests and convictions which followed, caused the suffragettes to adopt

271

violent and illegal methods. They broke shop windows and chained themselves to railings, shouting 'Votes for Women!', and soon they filled the jails. They then went on hunger strike, and were subjected to the painful and humiliating process of forcible feeding. When this led to public protests, the government released the hunger-strikers and then re-arrested them to complete their prison sentence when their hunger strike was over. This 'Cat and Mouse' Act aroused fresh protests from the supporters of the suffragettes.

By 1912 the movement was being directed by Mrs Pankhurst's daughter Christabel in Paris as a well-organised 'underground' revolutionary movement. Suffragettes dropped petrol bombs in letter boxes. One committed suicide at the Derby in 1913 by throwing herself in front of the king's horse as the horses passed Tattenham Corner, with the suffragette flag wrapped around her. Another slashed a famous portrait in the National Gallery. Others succeeded in burning down the country houses of Lloyd George and other Cabinet ministers.

Both the Irish crisis and the suffragette struggle were at their height when the First World War broke out in August 1914. Mrs Pankhurst, fearing to alienate all public sympathy if she continued the violence and sabotage in wartime, called off the campaign and placed the services of the suffragettes at the government's disposal. The Irish problem was shelved by passing the Home Rule Bill over the veto of the House of Lords under the provisions of the Parliament Act, but also enacting another statute which postponed indefinitely the date when it should come into operation. The leaders of the Irish Nationalist MPs accepted the compromise; the younger extremists in Ireland regarded it as another betrayal by the British Liberals.

Since the turn of the century, the British government had been alarmed at the growing naval strength of Germany, and at the aggressive intentions of the German emperor. They had therefore formed an alliance with France, who was also allied to Russia. The assassination of the Archduke Franz Ferdinand of Austria by Serbian nationalists at Sarajevo started a chain of events which led to the outbreak of war, with Russia, France, Britain, Belgium and Serbia fighting against Germany, Austria, Bulgaria and Turkey. In 1915 Italy, and in 1917 the United States, entered the war on the Allied side.

For several decades, the governments and experts had been worried about the increasing destructiveness of war, as new weapons and more powerful explosives were invented, and the defensive power began to prevail over the offensive. The number of casualties at Linden and Malplaquet had been surpassed in the Napoleonic Wars at Borodino, where the combined casualties on both sides were 74,000, the Russians losing one-third of their total force; the British army and navy lost only 20,000 killed in the course of the war from 1792 to 1815, 6,000 of these in the three days of the Waterloo campaign. The American Civil War had been very deadly, the total casualties in four years' fighting on both sides amounting to about 600,000.

The trench warfare on the Western Front in France led to a prolonged and bloody war which had not been expected by the officers and men who hastened to volunteer in August 1914 for fear the war would be over before they had time to reach the front line; but the British army leaders knew from the start that there would be heavy losses, and launched repeated recruiting campaigns. There was no longer any question of fighting the war with a small army of 'the scum of the earth' under the command of noblemen and gentlemen. The British people responded in a wave of patriotic enthusiasm to the call for volunteers. The officer corps was expanded to include a substantial proportion of the professional middle classes of military age, and the rank and file included even larger numbers of the respectable sections of the working class. But the losses were so heavy that, for the first time in English history since feudal times, compulsory military service was introduced.

On 1 July 1916 the French and British armies began an offensive on the River Somme. The British lost 60,000 in the first day's fighting. By the time that the offensive was broken off in October, the total casualties on both sides were over 1,300,000, of which the British share was 453,000. In the offensives in the eight months from April to December 1917, the British losses alone were three-quarters of a million, and by the end of the war they amounted to 2,700,000 – more than a hundred times the losses in the Napoleonic Wars, and more than had fallen in all the wars in which England had been engaged in the last fifteen hundred years. War had so recently been a romantic, if cruel, affair, with cavalry charges and the infantry heroically storming a height at bayonet point. But standing and sleeping for months in the mud of the trenches of Flanders, going over the top into the barbed wire entanglements and advancing a few thousand yards after weeks of fighting, with casualties so unprecedently high as to be beyond any comparison with former wars, caused an altogether different attitude towards war to spread among the soldiers at the front.

They also rather unfairly blamed their generals. If the Great War produced no military genius, this was chiefly because of the nature of the fighting. In the Napoleonic Wars and all the wars of the nineteenth century, the casualty rate among generals had been very high, as enemy snipers, recognising them by their splendid uniforms and epaulettes, picked them off. Even the commanders-in-chief were in danger; both Napoleon and Wellington saw their staff officers killed or severely wounded within a few yards of where they were standing. In the First World War the generals directed the war from headquarters several miles from the battlefield, running no risks whatever except the remote possibility of long-range bombardment or air raids. The soldiers, in the mud of the trenches and hanging on the wire in No-Man's-Land, thought bitterly of their commanders in the safety and comfort of some French château.

The idea of war as a fitting occupation for noblemen and gentlemen had gone. In the Crimean War, Lord Cardigan, risking his life in leading the charge of the Light Brigade, had encountered, when his men stormed the Russian position, a Russian officer whom he had known when he had been stationed in London, and he courteously saluted him. In the First World War, the people, indignant at the sufferings and casualties of their loved ones at the front, looked for the villains who were responsible for this wickedness. If war was a crime, not a career, someone must be punished for having caused it; and in the eyes of the British people, the German Kaiser and the German nation, the 'Huns', were responsible. The war would be continued until the Kaiser was overthrown, put on trial, and hanged; and future wars must be prevented by creating an international organisation which would make it impossible for anyone to start another war. The war was 'a war to end war'. It was being fought because 'the world must be made safe for democracy'; and as the soldiers who fought in it were heroes, Britain after the war would be 'a fit country for heroes to live in'.

In December 1916 the German government offered to open peace negotiations, and several peace feelers were put forward by both Germany and Austria during the next two years; but they were indignantly rejected by the Allies – not, as would have been the case in earlier wars, because they hoped to gain more advantageous peace terms by continuing military operations, but because public opinion demanded the complete destruction of the enemy. When Lord Lansdowne, in November 1917, wrote a letter to the *Daily Telegraph* suggesting the possibility of a negotiated peace, he was violently denounced almost as if he had been a traitor.

The national hatred of the enemy was fanned by the popular press which had developed in the last decade of the nineteenth century. William Howard Russell's dispatches from the Crimea were read by 50,000 readers of his newspaper, *The Times*, which had a very much higher circulation than any other daily newspaper. His revelations which shocked and changed public opinion were published in long and well-written articles of some 15,000 words, printed in unbroken columns in very small print with no sub-headings. By the time of the First World War, Alfred Harmsworth owned newspapers with a circulation of over two million, in which the news was announced in sensational headlines on the front page, with the articles consisting of no more than a few hundred words broken up into short sections by many sub-headings, and illustrated with photographs. The new format of the newspapers reflected a fundamental change in the editor's approach to his readers. He no longer aimed to convert by reasoned argument, but to create some vivid impression in the reader's mind; for the readers were not educated gentlemen who studied the newspaper at leisure, but men who glanced at it in the trains and buses on their way to work.

The war ended on 11 November 1918, when the Germans agreed to an armistice on terms which amounted to complete surrender, after a revolution had broken out in Berlin and the Kaiser had fled to Holland. At the Peace Conference at Versailles next year, the victorious Allies adopted the unprecedented course of refusing to admit the representatives of their defeated enemies to the conference table. The Allied statesmen discussed the peace terms amongst themselves for many weeks, and when the final treaty had been drafted, the German delegates were summoned and informed of the peace terms, and given the choice of either accepting them or facing a renewal of the war, which was out of the question, as the armistice terms had destroyed their capacity for making war. The terms included two other unprecedented provisions – a statement that Germany was guilty of the crime of starting the war, and an undertaking by the Allied Powers to require the Dutch government to surrender the Kaiser to them for trial as a war criminal. They also created the League of Nations, which was to consist of representatives of national governments who would take decisions, after public debates, by majority vote, and would prevent war by 'collective security' – a system under which all the member-states of the League would unite to stop any of their members who committed aggression against another member state, irrespective of whether such action was in the national interests of their countries.

The Russian Revolution of 1917 had as deep an effect on British political life as the French Revolution of 1789. The British people were hostile to Russian tsarism, having for nearly a hundred years disapproved of the Russian oppression of Poland, the treatment of Polish patriots and Russian opposition elements who were 'sent to Siberia' under terrible conditions, and of the pogroms and persecutions of Russian Jews. Their criticism was only temporarily suspended when Russia became Britain's ally in 1914; and the Liberals who played such a leading part in the Allied war effort felt that tsarist Russia was something of a blot on the otherwise spotless purity of the Allied cause. There was therefore general satisfaction in Britain when the revolution in Petrograd in March 1917 forced the tsar to abdicate and led to the proclamation of a Liberal democratic republic; and the public hostility to tsarism was so great that George V dissuaded his ministers from inviting the tsar to take refuge in Britain.

The Liberal Russian government continued the war on the side of the Allies; but the opposition to the war was strong in Russia, whose losses had been even heavier than those of the other armies engaged in the war; and the extreme socialists – the Bolsheviks under Lenin and Trotsky – made use of the opposition to the war to overthrow the Liberal government of Kerensky by a second revolution in November 1917. The Bolsheviks established a rigid dictatorship, and, like the French revolutionaries of 1792, called on the proletarians in all countries to overthrow their rulers by revolution. They invited all the belligerent powers to begin immediate peace talks; and when the Allies rejected this proposal, the Bolshevik government signed a separate peace with Germany under which Germany occupied large tracts of Russia and replenished her food stocks, severely affected by the Allied blockade, from the wheatfields of the Ukraine.

In July 1918 the Bolsheviks shot the tsar and his family to prevent them from being set free by counter-revolutionary forces. The indignation of the British government and Establishment against the Bolsheviks exceeded in vehemence and hysteria even that which they had shown against the Jacobins in 1793; and Churchill, who took the lead in the anti-Bolshevik campaign, used language as violent as Burke's 130 years before. On the other hand, the sympathy for the Bolsheviks in Britain was stronger than that felt for the French revolutionaries; they were able to enlist the support, not only of Communists and socialists, but of pacifists who had been disgusted by the First World War and who welcomed the Bolsheviks' denunciation of the 'imperialist war' and their call to all peoples to end it. When the Conservative press denounced the horrors of Bolshevism, the shootings of counter-revolutionaries as hostages, and the murder of the tsar and his family, the Bolshevik sympathisers retorted that less than 10,000 people had been shot by the Bolsheviks, compared with the 10 million killed by the 'capitalist governments' in the trenches in the Great War. They blamed the Bolshevik severities on the Allied governments who were supporting the counter-revolutionary 'White' armies in Russia with arms and men.

In 1918 British troops intervened in Russia, seizing Archangel in the north and Baku in the south, and were in action against the Bolshevik forces; and as the intervention continued in 1919 and 1920, after the war with Germany had ended, it was clear to the socialists in Britain that their government's object was not, as the government had claimed, to maintain the Eastern Front against the Germans, but to overthrow Communism in Russia by force.

In 1919 the socialists in the Labour Party, who had succeeded the radicals as the mouthpiece of left-wing dissent and the Nonconformist conscience in Britain, saw their government as the chief instrument of counter-revolution and the main supporter of oppression in Russia, Ireland and India. In Ireland, the younger Nationalist elements, disgusted with the postponement of Home

Rule in 1914 and with the Irish Nationalist MPs' support for the British war effort, formed a new revolutionary party, Sinn Fein, and its fighting body, the Irish Republican Army (IRA). These younger revolutionaries, together with a handful of old survivors of the Fenian movement of the nineteenth century, launched an abortive insurrection in Dublin at Easter 1916, which was suppressed by the British government and army with all the severity which had been shown by their predecessors in 1798, 1803 and 1848. The leaders of the revolt were tried by military courts and shot under martial law. Many more of the rebels were sentenced to imprisonment, or interned; but a year later they were all released, chiefly in order to placate the criticism in the United States, which had just entered the war on the Allied side.

Sinn Fein promptly began an effective guerrilla war against the British troops, in which a thirty-year-old office clerk, Michael Collins, showed outstanding gifts in planning the terrorist campaign of the IRA. The Sinn Feiners had such widespread support among the population that they were able to organise large-scale fund-raising activities and a very effective boycott of the British law courts by which litigants agreed to sue each other, not in the legal courts, but in the illegal courts organised by Sinn Fein. The British army retaliated against the IRA attacks by a policy of counter-terrorism, assassinating leading Sinn Fein supporters and sacking towns and villages which sympathised with the IRA. Collins's greatest *coup* was to organise the murder by his gunmen of fourteen British secret service officers in their lodgings in Dublin on the same Sunday morning in November 1920. That afternoon a British army unit marched to a football stadium in Dublin and opened fire without warning or provocation on the crowd who were watching the match, killing a dozen of the spectators and wounding many more.

In India, too, Britain faced a powerful movement for national independence in 1919, and fought it with stern repression. A spiritual leader, Mahatma Gandhi, launched a civil disobedience campaign in 1919 to compel the British to leave India. Against Gandhi's instructions, the movement turned violent, and in the town of Amritsar an Englishwoman, a missionary, was assaulted and seriously wounded by an Indian mob. When Gandhi's supporters in Amritsar, a few days later, held an open-air political meeting, which had been banned by the government, the British commander, General Dyer, surrounded the meeting place with his troops, and after sealing the exits from the ground to prevent the crowd from escaping, opened fire, killing 385 people. He also compelled the Indian inhabitants of the district to crawl on their bellies along the street in which the Englishwoman had been assaulted. When public opinion in India, and the Nonconformist conscience in Britain, protested against the massacre of Amritsar, the British government removed General Dyer from his command; but the London Conservative newspaper, the *Morning Post*, organised a public subscription for a gift to Dyer and collected £30,000 from English men and women in Britain and India who strongly approved of his action, which they believed had saved India from revolution and the British inhabitants there from the horrors of another Indian Mutiny.

There had been many precedents in the history of the British army, as in that of every other army, for the executions and shootings in Ireland and India; but it was almost the last occasion on which Britain acted ruthlessly to suppress a movement for national independence against its imperial authority. The Nonconformist conscience was gaining the ascendancy over policies 'as selfish as patriotism' in British ruling circles, though not among the population as a whole. The British Establishment were losing their self-confidence in their own power and self-righteousness, and in both Ireland and India the savagery of 1919–20 was replaced by a different policy.

In Ireland the British government, in the summer of 1921, made a truce with Sinn Fein, and opened talks in London with their representatives for a permanent political settlement of the Irish problem. The most prominent of the Sinn Fein delegates was Michael Collins, the supreme commander of the IRA. Many Conservatives denounced the talks as 'shaking hands with murderers'. By a mixture of threats and concessions, the British Prime Minister, Lloyd George, persuaded the Sinn Fein delegation to agree to a compromise under which Home Rule – which in practice meant independence – was granted to twenty-six of the thirty-two Irish counties; but six of the counties of Ulster in the north-east were to remain independent from the new Irish government in Dublin and under the rule of the United Kingdom Parliament in Westminster and of its own local legislative assembly.

A powerful minority of the Sinn Fein leadership, including its president, Eamon De Valera, repudiated the agreement reached in London; and when Michael Collins and his colleagues, who supported the treaty, formed the government of the Irish Free State in Dublin, the IRA split. A section of it launched an armed insurrection against their former leader and his government, and Collins was killed in the fighting before the revolt was suppressed with the help of artillery supplied by the British government and with methods more brutal than those which the British army had so recently used against both groups of combatants in the Irish Civil War.

In India the process was slower, but followed the same pattern of negotiation, repression and concession. Gandhi was alternately imprisoned for sedition and invited to the Viceroy's palace in Poona, or to London, for talks about progress towards Indian Home Rule. Then, after the police charges, the floggings and the sentences of imprisonment, by which the British Labour government broke the Civil Disobedience Campaign of 1930, came the grant of provincial self-government by the British Conservative-dominated National Government in 1935, in the face of strong opposition from a Right-wing Conservative group in Britain, of which Churchill was the leading spokesman. The delay in granting Home Rule led to a new Civil Disobedience Campaign during the Second World War in 1942, when the Japanese armies stood on the north-eastern frontier of India, and to the detention without trial of Gandhi, Nehru and other Indian nationalists. In 1947 the British Labour government granted independence to India, after appeasing the indignation of the powerful Muslim minority by creating the separate Muslim state of Pakistan.

The grant of independence was immediately followed by massacres of Hindus by Muslims and of Muslims by Hindus; and in the thirty-four years which have passed since the two states of India and Pakistan became independent, they have been in a state of almost constant hostility, and on two occasions have been at war. The brutal despotism of the governments in Pakistan, if not in India, remain, like the regime in the independent Boer republic of South Africa, a strange tribute to the achievement of the British Nonconformist conscience.

CHAPTER 16

THE
TWENTIETH
CENTURY:
DECLINE OR
PROGRESS?
(1922–79)

The social and economic system of Britain was not seriously undermined by the First World War. The development of the motor car, and to a lesser extent the aeroplane, made an important change in the appearance and the life of the towns and the countryside. By 1930 nearly all the upper and middle classes owned private motor cars; and though a car was to some extent a class symbol, and only a minority of the working classes owned one, cars were more common than private carriages had formerly been, and private transport had become far more widespread than before 1914. It did not, however, cause so profound an effect on social life as the development of the railways a hundred years earlier, which had liberated the common people from the confines of their parishes. Already by the end of the nineteenth century, before the appearance of the car, only a small minority of the inhabitants of Britain had never left their native village; large numbers of them already travelled regularly to the seaside for their summer holidays, and to other parts of the country to visit their relatives at Christmas.

Before the First World War, the telephone had changed the

281

way of life of the wealthier classes who could afford to possess one. The cinema developed as a mass industry at the beginning of the twentieth century, especially after the invention of talking pictures in 1928, and enabled people all over the country to see performances by leading actors and actresses who otherwise could be seen only in West End theatres in London, where the more comfortable seats cost about one-third of the weekly wage of the average working man. The cinemas to a considerable extent replaced the touring theatrical companies which had formerly performed plays at the local village halls. By 1930 nearly every large and small town in Britain had at least one cinema, and except in the remoter regions, such as the Scottish Highlands, most people lived less than ten miles from their local cinema, which was usually crowded to capacity on Saturdays. Most of the films were made in Hollywood in California, and showed the millions of people who saw them, in England as well as in Asia and South America, a way of life which they had not experienced – a world of material luxury, of male competitiveness, and of women liberated from the restrictions of the kitchen, of village life, and of parental control.

The position of women had greatly changed. In 1918 they were granted the vote at the age of thirty, and this discrimination between the sexes was removed in 1928, when they were allowed to vote, like men, at the age of twenty-one. The age for both sexes was lowered to eighteen in 1969. The Great War had accelerated the tendency to bring women into employment in offices; by 1920 most business firms employed more young unmarried women than men as secretaries and typists in offices. This practice became so well established that in 1979 an opponent of the Women's Liberation Movement argued that it was a law of nature that men should be miners and women should be secretaries, although until 1842 women worked in mines, and until about 1890 all secretaries were men.

The legal status of women had been improved by legislation which sometimes produced a change which was of more theoretical than practical importance. Until 1882, a married woman's property belonged to her husband in law; but it had long been the practice, in the property-owning classes, for the bride's father to settle her property on trustees holding on her behalf, thus giving her, and not her husband, complete control of the property. The Act of 1882, which permitted her to own property, gave legal effect to the long-standing reality. In 1840 the judges ruled that in certain circumstances a husband was allowed to imprison his wife in her room; in 1891, they held that he could not do so, even if he knew that she was planning to elope with her lover; and they also ruled that a husband was not allowed to beat his wife.

The conventional masculine view of women was changing. In nineteenth-century Britain – the tendency was less marked in France and other European countries – women were both despised and worshipped. They were regularly referred to as 'the weaker sex' and 'the gentle sex', who were to be protected from the harsh reality of the world. Though, as Marx and Engels pointed out in *The Communist Manifesto*, this attitude of the middle-class man towards women of his own class did not prevent him from exposing working-class women to the rigours and risks of life in his factories. The amendments of the criminal law in the early nineteenth century forbade the flogging of women, which had previously been common, and exempted them from the rigorous prison regime which was applied to men. If a man and a woman jointly committed a criminal offence, the man was nearly always punished much more severely than the woman, on the assumption that her weaker will had been influenced to do wrong by him; and this attitude of the courts still persists to a considerable extent today.

Not all the changes worked to the advantage of women. In 1882 the eminent barrister, Serjeant Ballantine, was concerned over the miscarriages of justice which could result from the fact that if a woman accused a man of rape or of indecent assault he was almost automatically convicted and punished by a long term of imprisonment; by 1930, advanced and sophisticated women were saying that they 'did not believe in rape', and ridiculing the idea that the man, not the woman, played the decisive part in a sexual relationship. In 1981 the Women's Liberation Movement complain of the difficulty of persuading juries to convict men who have committed the most brutal rapes, and of the leniency of the punishments imposed in the cases when a conviction is obtained.

In 1856, the *Times* leader-writer was horrified that audiences which included women should be permitted to see so immoral an opera as Verdi's *La Traviata*, which expressed sympathy for a courtesan. By 1893 Pinero, in his play *The Second Mrs Tanqueray*, was criticising the moral code which condemned the woman, but excused the man, who had been involved in an extra-marital relationship. By 1930, Bernard Shaw's *Mrs Warren's Profession*, which was banned in 1893, had been produced on the London stage.

The middle classes were still prosperous in the inter-war years. They lived in a style which surprised foreigners from Europe, in the middle-sized houses which were to be found on the outskirts of the villages all over England, but especially in the south-east – houses with fifteen or twenty rooms, surrounded by fifty acres of garden and fields, and manned by a staff of five or six women servants in the house, in addition to half-a-dozen gardeners and under-gardeners in the grounds. There were smaller houses occupied by the bank manager or local accountant, with only one maid to wait at table and do all the work in the house. In the larger town houses of the aristocracy and wealthy families, there was a regular hierarchy of servants presided over by butlers and valets who behaved in the manner portrayed by P. G. Wodehouse and in the TV series 'Upstairs, Downstairs'. This famous type of servant did not appear before the middle of the nineteenth century. Lord Malmesbury in 1861 disliked the new kind of suave and obsequious manservant; he much preferred the old sort who spoke to his master as man to man, and scolded him quite harshly in appropriate cases. He thought that his outspoken manservant Brenton was the last surviving servant of the good old school.

The upper and middle classes of the 1920s still retained their economic prosperity, but had already lost their sense of security. As the hopes of the League of Nations faded away, and it was clear that Britain had not become a land fit for heroes to live in, they reacted by living for the hour and hoping that the deluge would come after they had enjoyed a few more years of good living. Then, in the early 1930s, they were confronted with the economic depression – the 'Slump'. Unemployment rose sharply, and while the working classes, at least in the 'depressed areas', suffered severe poverty, the middle classes too were impoverished to some extent by the recession. They took fewer holidays abroad, and in some cases reduced the number of their servants. For the first time for several centuries – apart from wartime exigencies – the middle classes found themselves enjoying a substantially lower standard of living than ten years before. Their way of life was not radically altered, but their confidence was shaken.

They were also losing faith in the old ideals. They no longer boasted of English glory and of the innate moral superiority of the Englishman over the foreigner; and while they did not denounce the crimes of British imperialism, like the Communists and the Labour keepers of the Nonconformist conscience, they laughed at the British empire and at other established institutions, with their very popular playwright, Noel Coward, and enjoyed P. G. Wodehouse's ridicule of the silly young aristocrat, Bertie Wooster, who could be rescued from the consequences of his idiocy only by his manservant, Jeeves. When foreigners expressed surprise that they should thus denigrate their country and its traditions, they explained that this was the British sense of humour; but it was not the kind of joke that would have been appreciated by Palmerston and the boisterous humourists of his generation, who laughed at the *Mikado* and at the costumes and habits of Frenchmen and Asiatics.

The Labour Party, with its close organisational ties with the trade unions, made remarkable advances after the First World War. Fifty-seven Labour MPs were returned at the general election of 1918, and 142 in 1922. In 1923 191 Labour MPs were elected, and in January 1924 Ramsay Macdonald formed the first Labour government. Nine months later, he was defeated at a general election fought on the issue of Labour's sympathy for the Russian Bolsheviks after the Conservative newspaper, the *Daily Mail*, published a letter alleged to have been written by the Russian Communist leader, Zinoviev, in which he instructed the British Communist Party to support Labour against the Conservatives in the election. Although this was in fact the Communist policy which Zinoviev might well have formulated, the letter had been forged by Russian anti-Communist refugees in Berlin with the connivance of at least one prominent British Conservative. The 'Red Letter' was used to considerable effect by the Conservatives in the election campaign.

In 1926 the Trades Union Congress called a general strike in support of a strike by the miners against a reduction in wages. The Conservative government defeated the general strike with the help of thousands of middle-class volunteers who kept the public services running until the TUC called off the strike, nine days after it had started. In 1929 Ramsay Macdonald again formed a Labour minority government after winning the general election with 287 MPs; but the government fell when Macdonald split with most of his Cabinet colleagues and formed a coalition with the Conservatives during the Slump in 1931; and Labour was heavily defeated at the ensuing general election.

By 1932, 23 per cent of the labour force in Britain was unemployed, and the Labour Opposition was attacking the National government of Macdonald and the Conservatives with great bitterness. The Communists and the left wing of the Labour Party organised the 'hunger marchers' from the depressed areas of north-east England to walk to London, where they became involved in violent clashes with the police, in which the demonstrators were injured and arrested. There were further protests against the 'Means Test'. Hitherto an unemployed person who had paid his national insurance contributions was automatically entitled to relief; under the Means Test, he could not claim it if the earnings of other members of his family exceeded a certain sum. This was bitterly resented by the unemployed.

In January 1936 George V died, and was succeeded by his son, the very popular Prince of Wales, who became King Edward VIII. Before the end of the year he had abdicated, because the Establishment, and probably the majority of his subjects, objected to his marrying an American divorcee. As his title to the throne, like that of all British monarchs since 1701, depended on the doctrine of the sovereignty of Parliament and the provisions of the Act of Settlement, it was legally impossible for him to deprive himself of the crown by abdicating it; a new Act of Parliament, amending the Act of Settlement, was required. His Majesty's Declaration of Abdication Bill passed the House of Commons and the House of Lords; and at the moment when Edward VIII gave his royal assent to the bill, he ceased to reign. He was succeeded by his brother King George VI who, on his death in 1952, was followed by his daughter, Queen Elizabeth II.

The abdication crisis revealed the position of the monarchy in twentieth-century Britain – both its great popularity and its relative political unimportance. The abdication aroused far more interest among the mass of the British public than the shattering economic and international events of the 1930s; but it had no effect on either the slump or the growing threat of the Second World War. Politically, a new government has more effect than a new sovereign. The relationship of the queen to her Prime Minister today is almost exactly the reverse of what it was in the sixteenth and seventeenth centuries. Thomas Cromwell, Cecil, Strafford and Danby exercised great political influence by the advice which they tendered to Henry VIII, Elizabeth I, Charles I and Charles II; but the final decision was always taken by the sovereign. Today, the queen can exercise great political influence by her advice to the Prime Minister; but it is the Prime Minister who ultimately decides the policy to be adopted.

The economic situation began to improve, and the unemployment figures to fall, after 1933; and the political struggle switched to international affairs. The Labour Party had always been internationalist in outlook, and the First World War had produced a strong pacifist feeling in the party. Many party members had been conscientious objectors during the war, and had suffered imprisonment, and in some cases brutal ill-treatment. After the war, an influential pacifist movement arose in the country. It laid much emphasis on the terrible weapons that would be used in any future war, above all poison gas, which had been resorted to by the Germans in the First World War. The anti-war propaganda was disseminated in books and pamphlets which were read, if not by the great mass of the population, by hundreds of thousands of intellectuals and political activists. One of these publications predicted that if there were another war, the whole population of Britain would be killed by poison gas within twenty-four hours of the start of the war. These warnings were taken very seriously. The Reverend Dick Sheppard, a canon of St Paul's, founded the Peace Pledge Union, whose members signed a declaration: 'I renounce war, and never again, directly or indirectly, will I support or sanction another.' In 1933, the university students in the Oxford Union debating society caused a sensation by carrying a resolution that 'This House will in no circumstances fight for its king and country.'

In January 1933 Adolf Hitler came to power in Germany, and began a fierce persecution of Communists, suppressing the Communist Party and arresting its leaders and active members. He also attacked the Jews, continuing the tradition of the Russian

Whites and their supporters in Britain and elsewhere of denouncing Russian Bolshevism and international Communism as a Jewish conspiracy. The Communists and the Labour Party in Britain, who had strongly opposed the Fascist dictatorship which Mussolini established in Italy in 1922, were even more indignant and alarmed at the coming to power of Hitler and the Nazis in Germany, whom they regarded with as much horror as the British Conservatives viewed the Russian Communists. They launched a vigorous propaganda campaign exposing the cruelties committed by the Nazis against Communists, socialists, pacifists and Jews in the concentration camps where they were imprisoned, and the torture employed by the Nazi secret police, the Gestapo, to extract information from them. The British Conservatives were less concerned about the fate of German Communists and socialists, and some of them welcomed Hitler as a bulwark against Communism.

In 1931 the imperial government of Japan, which was a right-wing military dictatorship, invaded the Chinese province of Manchuria. This indirectly threatened the safety of Russia's far eastern provinces. China appealed to the League of Nations in Geneva; but the League made no attempt to help China by enforcing the doctrine of collective security. The Labour Opposition in Britain, supported by the Liberals and a few Conservatives, criticised the Conservative government for failing to urge the League of Nations to take action against Japan.

In 1935 Mussolini invaded Abyssinia (Ethiopia), which with Liberia was the only independent black state on the African continent. The British government at first took the lead at Geneva in persuading the League to apply economic sanctions against Italy; but these were limited to a boycott of Italian goods; and the government refused to agree to the demand of the Labour Opposition and their supporters in the other parties for the imposition by the League of an embargo on the supply of oil to Italy. The Conservatives argued that this would provoke a world war. In May 1936, after an eight months' campaign, the Abyssinian resistance collapsed, and Abyssinia was annexed to the Italian empire. The British government then persuaded the League to remove the economic sanctions imposed on Italy. The Opposition denounced this as a betrayal of the League and the principle of collective security.

A month after the League of Nations' 'surrender' to Mussolini over Abyssinia, the Spanish Civil War broke out, when General Franco and his right-wing supporters rose in revolt against the left-wing government which had won the recent general election. Political opinion in Britain was sharply divided, with the Liberals, socialists and Communists supporting the 'democratically elected government', and many Conservatives supporting Franco. While the British government adopted a policy of neutrality and non-intervention in Spain, there was large-scale intervention by Germany and Italy on Franco's side, and Russia sent a limited amount of aid to the left-wing government. The Labour Opposition in Britain, unlike the Communists, at first supported non-intervention, but afterwards denounced it as a trick by which the British government was facilitating the destruction of Spanish democracy by Fascist Italy and Nazi Germany. In March 1938 Hitler invaded and annexed Austria, and Britain took no action.

The aggressive foreign policies of Japan, Italy and Germany caused a complete reversal in the positions of the British Conservatives and socialists on pacifism and militarism. The socialists, who had always attacked the Conservatives as militarists, now demanded that Britain should resist the aggression of the three 'Fascist' powers; the Conservatives, who for the last sixty years had glorified the armed services and had denounced the socialists as pacifists, now preached the virtues of what their leader Neville Chamberlain, the Prime Minister, called the 'appeasement' of Germany, Italy and Japan, and warned the people that the socialist policy meant war. The anti-war propaganda which the socialists had formerly spread now proved an obstacle to them and an asset to the Conservatives, for the fear of another war was too widespread among the people for them to support firm action against the aggressors; and the socialists themselves were prevented by their anti-militarist tradition from supporting the demand for a rearmament programme to match the growing military power of Germany. At the same time as they were calling for resistance to Nazi aggression, the British Labour Party continued to call for disarmament.

A small minority of Conservative MPs, including Churchill and the rising politician, Harold Macmillan, opposed their government's foreign policy, and went as far as party discipline allowed in supporting the Labour Opposition's demand for firm action against the aggressors, though Churchill did not support the Labour attitude about the Spanish Civil War. Churchill and his group were joined by the Foreign Secretary, Anthony Eden, after his resignation from the government in February 1938. Unlike the Labour Party, Churchill strongly urged rearmament.

In September 1938 Hitler demanded that the Liberal government of Czechoslovakia should cede the Sudetenland, with its German-speaking population, to Germany. For a few days it seemed as if a European war was imminent; but Neville Chamberlain took the leading part in forcing the Czech government to capitulate and cede the province. He returned to London from his meeting with Hitler, Mussolini and the French Prime Minister at Munich, and told the crowds who cheered him in Downing Street, in Disraeli's words in 1878, that for the second time in a generation a British Prime Minister had returned from Germany having achieved 'Peace with honour'. He added that he had complete confidence in Hitler's promise not to claim any further territory in Europe, and foretold: 'I think it is peace for our time'. The Munich Agreement was strongly denounced by the Labour Opposition and by Churchill and his section of the Conservative Party; but for a few weeks Chamberlain was the hero of the British people, for they believed that he had saved them from war. The king praised 'the magnificent efforts of the Prime Minister in the cause of peace'; and The Times, hailing 'a new dawn', stated that 'no conqueror returning home from a victory on the battlefield has come home adorned with nobler laurels than Mr Chamberlain from Munich'.

Within less than six months Hitler had sent his troops into Prague and had divided the whole of Czechoslovakia between himself and his Hungarian and Slovak allies. While Mussolini annexed Albania, Hitler seized the town of Memel from Lithuania and demanded that Poland should cede Danzig. These events produced a change in Chamberlain's policy; he and his French ally made a military pact with Poland and opened negotiations to form the alliance with Russia which the socialists had been demanding for several years; but when it seemed as if the alliance was about to be concluded, the Russian dictator, Stalin, with a reversal of policy even more abrupt than Chamberlain's, signed a treaty of friendship with Hitler. When Hitler invaded Poland on 1

September 1939, Britain and France declared war, while Russia pursued a policy of neutrality which was more friendly to Germany than to the Western Allies.

The almost unbroken run of German successes in the first year, during which Poland, Denmark, Norway, Holland, Belgium and France were occupied by the German armies, forced the resignation of Chamberlain's government and the formation of a coalition with Churchill as Prime Minister, in which the Labour leaders, who had refused to serve under Chamberlain, took office. While the official right-wing leadership, and most of the Labour Party, supported the war, it was opposed by an active left-wing minority and by the Communist Party, who, having been the most ardent advocates of resistance to German aggression before the Hitler–Stalin pact, reverted in the autumn of 1939 to their former policy of opposition to 'imperialist war', only to change yet again and demand the opening of a second front in Europe after Hitler invaded Russia in June 1941.

In the summer of 1940, England faced a greater danger of invasion than in 1588 or 1805. In August, the German Air Force began an intensive attack on the airfields in south-eastern England as a preparation for an invasion by the land forces; and on 15 September – the most decisive day in English history – the Royal Air Force threw their last reserves into the battle. They won the day, and Hitler, abandoning his invasion plans, ordered his airmen to bomb London and other British cities in a bid to break the morale of the people. The morale held, and the most critical moment had passed. It was, in Churchill's words, the British people's 'finest hour'.

Britain, standing alone without allies against the full force of Hitler's Germany, had as its leader a statesman who combined both the oratory and the strategical gifts of the elder Pitt. He was deeply imbued with a consciousness of English history – he was himself a historian and a historical biographer – and he fought the war as another, and the greatest, struggle for king, country and empire. He had no sympathy with the ideological hatred of Fascism and Nazism which had always animated the socialists; and he had gone so far as to assure Mussolini that if he had been an Italian he would whole-heartedly have supported him 'in your triumphant struggle against the bestial appetites and passions of Leninism'. But when the test of war came, it was the

Conservatives – the party of appeasement, but also of nationalist and military tradition – and not the anti-Fascist but pacifist Labour Party, who played the more active part. A hundred and thirty-six of the 400 Conservative MPs joined the armed services during the war, as compared with 14 of the 180 Labour MPs; and although Labour voters and party members at the lower levels joined the forces, and the trade unions gave vital assistance to war production in the factories, the military direction of the war was in Conservative hands. Most of the leading socialist intellectuals were chiefly preoccupied, during the war, with the problems of post-war reconstruction. In Europe, it was a different matter: the Communist parties played by far the most active part in the underground resistance movement, and it was to them that the British authorities, at Churchill's orders, supplied arms and other assistance in their campaign of guerrilla warfare, sabotage and terrorism.

By the end of 1941, Britain, Russia and the United States were at war with Germany, Italy and Japan, and the three war leaders, Churchill, Stalin and President Franklin D. Roosevelt, popularly known as 'the Big Three', were settling grand strategy and the political future of the world at their wartime meetings. In the autumn of 1942 the tide of war was sharply reversed, both at Stalingrad on the Russian front and at El Alamein in Egypt; while the Japanese, after successes even more remarkable and rapid than the Germans' in Europe and North Africa, were held at the frontier of India.

An important part in the Allied counter-offensive was the use of air power to bombard the industrial centres of Germany. The bombing from the air of the civilian population had been regarded with special horror in the 1930s by the socialists and Liberals and the Nonconformist conscience. They had condemned the refusal of the British government in 1933 to agree to a proposal of the Disarmament Conference of the League of Nations to outlaw bombing from the air as a method of warfare; and the air raids on towns and villages in Spain by the German Air Force, when helping Franco in the Civil War, and on Warsaw, Rotterdam and Coventry at the start of the Second World War, as well as the Russian air raids on Helsinki during the Russo-Finnish War of 1939–40, had been condemned as acts of barbarism. By contrast, the British government had ordered the RAF to drop no bombs, but only leaflets, on German cities during its flights over Germany in the first winter of the war. But by 1943 the RAF was dropping bombs on German cities on a scale far beyond anything that the German, Italian or Japanese air forces had ever done, killing 90,000 civilians in the course of two hours at Hamburg in July 1943, and 135,000 in the same time at Dresden in April 1945.

By August 1945 the British Labour government was ordering a national holiday on 'VJ Day' (Victory over Japan Day) to celebrate the dropping of two atomic bombs on Hiroshima and Nagasaki, which, by killing 300,000 people and causing serious damage to the health of future generations, had forced the Japanese government to capitulate, and had ended the Second World War. The war against Germany had ended on VE Day (Victory in Europe Day) on 8 May 1945, with the unconditional surrender of the German armed forces after the Russian army had captured Berlin and Hitler had committed suicide.

In the Second World War, the aeroplane and the tank were the decisive weapons, and, unlike in the First World War, the offensive regained the ascendancy over the defensive. Because of this, the British people suffered fewer casualties than in the First World War; but on the Russian front, where large numbers of infantry forces were engaged, the two armies suffered 20 million casualties. The Germans and their anti-Semitic allies in the Ukraine and the Baltic territories also murdered nearly 6 million Jews in cold blood in extermination camps and in open spaces behind the front line between 1941 and 1945.

The Allied statesmen had announced in 1943 that they would not negotiate peace with either Germany or Japan, but would continue the war until it ended with the unconditional surrender of both powers; and when the surrender took place, both Germany and Japan were placed for a number of years under the direct government of the Allied armies of occupation. In both countries the defeated leaders were put on trial as 'war criminals' before Allied tribunals and hanged, after being convicted, not only of mass murder and crimes against humanity, but of waging aggressive war. No politicians or generals in history have more richly deserved their fate; but the Nuremberg and Tokyo trials violated all the established principles of justice and international law, without having the moral justification which they would have had if the criminals had been executed as an act of revolutionary justice of the peoples whom they had oppressed; for the trials were marred by the fact that the judges represented the governments of the victors who had themselves committed many of the crimes with which the defendants were charged and had at one time encouraged them in their plans to wage aggressive war. The mass murders in the extermination camps, and the hanging of defeated generals for the crime of planning an attack on an enemy country, took place during the lifetime of a generation who in their youth believed that the twentieth century would be free from all the cruelties of the past, and whose rulers had treated each other with courtesy both in peace and war.

In the summer of 1945 a general election was held in Britain. Contrary to what all observers expected, the great war leader, Churchill, and his Conservative Party were defeated, and a Labour government was elected with a large majority in the House of Commons. The people associated the Conservatives with the unemployment and the appeasement policy of the 1930s, and intended that the war should lead to a new society in which the common man should enjoy a far higher standard of living than hitherto, and in which the wealth of the rich should be redistributed for the benefit of the people. The chief method by which this was achieved was high taxation. During the first twenty months of the Second World War, income tax was increased from 5 shillings and sixpence to 10 shillings in the pound (from 27½ per cent to 50 per cent), and for ten years after the war neither Labour nor Conservative governments reduced it below 9 shillings (45 per cent). Surtax on larger incomes was much higher; and death duties, by which up to 80 per cent of a man's property was confiscated at his death, had the effect of substantially reducing the standard of living and the whole way of life of a rich family within two or three generations. The development of ingenious methods of tax avoidance by highly paid accountants and lawyers was only partly successful in slowing down the impoverishment of the aristocracy and landed gentry.

The Conservatives, though strongly opposing the Labour policy of nationalisation of industry, adapted themselves to the new situation and public mood after 1945 with the same readiness with which Peel and Disraeli in their times had changed the nature of the Conservative Party in the 1830s and 1870s. The implementation of this policy was largely due to the Conservative statesman, R. A. Butler. The similarity of his policy to that of the moderate Labour Party leader, Hugh Gaitskell, led to the invention of the word 'Butskellism' to describe the very similar social policy of the two great parties in the state. The Labour Prime Minister, Clement Attlee, stated in a private conversation that the difference between Labour and Conservative was that a Labour government went as far as public opinion allowed them to go, and a Conservative government as far as public opinion compelled them to go, towards the creation of the new society.

The basis of this policy was redistribution of wealth through high taxation; the protection of the working man from the effects of poverty, ill-health and his own follies and lack of foresight by a system of social welfare, financed in part from insurance contributions compulsorily collected from every individual in the country, and partly from government expenditure; the creation of greatly improved educational facilities, and a free state medical service; the prevention of unemployment at all costs, above all by the payments of subsidies from the government to unprofitable industries; and the development of a consumer economy by a rapid development of hire-purchase and facilities for buying on credit. The result was a great increase in the standard of living of the working classes; the Conservative Prime Minister, Harold Macmillan, could truthfully claim in 1957 that the British people 'have never had it so good'. Many members of the old ruling classes sold or sub-divided their large houses and dispensed with their staff of domestic servants, who no longer needed or wished to do this work, and applied for positions as directors or public relations officers in large businesses, with the 'perks' which they would thereby obtain. Every year, more working-class families owned a motor car, a refrigerator, a washing machine and a television set.

There was an even closer agreement between the Labour and Conservative parties in foreign policy. The victorious Allies had begun to quarrel amongst themselves even before they had hanged their enemies. Hitler's lifelong aim of destroying Bolshevism had resulted in the Russian armies occupying all Eastern Europe and East Germany and installing Communist governments there. But the United States could hold the Russian armies in check, and more than outmatch them, with the atomic bomb, which the United States alone possessed; and soon afterwards the United States developed the hydrogen bomb, a far more terrible weapon than the uranium atomic bomb, which could exterminate life for many miles from the place where it was detonated. It took Russia less than ten years to develop the atomic and hydrogen bombs, and for the next thirty years the two 'super-powers' faced each other, in a state of continual diplomatic tension, which at times improved almost to the point of friendship, and at other times deteriorated to such a degree that war seemed to be imminent; but open war between Russia and the United States was always avoided, and diplomatic relations were never severed.

In this situation, Britain abandoned the foreign policy which she had pursued for four hundred years. Ever since Elizabeth I severed the alliance with Philip of Spain in 1558, the foundation stone of English policy had been to keep free of irrevocable entanglements – 'We have no eternal allies', said Palmerston – and to preserve the balance of power by shifting from one side to the other in order to check the domination of the strongest nation. In 1946 Britain attached herself permanently to the American alliance, and became economically and militarily so closely linked with the United States that it became in effect impossible for her to pursue an independent foreign policy. It was at this moment that Britain ceased to be a great power. Since then she has inevitably shown all the symptoms of the satellite state which is dependent on a powerful ally, including an irritability against its protector and anxiety whenever this protector becomes too friendly with its great enemy.

The alliance with the United States against Russia was not hindered, but facilitated, by the fact that Britain had a Labour government during the years of decision after 1945. The Labour and Communist movements had grown out of the same socialist movement, and many Labour supporters, whose bitter memories of past struggles had left them with an intense hatred of 'the Tories', felt great sympathy with Bolshevik Russia and the British Communist Party. But though the differences between Labour and Communist supporters were originally seen as being only a question of the use of revolution or of the ballot-box as the method of achieving the same end, it had become clear by 1930 that there was a fundamental difference in objective; for the Communists aimed at the creation of a revolutionary dictatorship, while the Labour Party wished to become alternately government and Opposition in the British Parliamentary system.

The hostility between the two wings of the socialist movement grew even more bitter after the Communist governments in Eastern Europe suppressed political democracy and arrested or executed socialist opponents, and by 1950 the hatred between the right-wing Labour leaders and the Communists in Britain was as intense as that between the Presbyterians and the Independents three hundred years before. The appointment of the right-wing trade union leader, Ernest Bevin, as Foreign Secretary in the Labour government of 1945 led to an immediate change in the policy of the British diplomatic missions throughout the world and an ending of the collaboration with Russia which had been pursued under his Conservative predecessor, Anthony Eden; and it was not until after Churchill and a Conservative government had returned to power in 1951 that a slight relaxation of the tension was possible.

The new role of the trade unions, which had been noticeable as early as the 1890s, had gone a long way further by 1950. Trade union leaders were now knighted or given peerages for their services to trade unionism. Trade union representatives sat with representatives of the employers, along with lawyers or other impartial chairmen, on countless tribunals and government advisory bodies. The TUC, like the employers' Confederation of British Industries, was consulted by the government on all important questions of economic and social policy. During the years immediately following the Second World War, the trade union leaders were concerned above all in preventing and defeating unofficial strikes and in destroying the influence in the unions of the Communists who usually led these strikes. In 1949 and 1950 the Labour government regularly used troops to break unofficial strikes by dockers and power workers, and prosecuted the strike leaders in the criminal courts.

This state of affairs began to change in the 1960s. The disclosures in 1956 by the leaders of the Russian Communist Party of

297

the atrocities which had been committed under Stalin's govern-ment; the split between the two great Communist states, Russia and China; the armed intervention by Russian troops in Hungary in 1956 and in Czechoslovakia in 1968; and the growing in-dependence from Russia of the Communist Parties in Yugoslavia, Italy and other countries, all led to a great loss of influence by the Communist Party in Britain. By 1970 the radical and revolution-ary movements in Britain no longer had any sympathy or links with Russia or the Communist Party, but were far closer to international anarchist or terrorist groups, and to left-wing nationalist organisations in the Middle East, Africa and South America. The old type of trade union leader, determined above all to destroy the Communist influence in the trade unions, had been replaced by leaders who were eager to win higher wages and living standards for their members, irrespective of the effect on national and international affairs, and to show the power of the unions in political and economic life.

In 1970 the Conservatives won the general election and formed a government with Edward Heath as Prime Minister. He attempted to deal with the problem of the growing number of strikes, which were having a serious effect on British competition in international markets, by limiting the power of the unions to call strikes and by setting up the National Industrial Relations Court to regulate relations between unions and employers. This policy, which had been formulated by Conservative lawyers despite warnings from the employers' organisations, was adhered to with a mixture of obstinacy and weakness which was reminiscent of the policy of Charles I. Faced with the warnings and threats of the trade union leaders as to the consequences of introducing and enforcing this trade union legislation, the government resolutely declared that it would never surrender to threats; as soon as the threats were implemented, they took no action to deal with them, and prevented the prosecution of strikers who had broken the law.

In the winter of 1973–4 the miners, with the full support of the Labour Opposition, caused a serious economic crisis and great inconvenience to the public by a strike for a large increase in wages. In February the Heath government, after vacillating for several weeks, held a general election while the strike was in progress; and though they won a majority of the total votes cast, the distribution of the votes under the British Parliamentary system gave a very small majority in the House of Commons to Labour, who formed a government and secured a working majority at another general election eight months later.

The Labour government immediately granted the miners' wage demand, and other unions put forward new wage claims. These led to increased costs, price increases, and new wage demands; and inflation, which had started some years earlier in nearly every country in Europe, rose as high as nearly 30 per cent per annum in Britain. The British economy was injured by a series of strikes, chiefly in the nationalised industries, though one of the arguments which earlier socialists and trade unionists had advanced in favour of nationalisation was that this would prevent strikes, as the workers in the nationalised industries would then feel that they were working for themselves and the country and not for the profits of their employer. The Labour government claimed that their good relations with the trade unions would make them better able than the Conservatives to prevent strikes; but having encouraged the strikes in 1973, they were unable to prevent them in 1978. Their solution of the problem was to penalise employers who paid the wage increases demanded by the unions, and then to take no effective action to deal with the strikes which ensued when the employers complied with their wishes and refused to pay the increases.

The repeated strikes in transport and the power services, which prevented people of all classes from travelling, forced them to wait for hours on cold railway platforms, and deprived them of warmth and cooking facilities and water in their homes and of medical attention in hospitals, caused a strong public revulsion against trade unions and strikers which undoubtedly was the most important factor in securing the election of a Conservative government in May 1979 under Mrs Margaret Thatcher, the first woman to be Prime Minister in Britain.

Her policy has been to attempt to reduce inflation by restricting the supply of money, at the cost of tolerating a substantial increase in unemployment, a limitation of the social services, and a temporary fall in the standard of living of the people. This conflicts, at least to some extent, with the policy which the leadership of both the Conservative and Labour Parties have accepted for the last thirty-five years. It is too early to say whether this will be the beginning of a new attitude, and will lead to a new political and social system, or whether it will be a passing and forgotten interlude in the earlier contrary process.

The system which has existed in Britain since 1945 has been aptly called the 'Welfare State'. Other generations of Englishmen have devoted themselves to the glory of God, the establishment of the Protestant religion, imperial glory, or the winning of the right to free speech, the Parliamentary suffrage, or trade union freedom. The aim of the generation which governed Britain from 1945 to 1979 was to achieve the material welfare of the people, which to earlier generations was a desirable by-product, but not the main objective, of their efforts. Like other systems, the welfare state has its virtues and its faults; it has eradicated old evils and created new ones.

In the welfare state, no one has to work for eighteen hours a day in a mine or mill; but hard work, instead of being praised and rewarded, is ridiculed and even penalised. No one starves to death because Liberal economic theory prohibits the state from relieving distress; but initiative is stifled by pettifogging meddling from bureaucrats whose salaries and expenses are a burden on the taxpayers and ratepayers. A child of thirteen is not sent to jail for picking a flower for her aunt from an almshouse garden, as occurred in 1875; but men and women convicted of savage assaults on their children or of other crimes of violence receive trivial punishments, or often are not punished at all, while in the same court on the same day the next offender is heavily penalised for a much less serious crime, is fined for some technical motoring offence or breach of an unnecessary public health or town planning regulation, or for some action at a political demonstration after being convicted against the weight of the evidence.

When offenders are sent to prison, they are not forced to work on the treadmill; but they are locked for hours in their cells in very oppressive conditions, not as part of their punishment, but because their warders are taking 'industrial action' to get more money, and the authorities are as reluctant to punish the indiscipline of the prison officers as they are to impose harsh sentences on the criminals. The leniency of the courts in dealing with a certain type of offender has produced a situation which is almost comparable to that which existed in earlier times when weak and saintly kings allowed lawlessness to flourish in their realms, and their subjects longed for a strong ruler who, by hanging thieves and malefactors, would establish a state of affairs in which 'a woman with a new-born child could walk throughout the island from sea to sea and take no harm'.

The relative ease of modern life, with the reduction of the need for hard work and physical exercise, and of risks of premature death, have led to a decrease in physical and mental resilience, to drug-taking, and to a marked increase in mental illness in every part of Britain except Northern Ireland, where it has fallen sharply among a population which is constantly exposed to the risks of death from bombs. The advances in medical science and the development of a National Health Service have greatly reduced the cases of infant mortality and the death-rate among the working classes; but thanks to this greater knowledge, and also perhaps to a weakening of religious belief, many people have a morbid anxiety about their real or imaginary ailments, while well-meaning individuals and organised groups exert themselves to prevent others from risking their lives or health in adventures or pleasures.

The discovery of statistical proof that smoking is harmful to health, which had always been generally accepted, has led to a powerful campaign against smoking by enthusiasts who eclipse the temperance advocates of the Victorian era, Wilberforce's 'Clapham Saints', and the most ascetical medieval friar, in their zeal to deprive themselves and others of the joys of self-indulgence. As their claim that smoking causes 50,000 deaths a year means that the risk of death incurred by each of Britain's 20 million smokers is only one in 400 per annum, the danger to health is obviously not a logical reason, but is the excuse, for a fanatical campaign for self-abnegation which the twentieth-century Englishman, unlike his medieval ancestor, is unwilling to justify as an act of religious devotion. This asceticism has always been a tradition in English life, as opposed to the rival attitude held by the sixteenth-century Englishman who was famous as the biggest eater in Europe, and the eighteenth-century gentlemen who believed that the man who went to bed sober 'fades as the leaves do fade that drop off in October', whereas the man who went to bed 'half-seas over, will live until he die and then lie down in clover'.

301

Modern conveniences have freed millions of people from exhausting drudgery; but they have confronted the nation with new problems. The England of Alfred and Edward I, of Elizabeth I and Oliver Cromwell, and even of Palmerston and Disraeli, survived and prospered without any Middle Eastern or North Sea oil; the England of 1981 is absolutely dependent upon it to maintain the standard of living which people of all classes have come to expect.

The British empire has passed away, within eighty years of Disraeli's Guildhall speech in 1878 and within twenty years of Churchill's declaration on the same occasion in 1942 that he had not become the king's first minister in order to preside over the liquidation of the British empire. Having granted independence to India, Pakistan and Burma after the Second World War, Britain, under her Conservative governments in the 1950s, made an attempt to repress the nationalist movements in Cyprus, Kenya and Nyasaland, in all of which there were occasional incidents which shocked the Nonconformist conscience; but in 1960 Macmillan, declaring that the 'wind of change' was sweeping through Africa, initiated a policy which resulted in all Britain's African colonies being granted independence before the end of the next decade. But any goodwill which this might have won for Britain among the black African peoples was forfeited by the fact that, for financial and strategical reasons, the British government generally gave diplomatic support to the racialist Boer police state in South Africa and discouraged all attempts to injure South Africa by a policy of economic sanctions.

Further difficulties arose in the colony of Rhodesia, which Cecil Rhodes had founded in 1890. The British Conservative government in 1953 formed the Central African Federation, consisting of Northern Rhodesia, Southern Rhodesia, and Nyasaland, with a constitution which gave political control to the white British immigrants of Southern Rhodesia; but ten years later the Federation was dissolved by Britain because of the opposition of the black political organisations, and Northern Rhodesia and Nyasaland were given independence as the black states of Zambia and Malawi. The whites in Southern Rhodesia then announced their intention of proclaiming their independence from Britain and setting up a white-dominated state. The British Labour Prime Minister, Harold Wilson, took the extraordinary step of announcing that if the white settlers proclaimed their independence they would be guilty of treason, but that no measures would be taken to suppress their rebellion by armed force. Not surprisingly, the leader of the white settlers, Ian Smith, thereupon proclaimed the independence of Rhodesia in November 1965.

The British government asked the other governments of the world, at the United Nations, to impose economic sanctions against Rhodesia; and when they agreed to do so, Wilson expressed his confidence that the 'rebel regime' in Rhodesia would be forced to capitulate in 'weeks, not months'. But the rebel regime, sustained by the government of South Africa and by the Portuguese colonial authorities in Mozambique, remained in power for fourteen years. Only twenty years after Britain emerged triumphant from the Second World War as one of the four great powers in the world, a British government could think of no other way to suppress what it called a revolt in its colonies than to ask other nations to impose a trade boycott against the colony, while at the same time successive British governments continued to claim that Britain alone was the sovereign power in Rhodesia and that no one else had the right to decide the future of the territory. Meanwhile Britain took no effective steps to intervene in the guerrilla warfare which was raging in Rhodesia or in the raids made by the armed forces of the white settlers on the neighbouring black states. All this was nearer to the world of comic opera than to the world of Palmerston.

The rebel government of Rhodesia was eventually overthrown, not by the British government, but by the successes of the black guerrillas; by the collapse of Portuguese rule in Mozambique after the end of Salazar's dictatorship in Portugal, and the installation of an independent Marxist black government there; and, above all, by the action of the United States. In 1976 the American government, hoping to forestall the danger of the blacks in Africa enlisting Russian help, put pressure on the government of South Africa to threaten to abandon the Rhodesian whites unless they made political concessions to the blacks. The formation in Rhodesia of a coalition government of blacks and whites under a black Prime Minister, Bishop Muzorewa, failed to defeat the guerrillas. At this juncture the Conservative election victory in Britain brought Mrs Thatcher to power. Her government pursued a far more positive policy than her predecessors' had done, and was at least able to save British face by gracefully presiding at the transfer of political power to the Marxist black guerrillas of Robert Mugabe in Rhodesia.

On two occasions Britain attempted, by a show of strength, to assert her position in international affairs; but on both occasions she failed disastrously. In 1956, without consulting its American ally, the British Conservative government invaded Egypt in order to prevent the Egyptian government from nationalising the Suez Canal; but a threat from the United States government to cease financial aid was sufficient to induce Britain to withdraw the troops immediately. In 1975 Icelandic gunboats began harassing British ships on the high seas in order to prevent cod fishing within the 200-mile territorial limit claimed by Iceland, but outside the 12-mile limit recognised by Britain. The British Labour government sent the navy to protect the British fishermen; but the conflict ended with Britain accepting terms considerably worse than those which Iceland had offered before the 'cod war' began.

The reason for the sharp decline in British power is not primarily military or economic. Britain, which is one of the few powers in the world to possess the hydrogen bomb, is militarily as strong as Israel, Tanzania, India or Cuba, but, unlike these powers, is psychologically incapable of pursuing a forward policy. She carries this to the point, not only of refraining from committing military aggression, but of submitting to affronts which few other powers would tolerate. Britain is ready to go to war, under American leadership, to defend a right-wing dictatorship in South Korea from invasion by a Communist dictatorship in North Korea, but not to intervene when her fishermen are attacked on the high seas by Icelandic gunboats. This is the length to which the Nonconformist conscience has gone in its reaction to the high-handed Palmerstonian policy.

It is difficult to know how far these trends in national policy represent the true feeling of the English people; for in many ways there is a greater conflict than at earlier periods between the outlook of the Establishment and the man in the street. The British system of Parliamentary democracy is not designed to allow public opinion to prevail. The political influence of the ordinary voter is limited to deciding every four or five years which of two or three professional politicians shall represent him in the House of Commons, and whether the leader of the Conservative Party or of the Labour Party shall be the next Prime Minister, although possibly he has the lowest opinion of both of them. The pretence that a Prime Minister has a 'mandate' to introduce the measures in his party's election manifesto is a farce, as the manifesto has probably been read by less than one per cent of the electorate, and many of these may agree with some points in it, and disagree with others. On several matters, for example capital punishment, and the attempts to pressurise British athletes into making the utterly pointless gesture of boycotting the Olympic Games in Moscow, most of the people are completely opposed to the views of the majority of their elected representatives; but only in exceptional circumstances is the pressure of public opinion on MPs strong enough to counter the other pressures of party loyalty and personal political prospects. It has been shown statistically that the people have a greater contempt for MPs than for any other professional group.

There are, however, indications that the popular attachment to past traditions is weakening. England, which for so long had a reputation for insular prejudice and aversion to change, has since 1950 shown the greatest eagerness to abandon her national peculiarities and traditions. She has accepted with only limited protest the introduction of the decimal system, which her Victorian ancestors firmly refused to do. When France 'went metric' in 1790, the French people continued for nearly two hundred years to do business in the old pre-metric coinage, and to speak of *sous*, not of *centimes*, until inflation made the term meaningless; when England went metric in 1971, it took only a few weeks before the English people ceased to talk about the sixpence and the half-crown. In 1973 the counties of England were revised, having stood virtually unchanged for over a thousand years. There were administrative advantages in changing some of the county boundaries; but in any earlier period of English history, these advantages would somehow have been introduced without radically altering the ancient boundaries and names. Now the officials who decide such matters welcome the opportunity to introduce the changes. It remains to be seen how long the English will continue to talk about the old counties, as the French still do about the provinces in France which were abolished in the Revolution of 1789.

The English common law has been transformed almost beyond recognition, more changes having been introduced since 1945 than in the previous eight hundred years. New models of cars and washing machines come on to the market and disappear again within a few years of months.

In 1973, after delaying the decision for twenty years, Britain joined the European Economic Community, by which many aspects of its economic policy is decided by the ministers and bureaucrats of the EEC in Brussels. It is not surprising that there should have been more opposition in Britain to joining the Common Market than in most other countries. This is not the first time in history that the inhabitants of Britain have been governed from somewhere in Europe – from Rome by the Caesars, from Roskilde by Cnut, from Rouen by William the Conqueror, from Poitiers by Richard Coeur de Lion. But English power and glory have always flourished most when England was free from Europe and was defying it – in 1559 and 1588, in 1805, in 1940. The greatest moments in English history have been when they were looking across the Channel at their foes. Yet the British people have accepted membership of the EEC by a substantial majority; it is in fact the only issue which can definitely be said to have been approved by the people, who decided it by referendum.* The dissatisfaction with the Common Market which exists today comes not from opposition to co-operation with Europe, but from resentment at the constant meddling of bureaucrats in Brussels, and from the feeling that its representatives, unlike those of the other members of the EEC, cannot be relied upon to struggle for its national interests inside the Community. English public opinion certainly does not reject the possibility that union with Europe may replace union with its former empire, even if it would prefer a political union in which the inhabitants of English villages were free to eat whatever butter and ice-cream they preferred in packages of their own choice, not in those prescribed for them by officials who do not properly understand their language.

This is the moment in time which English history has now

* It should however be remembered that at the referendum of 1975 the British electorate were merely asked to approve a *fait accompli*, Britain having joined the EEC two years earlier without a referendum.

reached. It is pointless to attempt to speculate as to what will happen in the future. The men who fought in the Wars of the Roses could not foresee that their children would witness the Protestant Reformation, and that their grandchildren would applaud the victories of English seamen over the Spaniards at Cadiz and in the Caribbean. Nor can we today foresee the events which will confront our children and grandchildren in the twenty-first century. Is the loss of national confidence the beginning of a permanent decline? This is not impossible, for Britain's international position today, thirty-five years after 1945, is as low as Spain's thirty-five years after Philip II, as Holland's thirty-five years after William III, and as Sweden's thirty-five years after Charles XII, if better than India's thirty-five years after Aurangzeb. Yet everyone who considers the history of England, the resilience of the English nation, and the difference between the attitude of the people and those leaders whom its modern Parliamentary system brings to the fore at all times, except at moments of acute national crisis, must feel in his bones that the eclipse is only temporary, and that a national revival is at hand.

INDEX

309

**THE LIVES OF THE
KINGS AND QUEENS OF ENGLAND**

Edited by Antonia Fraser

From William the Conqueror to Elizabeth II ten
dynasties of English monarchs have made, marked
and marred the saga of England's realm — a saga of
wars and glory, conquest and exploration, usurpation
and murder.

Here is the whole sweep of English history told
through the lives of England's many monarchs by
eight specialist historians who bring alive the
complex characters both of well-known and loved
monarchs like Victoria and of the fascinating,
enigmatic figures of medieval England.

'Lively . . . bursting with colour . . . demonstrates not
only the way to enjoy history but also the way to
marshall a mass of facts'
The Economist

'Lively writing . . . a comprehensive history of
England in biographical form'
Sunday Telegraph

Futura Publications
Non-Fiction/History
0 8600 7449 8

KING CHARLES II

Antonia Fraser

'The fullest and most sophisticated account to date of
the most charming and approachable of English
Kings.'
The Observer

By the author of the bestselling *MARY, QUEEN OF
SCOTS* and *CROMWELL, OUR CHIEF OF MEN*, a
lively and authoritative biography of the popular
Charles II. The King whose youth was spent in
poverty-stricken exile after his father's execution,
who was restored to his throne in triumph after
Cromwell's death and whose reign gave its name to
an entire society and culture.

'Well planned, thorough, superbly illustrated, well
produced . . . and Lady Antonia is at her best.'
Daily Telegraph

'a rich feast of instruction, drama and entertainment
based on a most thorough investigation of available
material'
Times Literary Supplement

'detailed, sympathetic and admirably readable'
The Economist

'Her graceful style makes this a book for every kind
of reader'
Daily Mail

A Contact Book/Futura Publications
Non-Fiction/Historical
0 7088 1933 8

TALES FROM THE NEWGATE CALENDAR

Rayner Heppenstal

The original Newgate Calendars were published in the 18th and 19th centuries and chronicled infamous crimes and their punishment, usually by hanging, at London's Newgate prison.

From these Calendars, the bestsellers of their time, the writer Rayner Heppenstal has distilled an account of the most colourful figures in the annals of crime. Here are the stories of Captain Kidd and Dick Turpin, the Fourth Earl Ferrers and the bigamous Duchess of Kingston, and of the three men who survived the Newgate rope. All part of the story of London's teeming underground of crime which the author so brilliantly captures in *TALES FROM THE NEWGATE CALENDAR*.

Futura Publications
Non-Fiction
0 7088 2274 6

A SHEPHERD'S LIFE

W. H. Hudson

In the 1920s W. H. Hudson was regarded alongside
Joseph Conrad as Thomas Hardy's natural literary
heir. His books about the English countryside are first
class but of them all, *A SHEPHERD'S LIFE* stands out
as a classic.

In this book Hudson recreates the life of a Wiltshire
village in the last century, and he does so by telling
the story of one man, the remarkable shepherd,
Caleb Bawcombe. Bawcombe has now been
identified as one James Lawes, the village of
Winterbourne Bishop as Martin, on the borders of
Wiltshire, Hampshire and Dorset. Hudson gave them
both aliases but the stories he told about them were
unmistakably authentic and make *A SHEPHERD'S
LIFE* the most poignant portrait of country life to
appear in paperback since Flora Thompson's
LARKRISE TO CANDLEFORD.

Futura Publications
Non-Fiction
0 7088 1532 4

PLAIN TALES FROM THE RAJ

Edited by Charles Allen

'One of the most enjoyable books I have read this
year . . . by turns informative, funny and deeply
touching. It is an authentic record of the survivors of
British India . . . a book which takes on where Kipling
left off.'
Antonia Fraser

'That extraordinary world of crows and dust sunsets,
of dinner parties that started with anchovy toast
(always) and ended seven courses later with little
glass bowls full of water and hibiscus flowers to
wash the fingers in; of cane chairs on club
verandahs, and damp sugar full of ants; of shining
Indian rivers and beautiful women . . . Pure nostalgia
and irresistible.'
Scotsman

'Britons ruled for almost three centuries creating a
society the like of which will never be repeated. The
flavour of the era is captured in *PLAIN TALES FROM
THE RAJ*.'
Daily Mirror

Futura Publications
Non-Fiction
0 8600 7455 2

TALES FROM THE DARK CONTINENT

Charles Allen

The bestselling collection of reminiscences from the famous BBC Radio 4 series.

Small boys and sleeping dictionaries, bush camps and blackwater fever, mosquito-boots and mammy-chairs – the vanished world of British Colonial Africa captured in the vivid stories and recollections of the pioneering men and women who lived and worked there.

'Even more successful than its predecessor (*PLAIN TALES FROM THE RAJ*). The individual officer's devotion to his little corner of Africa is as heart-warming as anything from India.'
Sunday Telegraph

'A rich treasure-house of the Empire . . . The great thrill is to know that the memories you read are coming from people who are still alive – what they have lived through is so far removed from English life as to be barely credible.'
Spectator

Futura Publications
Non-Fiction
0 7088 1930 3

All Futura Books are available at your bookshop or newsagent, or can be ordered from the following address:
Futura Books, Cash Sales Department,
P.O. Box 11, Falmouth, Cornwall.

Please send cheque or postal order (no currency), and allow 45p for postage and packing for the first book plus 20p for the second book and 14p for each additional book ordered up to a maximum charge of £1.63 in U.K.

Customers in Eire and B.F.P.O. please allow 45p for the first book, 20p for the second book, plus 14p per copy for the next 7 books, thereafter 8p per book.

Overseas customers please allow 75p for postage and packing for the first book and 21p per copy for each additional book.